W9-BWS-929

Planning Curriculum in Science

Shelley A. Lee
Science Consultant

Elizabeth Burmaster, State Superintendent
Wisconsin Department of Public Instruction

Madison, Wisconsin

This publication is available from:

Publication Sales
Wisconsin Department of Public Instruction
Drawer 179
Milwaukee, WI 53293-0179
(800) 243-8782 (U.S. only)
(608) 266-2188
(608) 267-9110 Fax
www.dpi.state.wi.us/pubsales

Bulletin No. 2046

© January 2002 Wisconsin Department of Public Instruction

ISBN 1-57337-100-9

Printed on recycled paper

Foreword

Science and discoveries in science have changed our lives in ways unimaginable to previous generations. As educators it is our goal to understand those changes, to teach our young students to think scientifically, and to prepare them for even more unimaginable and unpredictable changes in science in the future. It is our task to prepare them for a global future by educating them about science so they can use science and scientific evidence to make choices. As adults our students must be able to engage intelligently in public discourse and debate important issues in science and technology. And *all* Wisconsin students must be able to share in the joy and wonderment of learning about nature and the natural world.

Planning Curriculum in Science has at its foundation, *Wisconsin Model Academic Standards for Science* — what we expect *all* students throughout Wisconsin to know and be able to do in science. This new guide has been developed to assist school districts with the design of a science program that meets or exceeds the expectations of the science standards and achieves scientific literacy for *all* students. The guide uses the standards for science as a springboard to suggest ways in which students can make connections in science, to become scientifically literate, and to understand the role scientific literacy plays in the workforce and in their daily lives.

Wisconsin science teacher Joe Riederer wrote *A Central Wisconsin Love Story*. In the story, Corey was curious about the world around him. This curiosity led him to seek answers to his questions by inquiring and investigating about many things in nature. During his investigations he was able to learn much about his world and even about science. One day he came across a pair of sandhill cranes and he began to make observations about the pair. Through these observations, he learned about the plight of the cranes, which led him to take action. While each student taking science in Wisconsin will not have Corey's experiences, each student can experience the same curiosity, inquiry, and the same quest for knowledge within the science classroom.

This guide is designed to assist districts and teachers of science establish a science program that allows students to explore science, to investigate nature, to ask questions, and to find answers to those questions. Further, the guide is designed to assist the teachers in developing the habits and practices that allow students to construct their own knowledge about science.

My predecessor, former state superintendent John T. Benson, appointed the task force for this guide. I am highly appreciative of his initiative, his foresight, and his understanding of the type of support school districts have come to expect from the Wisconsin Department of Public Instruction. His work is to be applauded.

I am proud of the work of the task force and authors of this guide, so on behalf of them I hope that each teacher of science will become involved in developing a science program that is described in this guide. I will continue to give my support to curriculum development at the Department of Public Instruction. I know that *Planning Curriculum in Science* will be an invaluable planning tool in every school district throughout Wisconsin.

Elizabeth Burmaster
State Superintendent

A Central Wisconsin Love Story

by Joe Riederer

The two had been together for three years and would stay together for the rest of their lives. To the scientist, it was nothing more than a preprogrammed, biochemical response. Love was a word for the poet. This was how it was and any talk of emotions just muddied the picture.

As the pair walked through the tall grass of a Central Wisconsin September, swallows gathered in large flocks on the telephone line. Somewhere to the east, a truck hauling potatoes to a processing plant in Plover loudly downshifted. To the west, sandstone hills towered over the otherwise flat landscape. The sights and sounds of late summer meant nothing to the two of them. They focused on only one task, preparing for the long trip back to Florida. A leopard frog darted between them. She missed it— he didn't. With an archer's precision he grabbed the startled frog just behind the front legs and swallowed it whole. A stretch of wings, a short run, and the pair of cranes flew to another field.

Sandhill cranes had been coming to Central Wisconsin for thousands of summers. Parents showed the way to their offspring, and the cycle continued. If culture is the passing of wisdom from one generation to the next, crane culture is surely as old as any on the continent.

The mix of prairie, marsh, and pine barrens found here provided the diversity of habitat needed for cranes to raise their young. As agriculture expanded into the area, the cranes adapted. Their love of tender corn seedlings did not endear them to people trying to eke out a living by farming. At the same time, most people overlooked the benefits provided when the cranes ate grasshoppers, mice, and other crop pests. This area was a perfect place for cranes to spend the summer. It was not, however, any place for a crane to be in the winter.

A ground-fog hung in the air as the sun climbed the eastern horizon. The chill of the morning left no doubt that their time in the north was almost over. Feeding on corn that had been missed during the harvest, they stayed in sight of each other. Whether it was the scientist's "instinct" or the poet's "love," didn't matter. They had become a single functioning unit. Neither would be complete without the other.

A flash of brown fur was the first thing he saw. This was followed immediately by his mate's bugling alarm and the dog's angry growl. Next came the hot canine breath and a sudden loss of balance. The dog's yellow teeth firmly grasped the large bird's wing as they tumbled together to the ground. The kicks from the fragile legs of the crane were futile. His beak, however, found its mark just above the dog's left eye socket. Stunned and in pain, the dog ran off with blurred vision and its tail firmly between its legs.

The wounded crane struggled to return to his feet. He kept one wing neatly folded. The other wing was bent out and forward, dripping blood. His mate, having taken to the air to avoid the beast, returned cautiously. Still wary of the danger that lurked in the farmyard nearby, she jumped into the air and flapped her wings, trying to encourage her mate to leave. This field was too dangerous for an injured crane. He too jumped into the air, but could only move one wing. Both the poet and the scientist would have agreed that cranes were able to feel pain.

Their first need was cover. They slowly made their way from the cornfield to the adjacent stand of jack pine and scrub oak. She flew over the barbed-wire fence. He tried, but instead only managed to scrape himself on the rusty steel. A second try, this time more of a hop than a flight, got him safely to the other side.

The bleeding had stopped, leaving a crust of dried blood on his now useless wing. The pain continued through the night. Morning came and other cranes called from distant fields as they began to congregate into larger flocks. She flew over the fence, landed in the corn stubble, and then called back to where he was standing. He didn't join her. She called again, but the result was the same. A slow and low flight took her back to where he spent the night with his injured wing. She called and flew back to the field, but again, he did not follow. Finally, after a fourth call he managed to jump the fence and feed on the corn.

Their days went by in much the same fashion for the next several weeks; staying as far away from the farmyard as possible, hiding near the trees at night and eating any food they could find. Three days of cold weather and an early dusting of snow sent most of the other cranes heading south. Twice she tried encouraging him to fly but failed both times. Conflicting needs frustrated her. She knew they should leave before the weather closed in. She also knew that she could not leave her mate.

Changes in ocean currents on the other side of the planet helped to put the crisis on hold for weeks. The warmest fall in years kept the fields open and their limited food supply uncovered well into November. Almost all of the other cranes had left. As they flew overhead, she would take flight to join them, only to circle back when she saw that her mate had not followed.

The muscle tissue in his wing had healed, but the wing itself was no longer the correct shape for sustained flight. He had managed to make a few short trips. He was even able to move to a nearby field and a replenished food supply. Migration, however, was out of the question.

Cold nights and a dwindling cache of food put both birds on edge. Weather had become the most threatening predator. The other predator, the dog, had not returned since the attack.

Cautiously moving through the tall grass and scrub oak along the edge of the field, both birds stopped suddenly. A subtle noise or a slight movement caught their attention. Necks upright, heads turning to scan the surroundings, they were not going to get surprised again. A thirteen-year-old boy stepped out of the woods only a few yards from where the cranes were hiding. Both cranes bugled a startled alarm and the boy screamed. The birds flew north to the other end of the field. The boy ran south into the woods, stopped, and then slowly crawled back to the edge of the cornfield.

In the days that followed, the weather started to change. Cirrus clouds filled the sky, followed by ever darkening stratus clouds. The cold wind shifted directions and the birds could sense a drop in air pressure. There was a storm on the way. A heavy snow could make finding food difficult, but they'd been through that before. Nearly every April a late snowstorm blanketed Central Wisconsin, but the heavy snow never lasted long. In an early December blizzard, it was the starving cranes that wouldn't last long.

The storm began as heavy wet snow and the birds took cover in the scrub oak. Then the worst possible turn of events, the air temperature climbed to 32 degrees and the snow turned to freezing rain. Birds near starvation must stay dry. Wet feathers wouldn't insulate properly and much needed energy would be wasted.

The rain continued through the night. Crusts of ice formed on the backs of the cranes, only to crack and fall when they walked. His broken wing seemed to collect water, making warmth even less of a possibility.

By sunrise the storm had passed, leaving the world encased in a clear crystal coat. The wintry blast left grasses, soil, and even barbed wire fences covered with a thick layer of ice. The sounds of tree limbs, cracking from the weight of the frozen water, shot through the cold air. With the last of their strength, the two birds carefully made their way to the center of the field. What they needed most was food. They saw the corn that could keep them alive for a few more days, but the ice was too thick. The birds walked slowly, picking hopelessly at the ice-covered corn. Occasionally they found a defect in the ice and earned a few kernels.

Each night the clear sky sent the temperature dropping. Each morning their food, still clearly visible, was impossible to get. Starvation was a cruel predator. The same bond that kept them together for nearly three years was now only days, maybe hours, from causing them to die together.

From the far side of the field, she saw two people running towards them. Both cranes made a feeble attempt at escape. The humans, closing in fast, began shouting and flailing their hands over their hands. With the last of their strength, the birds headed for the shelter of the scrub oak less than a hundred yards away.

Suddenly, as if from nowhere, two more humans jumped up from the very spot the birds had counted on for safety. Escaping between the humans, both birds hit the net and fell to the ground, entangled in a mesh of nylon. Humans quickly surrounded her and held her to the ground. He struggled briefly, re-injuring the muscle tissue that had taken so long to heal, before the humans wrestled him to the ground also.

"Cover their eyes!" a woman in khaki canvas overalls, shouted. "And stay clear of those beaks."

Six hearts pounded with adrenaline—four human, two avian. One belonged to the thirteen-year-old boy who had been watching and worrying about this pair of sandhill cranes for over a month.

"Nice work, Corey," said the man from the wildlife hospital. "Another day or so and these two wouldn't have made it."

"Are they going to be alright?" asked the boy.

"That's hard to say at this point, I can tell you this much though, they'll have a much better night tonight than they did last night."

◆———————◆

SANDHILL CRANE FACTS
- Scientific name: *Grus canadensis*
- Cranes can be 48" tall, with a wingspan of 80".
- Cranes fly with an outstretched neck, while herons fly with their neck bent into a "U" shape.
- Sandhills have the oldest fossil record of any living bird … about 60 million years.
- The International Crane Foundation's 1999 Crane Count reported 10,626 sandhill cranes in Wisconsin.

Reprinted with permission of Big Bluestem Press
Copyright ©1999 Big Bluestem Press
12321 87th Street South
Wisconsin Rapids, Wisconsin 54494

Science Guide Task Force and Contributing Authors

This team of dedicated science educators spent many hours developing both the content and the context for *Planning Curriculum in Science*. The team committed their personal time, energy, and expertise to the project through both face-to-face meetings and electronic communication and worked tirelessly toward the goal of *science education for all students in Wisconsin*. The department expresses the utmost appreciation and thanks to the task force for taking the personal time and energy to make their goal a reality. Indeed, students in Wisconsin are lucky to have such a dedicated team of authors working for them on this guide.

Rhulene Artis
Director, Milwaukee Urban Systemic Initiative
Milwaukee Public Schools
Milwaukee, Wisconsin

Mark Klawiter
Science Teacher
Ladysmith High School
Ladysmith, Wisconsin

LeRoy Lee
Science Education Consultant
DeForest, Wisconsin

Wayne LeMahieu
WEST Executive Secretary
Sheboygan Falls, Wisconsin

Pat Marinac
Science Program Leader
Appleton Area School District
Appleton, Wisconsin

Tim Peterson
Science Program Leader
Marshall Public Schools
Marshall, Wisconsin

Paul Tweed
Science Teacher and Department Chairperson
Augusta High School
Augusta, Wisconsin

Lisa Wachtel
Science Coordinator
Madison Metropolitan School District
Madison, Wisconsin

Sue Whitsett
Science Teacher
Fond du Lac High School
Fond du Lac, Wisconsin

John Whitsett
Science Teacher
Fond du Lac High School
Fond du Lac, Wisconsin

Paul Williams
Professor Emeritus
University of Wisconsin–Madison
Madison, Wisconsin

Frank Zuerner
Science Teacher and Department Chairperson
Memorial High School
Madison, Wisconsin

Reviewers for the Guide

Special appreciation and recognition go to the reviewers of this guide. These individuals were asked to read and comment on the draft of the guide. Each was willing to give of his or her personal time to review and endorse the work of the task force and authors.

Abdallah Bendada
Eisenhower Coordinator
Department of Public Instruction
Madison, Wisconsin

Perry Cook
Associate Professor of Science Education
University of Wisconsin–Stevens Point
Stevens Point, Wisconsin

Harvey Hayden
Science Teacher and Science Coordinator
Wisconsin Rapids Public Schools
Wisconsin Rapids, Wisconsin

Robert Hollon
Professor of Science Education
University of Wisconsin–Eau Claire
Eau Claire, Wisconsin

Melody Orban
President, Wisconsin Elementary and Middle
    Level Science Teachers Association
Science Resource Teacher
Kenosha Unified School District
Kenosha, Wisconsin

Billie Earl Sparks
Professor of Mathematics
University of Wisconsin–Eau Claire
Eau Claire, Wisconsin

Julie Stafford
Project Director, Wisconsin Academy Staff
    Development Initiative
Wisconsin Educational Partnership Initiative
Chippewa Falls, Wisconsin

Peter Watts
President-Elect, Wisconsin Society of Science
    Teachers
Science Teacher
Watertown Public Schools
Watertown, Wisconsin

Pam Williams
Science Teacher
John Edwards High School
Port Edwards, Wisconsin

Acknowledgments

A special thanks goes to many individuals at the Wisconsin Department of Public Instruction and specifically to Lisa Albrecht, Beverly Kniess, Peggy Solberg, John Fortier, and Sue Grady. Each spent many extra hours assisting with the development of this guide, and without their dedication and energy, this guide would not have been possible.

Division for Academic Excellence

Jack Kean, Assistant State Superintendent
John Fortier, Assistant State Superintendent (Retired)
Sue Grady, Director, Content and Learning Team
Gerhard Fischer, Education Program Coordinator
Beverly Kniess, Program Assistant

Division for Reading and Student Achievement

Lisa Albrecht, Office of Educational Accountability
Maggie Burke, Assistant Director, Office of Educational Accountability
Peggy Solberg, Education Specialist, Office of Educational Accountability

Division for Learning Support: Equity and Advocacy

Barbara Bitters, Equity Team Director

Division for Libraries, Technology and Community Learning

Calvin J. Potter, Assistant State Superintendent
Kay Ihlenfeldt, Library Consultant

Office of the State Superintendent

Victoria Horn, Graphics Designer
Mark Ibach, Publications Editor
Sandi McNamer, Publications Director

The sandhill crane photograph is courtesy of Kate Fitzwilliams of the International Crane Foundation.
All photographs are courtesy of Robert Queen, Wisconsin Department of Natural Resources.
Bruce A. Brown of the Wisconsin Geological and Natural History Survey spent many hours preparing the captions for the chapter photographs.
Impressions Book and Journal Services, Inc., provided editing services for this publication.

Copyrighted Materials

Contents

Introduction

They put safety goggles on. Ziploc® bags are passed out, and the mystery compounds are on the supply table ready for use. Safety considerations are reviewed. "Using the two mystery compounds, water, and the Ziploc® bag, develop an investigation to uncover as much as you can about your mystery compounds. Keep a record of all observations," are both written on the board. The students begin to think, discuss, and work. "Check this out, It's getting hot, My bag is inflating," can be heard within the buzz of working chemistry students. The teacher circulates, asking students to explain what they are observing.

The next day two new instructions are on the board: "Ask a few questions about your observations of this reaction." "Develop a hypothesis to guide you in designing an experiment to try and answer one of your questions." This vignette, as described by task force member Paul Tweed, is a classroom example of the science represented in this guide. The vignette focuses on how students learn science concepts while actively engaged in doing science.

The *Guide to Planning Curriculum in Science* is designed as a tool to assist science curriculum committees and individuals plan a "science program."[1] The guide offers methods for a local committee to use when developing the curriculum for the program. The guide embraces *Wisconsin's Model Academic Standards for Science* published by the Department of Public Instruction (DPI 1998) and the *National Science Education Standards* published by the National Research Council (NRC 1996).

The task force made several fundamental assumptions while developing the guide. It is important that the district science committee or anyone using this guide agree with the following assumptions:

- Science education is for all students and all students must receive equal instruction in science.
- Science instruction must be guided by inquiry.
- Students learn science best when they can actively construct their own science concepts.
- Science concepts must be built grade-by-grade, from kindergarten through grade 12.
- Students must make connections among the concepts in order to understand science.
  Adopted by the Wisconsin Department of Public Instruction (DPI) Science Task Force, January 2000.

Throughout the guide a district science curriculum committee is called the "district team." Science concepts to be taught in kindergarten through grade 12 are thought of as the "curriculum." A glossary is provided for the dis-

[1] "Science program" is a term used by the science task force and means a K–12 science program that embraces the philosophy and concepts of the state and national science education standards. A science curriculum is part of that program.

trict team to refer to as they use the guide. A reference section is provided at the end of the guide, in addition to references and suggested further readings at the end of each chapter. A program evaluation tool has been developed and included to assist with improving the science program. The guide suggests ways to select science products, including textbooks, for a specific grade or grades. Classroom assessment is addressed as both a district and a classroom strategy that reveals how students are learning science to parents and teachers. Perhaps most importantly, this guide is built upon current research in science and science education. The guide presents the following chapters:

1) District vision about how students learn science that includes understandings about science and scientific literacy

2) A common understanding of what is meant by a K–12 standards-led science program

3) A coherent and focused curriculum that is linked to *Wisconsin's Model Academic Standards for Science*

4) Instructional practices that support students learning science

5) Assessment practices that are aligned with the curriculum and with teaching practices in a K–12 standards-led science program

6) Professional development for teachers of science and district professional development for all staff teaching science

7) Facilities and instructional resources needed to support the K–12 standards-led science program

8) Program evaluation that provides feedback for the K–12 standards-led science program

9) The future of science education.

Adopted by the Science Task Force, January 2000

Throughout the guide the science task force compares the K–12 science program to that of a jigsaw puzzle with each piece of the puzzle representing a chapter in the guide and symbolizing the interlocking nature of the science program. Each piece also represents the idea that the picture that emerges from the puzzle is incomplete unless all the puzzle pieces are joined together. As a special feature, a photograph representing a geological feature in Wisconsin accompanies each chapter. "Each geological feature is different and unique and is designed to provide a photographic mosaic of Wisconsin geology," indicated Bruce A. Brown, senior geologist for the Wisconsin Geological and Natural History Survey (WGNHS).

Finally, the guide presents a journey about teachers and teaching, learners and learning, the reform practices that are fundamental to the national and state standards for science, and the implementation of reform science at the local level.

References

National Research Council. 1996. *National Science Education Standards*. Washington, D.C.: National Academy Press.

Wisconsin Department of Public Instruction. 1998. *Wisconsin's Model Academic Standards for Science*. Madison, Wis.: Wisconsin Department of Public Instruction.

Chapter 1
Essential Components of a K–12 Science Program

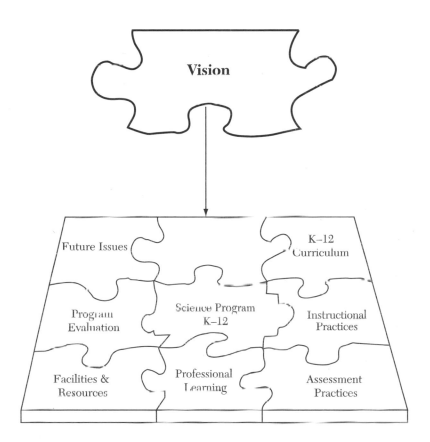

The figure illustrates the interlocking nature of the components of the standards-led science program. The power of the K–12 standards-led science program emerges when all the pieces of the program are present. Chapter 1 develops the vision for the standards-led science program, the first step toward scientific literacy.
Science Task Force, May 2000

How Do We Achieve Scientific Literacy for All Students?

The Vision

This scenic rock formation is an example of 1 billion-year-old Precambrian Lake Superior sandstone: Bruce A. Brown of the Wisconsin Geological Natural History Survey (WGNHS). Wisconsin Department of Natural Resources (DNR) photo.

Change is one of the most consistent factors of modern society. What the coming decades hold is difficult to imagine and impossible to predict. Today's students face a world that grows increasingly complex. Their futures will likely include dramatic changes that influence their schooling as well as the careers they pursue.

Educating our students has no higher purpose than providing a solid foundation for this future. Participating in quality programs will prepare students to lead personally fulfilling and socially responsible lives that encourage independent thinking and informed decision making. Science education plays an integral role in preparing and providing students with the essential knowledge and skills necessary for scientific literacy to construct this solid foundation.

"However, most Americans are not science-literate" (Rutherford and Ahlgren 1990). The *Third International Mathematics and Science Study* (NCES 1996) bears this out. These studies indicate that the achievement levels of American tenth graders taking science from the 1970s through the 1990s were equal only to those of developing countries. Findings from the *Third*

International Mathematics and Science Study-Repeat reinforce that little progress has been made toward the goals of scientific literacy (NCES 2000). Although Wisconsin students have demonstrated strong achievement in the past, one cannot be so complacent to assume this trend will continue.[1] Science educators must pay close attention to the information in each of those studies on scientific literacy to prepare our students for their global future.

This chapter provides guidance for establishing a science program that embodies high standards and excellence. Included in this chapter is summative research that will assist and support the *district team* in establishing a vision promoting scientific literacy for all students. Specifically, this chapter addresses the following questions:

- Why is science important to all students?
- How do students learn science?
- How does research on how students learn science impact the K–12 science program?

Why Is Science Important to All Students?

First, science is important to students because an understanding of science addresses a fundamental human trait—curiosity: the need or desire to know. Science can give students a way to interpret what they see in the natural world; it provides a means for understanding that world and provides a vehicle for incorporating that understanding into their everyday lives. The study of science satisfies and validates students' curiosities and provides the answers to many of their questions.

Science is a quest or journey that expands the realm of students' knowledge in numerous ways. Some of these ways are a system of active investigations; opportunities for students to use their senses; engaging students in observations; and evoking a sense of wonder, prompting more questions and further investigation. Through investigations, questions are asked, and models or ideas are developed and tested. Models or ideas are accepted or refuted based on their abilities to predict the behavior of natural or human events.

Science develops theories that provide a context for understanding and predicting the behavior of nature. These theories are based on facts collected through observation and experimentation. They are not wild guesses or unsubstantiated ideas; they are explanations of how nature works. Theories change when observations contradict them.

Many other fields of study are based on the principles of observation, rational argumentation, and logic, but they do not include principles of prediction, experimentation, and validation of prediction. Science gives students the capacity to deepen their understandings of the natural world, thereby helping to bridge the gap between the realms of believing and knowing. Without the ability to know and confidently predict the behavior of nature, students would be left with only belief and superstition. An argument based on verifiable evidence is

---

[1] Wisconsin student achievement data from NCES (1998).

different from one based on metaphysics or other ways of knowing. Science allows students to know something with an acceptable level of certainty.

Second, science is important to students because an understanding of science leads to scientific literacy, a prerequisite for functioning in modern society, and prepares students for their futures. The National Research Council (NRC 1996, 22) provides the following definition of scientific literacy. "Scientific literacy means that a person can ask, find, or determine answers to questions derived from curiosity about everyday experiences. It means that a person has the ability to describe, explain, and predict natural phenomena. Scientific literacy entails being able to read with understanding articles about science in the popular press and to engage in social conversation about the validity of the conclusions. Scientific literacy implies that a person can identify scientific issues underlying national and local decisions and express positions that are scientifically and technologically informed. A literate citizen should evaluate the quality of scientific information on the basis of its source and the methods used to generate it. Scientific literacy also implies the capacity to pose and evaluate arguments based on evidence and to apply conclusions from such arguments appropriately."

From this definition of scientific literacy, there are recognized attributes that describe scientifically literate people:

Our vision is a scientifically literate society.

Science Task Force, February 2000

- They use scientific knowledge, problem-solving skills, and informed attitudes in making responsible everyday decisions.
- They understand how society influences science, as well as how science influences society.
- They understand that society limits science through the allocation of resources.
- They recognize both the potential and limitations of science in advancing human and ecological welfare.
- They have a broad understanding of the conceptual schemes of scientific knowledge and are able to apply the understanding in various situations.
- They have an intellectual interest in science.
- They are curious about the natural world.
- They understand that new scientific knowledge results from inquiry that uses prior knowledge.
- They distinguish between scientific knowledge and personal opinion.
- They recognize the origins of scientific knowledge and understand that scientific knowledge is subject to change.
- They have a richer, more exciting view of the world. [2]

How Do Students Learn Science?

To achieve scientific literacy, it is important to consider findings in the research on how students learn. Knowing about student learning will enable the

[2] Attributes were adapted from DPI (1993).

district team to develop a K–12 standards-led science program that links curricular goals to student learning.

Yager (2000) summarized Simpson's 1963 article on the nature of science as consisting of four facets:

1. Wondering about and questioning events and objects in the natural world
2. Offering explanations about the objects and events encountered
3. Designing experiments as a means of collecting evidence to see if explanations have validity
4. Communicating the evidence collected to others with the hope that they will agree with the explanation and accept the evidence provided.

Simpson's four facets of science still hold true today and account for much of how students should learn science. Learning in science is not just about reading a textbook or memorizing facts. Learning in science is about having the opportunity to rely on one's own knowledge to construct new scientific understandings and concepts. Learning in science is about being able to rely on prior knowledge and transferring knowledge gained to new situations. This clearly means that students should participate actively in the acquisition of scientific knowledge.

One area of research examining how students learn in science is called *expert/novice* studies. Although these studies are usually conducted with adults, Gobbo and Chi (1986) have examined the research with children who were categorized as experts or novices, based on knowledge. Their research has identified several important differences between the knowledge of experts and the knowledge of novices. First, as might be expected, experts have substantially more and deeper factual knowledge than do novices. More importantly, this knowledge exists in a conceptual frame. This means that experts think contextually, whereas novices tend to think by relying on surface and isolated facts. Second, experts group their knowledge more effectively than novices, thus making it easier to retrieve when needed to solve domain problems, which experts can do better than do novices (Gobbo and Chi 1986).

Lowery (2000) agreed with Gobbo and Chi's findings when he applied expert/novice research to the science classroom. He stated that the typical student begins to learn science at the novice level and then, through the learning process, can become an expert learner on the science being taught. Lowery proposes three formats for learning science: hands-on, pictorial/ representational, and symbolic/narrative. Hands-on learning, says Lowery, allows students to use as many senses as possible. Pictorial/representational learning, sometimes referred to as passive learning, restricts the number of senses used by students, according to Lowery. He considers symbolic/narrative learning to be abstract and difficult for students because they typically can use only the sense of sight during the learning process.

Science classroom activities where students are actively exploring science (hands-on science) provide opportunities for students to become experts on the science being studied. Pictorial/representational classroom activities include using videos or simulations to represent science for the students, which may or may not allow students to become experts in the knowledge being presented. An example of a symbolic/narrative science activity is having students read science textbooks and memorize science content for a particular test or classroom event. This type of activity provides little or no opportunity for students to develop expertise in the science being studied. All three types of learning have a place in the science classroom, according to Lowery. However, he cautions that using only one type of learning may not give students the opportunity to become expert learners in the subject being studied.

Another area of research that examines how students learn is called *learning and transfer*. Research in this area found that students learned best when they had opportunities to experience and then transfer knowledge to familiar situations, because all new learning involves transfer. An example of learning and transfer was found when Hallinger and Williams stated that attempts to make schooling more relevant to the subsequent workplace have also guided the use of case-based learning in business schools, law schools, and schools that teach educational leadership (NRC 1999).

Learning and transfer research has direct implications for science education. Several critical factors must be considered: (1) Students learn best when motivated to spend the time needed to learn the complex subject matter found within science and to solve problems they find interesting. (2) The type of initial learning that engages students is a major factor in determining the development of expertise and transfer of the knowledge. (3) Students must be given opportunities to create and use the knowledge in a new situation. (4) Students must be given the time to learn for understanding and the opportunity to transfer this learning (NRC 1999).

Included in research on how students learn science is the work of Piaget. Piaget's research led to the constructivist philosophy prevalent in science education today. According to this philosophy, "learners bring their personal experiences into the classroom, and these experiences have a tremendous impact on students' views of how the world works" (Schulte 1996, 25). This means that knowledge exists within students', and that they must be able to construct their own meanings and understandings when learning science concepts.

The context for learning science is important for promoting and transferring knowledge. If students are to learn science this way, their metacognitions must be taken into account, they must be allowed to develop problem-solving tools for classroom learning, and, ultimately, they must have opportunities to transfer their understandings and skills to everyday environments.

Additional research on learners and learning includes that of Gardner's (1983) on multiple intelligences, which first appeared in his book *Frames of Mind*. Through his research, Gardner has hypothesized that human potential encompasses eight intelligence types: spatial, musical, kinesthetic, interpersonal, intrapersonal, verbal, mathematical, and naturalist. Information on how to apply Gardner's work in the classroom can be found in *Multiple Intelligences in the Classroom* by Thomas Armstrong.

Summative research on how students learn science is presented in the key findings from *How People Learn: Bridging Research and Practice* (NRC 1999).

Students come to the classroom with preconceptions about how the world works. If their initial understanding is not engaged, they may fail to grasp the new concepts and information that are taught, or they may learn them for purposes of a test but revert to their preconceptions outside the classroom.

(NRC 1999b, 10)

The understandings that students bring to the classroom are based on experiences that are built from the moment a child is born and added to each day. Building from these personal experiences is an important aspect of learning. If these experiences are not related to the concept being studied, the student will learn the concept for a short period of time but not retain the concept. This is often the case when students do well on short unit tests, but score poorly on culminating course exams.

Often these personal experiences lead to misconceptions about science. Those student-held misconceptions must be revealed to the teacher. By understanding the students' misconceptions, the teacher can provide instruction to replace the students' incorrect understandings with correct understandings. If the teacher allows the students to draw from their experiences to reveal misconceptions, they can replace the misconceptions with the correct understandings and then the correct understandings in science will then be retained. *Making Sense of Secondary Science: Research into Children's Ideas* is a publication dedicated solely to revealing students' misconceptions from international research studies and the *district team* may consider this an excellent source for science misconception. *A Private Universe* video and accompanying teacher workshop guide provide discussion topics for teachers of science on misconceptions that can develop in the science classroom.

To develop competence in an area of inquiry, students must: (a) have deep foundations of factual knowledge; (b) understand facts and ideas in the context of a conceptual framework; and (c) organize knowledge in ways that facilitate retrieval and application.

(NRC 1999b, 12)

This idea about students developing the ability to inquire within science emerges from research that encompasses the findings from expert and novice studies. Expert learners have the ability to draw from a richly structured information base and are able to make sense of facts and place them into a larger context. On the other hand, novice learners cannot complete this transfer of knowledge, and facts remain disconnected.

A "metacognitive" approach to instruction can help students learn to take control of their own learning by defining learning goals and monitoring their progress in achieving them.

(NRC 1999b, 13)

"Metacognitive" activities are ones in which students are allowed to verbalize their thinking as they work, monitor their own understanding carefully, and make note of when additional information is required for understanding.

Typically, metacognition takes the form of an internal conversation. Example: If the students know what they are attempting to learn or do, they can consciously assess whether learning is happening and in what way. It is often important and useful for the students to talk through this process. These "think aloud" protocols can also provide the teacher with valuable information about what and how the student is learning.

Students create and retain new knowledge when teachers design learning experiences in a manner that is consistent with how children naturally learn science. Through the acquisition of new knowledge, students can continually modify existing knowledge throughout their life. As more learning occurs, more concepts are modified and the learning (cognition of the learner) becomes more and more inclusive. As students move from grade to grade, science concepts become more highly organized and complex. Students are then able to think more abstractly and independently and formulate solutions to complex problems. Thus, students acquire the capacity to understand science and become scientifically literate citizens.

How Does the Research on How Students Learn Science Impact the K–12 Science Program?

Decisions about science programs must give full consideration to both the content that is to be taught and how students learn and develop understandings in science. Science-program decisions must be compatible with students' physical and intellectual development. The science task force agreed with the findings from *How People Learn: Brain, Mind, Experience, and School*, that successful science programs keep in mind the following:

- Understandings of how students learn science have changed over time as new research has been developed.
- Classroom practices and environments should reflect contemporary research and understandings of how students learn science.
- Assessment is a tool and an aid to understanding what students are learning in science as well as a guide to improve the teaching and learning process in science.

Decisions about the science program must promote the development of a learning community. Essential elements of a learning community in a science program include the following:

- *Classrooms where students are the focus.* Madrazo and Rhoton (2001) believe that because classrooms are becoming more ethnically and culturally diverse, it is essential that classrooms become more student centered. Additionally, St. John (2001) stated that students and teachers must work together to create a learning community. He described the learning community as one where everyone interacts and works together cooperatively to learn science.

■ *Classrooms that connect science to the broader community*. Recent research (NRC 1999) shows that classrooms throughout a K–12 science program must be connected to a broader community. This community includes homes, businesses, the geographic area a student is most familiar with, and the culture or cultures of that broader community. This community-centered approach to learning acknowledges that children learn from one another and that students bring knowledge from the broader community into the classroom.

■ *Classrooms that value the search for understanding in science*. Learning happens in classrooms where the search for understanding is valued and students and teachers have the freedom to make mistakes in order to learn. In contrast, in a classroom where the teacher tolerates no mistakes or incorrect answers, a student's willingness to ask questions is hindered. Students fear asking questions when they do not understand the material, limiting their search for scientific understanding. However, when the teacher uses statements or questions that encourage students to develop new ideas and pose new questions, engagement and the search for a deeper understanding soon follow. Meaningful learning occurs in classrooms where students can explore and test the validity of their statements or beliefs and, at the same time, challenge misconceptions that they might have. Through experiencing these types of activities, students are more likely to truly learn essential science content and concepts.

The following vignette (NRC 1999a, 164–165) provides an example of a science classroom where the students are the center of the activity and able to learn science content in a meaningful way.

The degree to which learning environments are community centered is important for learning.

Rhulene Artis
(Science Task Force member), 2000

Which Water Tastes Better?

The seventh- and eighth-grade students in the Haitian Creole bilingual program wanted to find the "truth" of a belief held by most of their classmates: that drinking water from the fountain on the third floor, where the junior high was located, was superior to the water from the other fountains in their school. Challenged by their teacher, the students set out to determine whether they actually preferred the water from the third floor or only thought they did.

As a first step, the students designed and took a blind taste test of the water from fountains on all three floors of the building. They found, to their surprise, that two-thirds of them chose the water from the first-floor fountain, even though they all said that they preferred drinking from the third-floor fountain. The students did not believe the data. They held firmly to their beliefs that the first-floor fountain was the worst because "all the little kids slobber in it." (The first-floor fountain is located near the kindergarten and first-grade classrooms.) Their teacher was also suspicious of the results because she had expected no differences among the three water fountains. These beliefs and suspicions motivated the students to conduct a second taste test with a larger sample drawn from the rest of the junior high.

The students decided where, when, and how to run their experiment. They discussed methodological issues: How to collect the water, how to hide the identity of the sources, and, crucially, how many fountains to include. They decided to include the same three fountains as before so that they could compare results.

They worried about bias in the voting process: What if some students voted more than once? Each student in the class volunteered to organize a piece of the experiment. About 40 students participated in the blind taste test. When they analyzed their data, they found support for their earlier results: 88 percent of the junior high students *thought* they preferred water from the third-floor fountain, but 55 percent actually chose the water from the first floor (a result of 33 percent would be chance).

Faced with this evidence, the students' suspicions turned to curiosity. Why was the water from the first-floor fountain preferred? How can they determine the source of the preference? They decided to analyze the school's water along several dimensions, among them acidity, salinity, temperature, and bacteria. They found that all the fountains had unacceptably high levels of bacteria. In fact, the first-floor fountain (the one most preferred) had the highest bacterial count. They also found that the water from the first-floor fountain was 20 degrees (Fahrenheit) colder than the water from fountains on the other floors. Based on their findings, they concluded that temperature was probably a deciding factor in taste preference. They hypothesized that the water was naturally cooled as it sat in the city's underground pipes during the winter months (the study was conducted in February) and warmed as it flowed from the basement to the third floor.

Reprinted with permission of National Research Council 1999a.

This vignette illustrates the need for students to have rich experiences that lead them to wonder and pose questions about their environment. Students need time for exploration. This is true of all students, regardless of family background, culture, or educational needs. Children are problem solvers and their curiosity generates questions and problems. Children attempt to solve problems presented to them and also seek novel challenges. They persist because success and understanding are motivating in their own right (NRC 1999). A learning community rich in sensory experiences and opportunities for expression cultivates new avenues of learning and continuously expands students' learning capacities.

Conclusion and Implications

The vision for any science program is that students become scientifically literate. The preceding vignette provides a glimpse into a classroom founded on that vision, and this chapter provides the foundation for achieving it. The district team should use the information in this chapter to guide them through the process of developing a science program capable of meeting state and national science education standards.

The task force compared the work of developing a standards-led science program to a journey. The journey begins with the end in mind: the attainment of scientific literacy for all students by the time they graduate from the district program. Chapter 2 begins to develop the road map the district must use throughout the journey and maps out strategies for formulating a K–12 standards-led science program.

References

Appendix A.

Armstrong, Thomas. 1994. *Multiple Intelligences in the Classroom*. Alexandria, Va.: Association for Supervision and Curriculum Development.

Gardner, Howard. 1983. *Frames of Mind: The Theory of Multiple Intelligences*. New York: Basic Books.

Gobbo, C., and M. Chi. 1986. How Knowledge is Structured and Used by Expert and Novice Children. *Cognitive Development* 1: 221–37.

Lowery, Lawrence F. 1998. *The Biological Basis of Thinking and Learning*. Berkeley, Calif.: FOSS.

Lowery, Lawrence F. 2000. Presentation at the Cutting Edge Conference, 13–15 July at Chippewa Falls, Wis.

Madrazo, Gerry M. Jr., and Jack Rhoton. 2001. Principles and Practices in Multicultural Science Education: Implications for Professional Development. In *Professional Development Leadership and the Diverse Learner*, Arlington, Va.: National Science Teachers Association Press.

NCES (National Center for Education Statistics). 1996. *Pursuing Excellence: A Study of U.S. Eighth-Grade Mathematics and Science Teaching, Learning, Curriculum, and Achievement in International Context, Initial Findings from the Third International Mathematics and Science Study (TIMSS)*. Washington, D.C.: U.S. Department of Education.

———. 1998. *Linking the National Assessment of Educational Progress and the Third International Mathematics and Science Study: Eighth-Grade Results*. Washington, D.C.: U.S. Department of Education.

———. 2000. *Highlights from the Third International Mathematics and Science Study-Repeat (TIMSS-R)*. Washington, D.C.: U.S. Department of Education.

NRC (National Research Council). 1996. *National Science Education Standards*. Washington, D.C.: National Academy Press.

———. 1999a. *How People Learn: Brain, Mind, Experience, and School*. Washington, D.C.: National Academy Press.

———. 1999b. *How People Learn: Bridging Research and Practice*. Washington, D.C.: National Academy Press.

Rutherford, F. James, and Andrew Ahlgren. 1990. *Science for All Americans*. New York: Oxford University Press.

Schulte, P.L. 1996. A Definition of Constructivism. *Science Scope* 20(3): 25–27.

St. John, Mark. 2001. Presentation to the Council of State Science Supervisors, 26–28 January at Washington, D.C.

Wisconsin Department of Public Instruction. 1993. *A Guide to Curriculum Planning in Science*. 1986. Reprint. Madison, Wis.: Wisconsin Department of Public Instruction.

———. 1998. *Wisconsin's Model Academic Standards for Science*. Madison, Wis.: Wisconsin Department of Public Instruction.

Yager, Robert. 2000. Real-World Learning: A Necessity for the Success of Current Reform Efforts. *ENC Focus* 7 (3): 18–19. Summarizing from Simpson, G.G. 1963. Biology and the Nature of Science. *Science* 139(3550): 81–88.

Additional Reading

NCES (National Center for Education Statistics).1998. *Linking the National Assessment of Educational Progress and the Third International Mathematics and Science Study: Eighth-Grade Results*. Washington, D.C.: U.S. Department of Education.

NRC (National Research Council). 1999. *Global Perspectives for Local Action, Using TIMSS to Improve U.S. Mathematics and Science Education*. Washington, D.C.: National Academy Press.

Misconceptions in Science:

Appendix A.

Driver, R., Ann Squires, Peter Rushworth, and Valerie Wood-Robinson. 1994. *Making Sense of Secondary Science. Research Into Children's Ideas*. London: Routledge.

Annenberg/CPB Corporation. 1995. Math and Science Collection. *A Private Universe* video and *The Private Universe Teacher Workshop Guide*. Harvard Smithsonian Center for Astrophysics at Harvard University.

Chapter 2
Essential Components of a K–12 Science Program

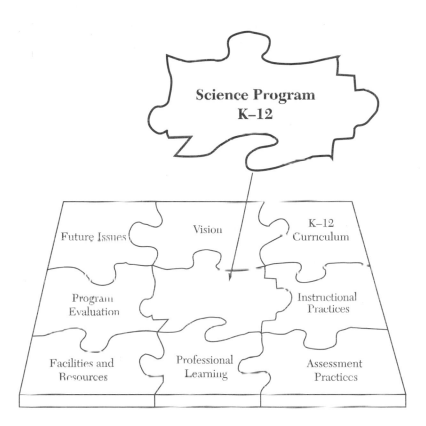

The figure illustrates the interlocking nature of the components of the standards-led science program. The power of the K–12 standards-led science program emerges when all the pieces of the program are present. Chapter 2 provides an overview of the science program.

Science Task Force, May 2000

What Does a Standards-Led Science Program Look Like?

Planning for the Change

Stream flowing over Precambrian basalt flows, Copper Falls State Park: Bruce A. Brown of the WGNHS. Wisconsin DNR photo.

Children take to science naturally. The many wonders of science and nature provide curiosity for all children. They seek answers to questions such as "How does a cloud form?" and "Why does it rain?", and they ask questions about their world before ever stepping into a formal classroom.

School districts and teachers strive to foster and develop children's natural curiosities and to ground that curiosity in the context of science. In short, this is schooling that is led by the standards, and implementing this process is not an easy task.

Developing a standards-led science program requires changes in planning science and changes in thinking about how science should be taught. Developing a standards-led science program requires new conversations that include staff members responsible for science education, parents, and students taking science. Standards-led science programs call for new conversations about how students learn science, acquire skills and knowledge in science, and gain access to science information. Finally, standards-led science programs require new types of professional development to guide the district through program implementation. This chapter will focus on the essential questions that *district teams* need to consider while planning a standards-led science program.

Specifically, the chapter will provide answers to the following questions:

- What is a standards-led science program?
- What principles should guide the district team as they develop a standards-led science program?
- How does a district team develop a K–12 standards-led science program?
- What if the district team wants to examine one part of the district science program, such as one grade or one course?

What Is a Standards-Led Science Program?

A standards-led science program, as defined by the science task force, is a K–12 science program that embraces the philosophy and concepts of the state and national science education standards. The publication, *Designing Mathematics or Science Curriculum Programs* (NRC 1999) compares the development of a K–12 standards-led science program to that of a story that develops over days, months, and even years. The story may include many other stories, some told simultaneously and some told over time with interdependence between them. Some of the stories unfold progressively, with the levels of complexity and conceptual understanding increasing from one segment to the next. Teachers and students are experiencing the stories together, and the stories continue from grade to grade until each student completes the formal part of the story by graduating.

The *National Science Education Standards (NSES) Program Standards* (NRC 1996) provide the criteria for the quality and conditions for development of a district standards-led science program. The program standards focus on the issues at the district level that relate to opportunities for students to learn science. They provide the foundation for the development of a district standards-led science program. The program standards are rooted in the assumption that district design and implementation of standards-led science programs are necessary to provide comprehensive and coordinated experiences for all students in all grades. Through these coordinated and comprehensive experiences, students learn science more effectively.

As the district team moves forward with the development of the K–12 science program the *NSES Program Standards* (NRC 1996, 209–225) are an excellent source of guidance. To assist the district team, a list of the program standards follows.

Program Standard A

All elements of the K–12 science program must be consistent with the other *National Science Education Standards* and with one another and developed within and across grades to meet a clearly stated set of goals.

- In an effective science program, a set of clear goals and expectations for students must be used to guide the design, implementation, and assessment of all elements of the science program.
- Curriculum frameworks should be used to guide the selection and development of units and courses of study.
- Teaching practices need to be consistent with the goals and curriculum frameworks.
- Assessment policies and practices should be aligned with the goals, student expectations, and curriculum frameworks.
- Support systems and formal and informal expectations of teachers must be aligned with the goals, student expectations, and curriculum frameworks.
- Responsibility needs to be clearly defined for determining, supporting, maintaining, and upgrading all elements of the science program.

Program Standard B

The program of study in science for all students should be developmentally appropriate, interesting, and relevant to students' lives; emphasize student understanding through inquiry, and be connected with other school subjects.

- The program of study should include all of the content standards.
- Science content must be embedded in a variety of curriculum patterns that are developmentally appropriate, interesting, and relevant to students' lives.
- The program of study must emphasize student understanding through inquiry.
- The program of study in science should connect to other school subjects.

Program Standard C

The science program should be coordinated with the mathematics program to enhance student use and understanding of mathematics in the study of science and to improve students' understanding of mathematics.

Program Standard D

The K–12 science program must give students access to appropriate and sufficient resources, including quality teachers, time, materials and equipment, adequate and safe space, and the community.

- The most important resource is professional teachers.
- Time is a major resource in a science program.
- Conducting scientific inquiry requires that students have easy, equitable, and frequent opportunities to use a wide range of equipment, materials,

supplies, and other resources for experimentation and direct investigation of phenomena.

- Collaborative inquiry requires adequate and safe space.
- Good science programs require access to the world beyond the classroom.

Program Standard E

All students in the K–12 science program must have equitable access to opportunities to achieve the *National Science Education Standards*.

Program Standard F

Schools must work as communities that encourage, support, and sustain teachers as they implement an effective science program.

- Schools must explicitly support reform efforts in an atmosphere of openness and trust that encourages collegiality.
- Regular time needs to be provided and teachers encouraged to discuss, reflect, and conduct research around science education reform.
- Teachers must be supported in creating and being members of networks of reform.
- An effective leadership structure that includes teachers must be in place.

Reprinted with permission of the National Research Council.

Table 2.1 (NRC 1996, 224) categorizes the positive influences the program standards can have on district science programs and should be used by the district team during their work on the K–12 standards-led science program. The left side of the table presents an interpretation of a more traditional science program. The right side presents a science program influenced by implementing the program standards, resulting in a standards-led science program.

The National Research Council (NRC) provides additional research about standards-led science programs. The NRC (NRC 1999, 9–10) states that standards-led science programs must achieve the following:

1. Focus on the important ideas and skills that are critical to the understanding of important phenomena and relationships and that can be developed over several age levels.
2. Help students develop an understanding of these ideas and skills over several years in ways that are logical and that reflect intellectual readiness.
3. Explicitly establish the connections among the ideas and skills in ways that allow students to understand both ideas and the connections among them.

TABLE 2.1 **Changing Emphases in K–12 Science Programs**

Less Emphasis On	More Emphasis On
Developing science programs at different grade levels independently of one another	Coordinating the development of the K–12 science program across grade levels
Using assessments unrelated to curriculum and teaching	Aligning curriculum, teaching, and assessment
Maintaining current resource allocations for books	Allocating resources necessary for hands-on inquiry teaching aligned with the *Standards*
Textbook- and lecture-driven curriculum	Curriculum that supports the *Standards* and includes a variety of components, such as laboratories emphasizing inquiry and field trips
Broad coverage of unconnected factual information	Curriculum that includes natural phenomena and science-related social issues that students encounter in everyday life
Treating science as a subject isolated from other school subjects	Connecting science to other school subjects, such as mathematics and social studies
Science learning opportunities that favor one group of students	Provide challenging opportunities for all students to learn science
Limiting hiring decisions to the administration	Involving successful teachers of science in the hiring process
Maintaining the isolation of teachers	Treating teachers as professionals whose work requires opportunities for continual learning and networking
Supporting competition	Promoting collegiality among teachers as a team to improve the school
Teachers as followers	Teachers as decision makers

Reprinted with permission of National Research Council.

Quality science programs (standards-led programs) are student focused.

Science Task Force, March 2000

4. Assess and diagnose what students understand to determine the next steps in instruction.

Using the *NSES Program Standards* and the NRC research, the science task force established the following essential components for a standards-led science program:

- District vision about how students learn science that includes understandings about science and scientific literacy
- A common understanding of what is meant by a K–12 science standards-led science program
- A coherent and focused curriculum that is linked to the state academic standards
- Instructional practices that support students learning science
- Assessment practices that are aligned with the curriculum and with teaching practices in a K–12 standards-led science program

- Professional development for teachers of science and district professional development for all staff teaching science
- Facilities and instructional resources that support the K–12 standards-led science program
- Program evaluation that provides feedback for the K–12 standards-led science program
- The future of science education
  Adopted by the Wisconsin Department of Public Instruction (DPI) Science Task Force, March 2000.

A standards-led science program is like a jigsaw puzzle, in that the true picture is not fully known until each puzzle piece is in place. If one piece is missing, the puzzle's picture is incomplete. Pat Marinac of the task force illustrated the analogy of a standards-led science program in Figure 2.1. The diagram illustrates the interlocking nature of the components of the standards-led science program. The power of the K–12 standards-led science program emerges when all of the pieces of the program are present.

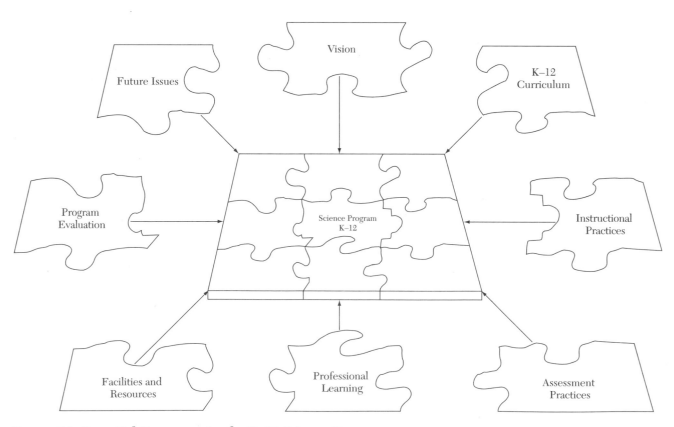

FIGURE 2.1 **Essential Components of a K–12 Science Program**

What Principles Should Guide the District Team As They Develop a Standards-Led Science Program?

To make the job of developing the science program easier, the district team should develop or adopt guiding principles. These principles should align with the district goals and mission statements and guarantee science education for all students.

To assist the district team in this endeavor, the science task force has provided a number of guiding principles. Collectively, these principles give the district team the foundation necessary to ensure a high-quality standards-led science program for all students. The principles range from what is meant by science education and scientific literacy, mapped out in Chapter 1, to more complex concepts about how students successfully learn science.

Some of the guiding principles are obvious; some are not. Sometimes it will be difficult for the district team to agree with all of the principles about school science, but agreeing on a common set of principles is essential to the success of a standards-led science program. The science task force drafted the following principles in March 2000:

1. Science education is based on agreed upon definitions of science and scientific literacy.
2. All students must achieve scientific literacy[1] by the time they complete the K–12 science program.
3. The science program must be focused on the learner.
4. *Wisconsin's Model Academic Standards for Science (WMASS)* are the cornerstones for the standards-led K–12 science program and provide the fundamental knowledge students need to be science literate.
5. Each of the eight content standards in science must be taught in all science classes and science courses.
6. The science program must provide adequate time for teaching science at all grades.

Each of these principles is explicated in greater detail below to help the district team develop guiding principles:

1. *Science education is based on agreed-upon definitions of science and scientific literacy.* The belief that the natural world is explainable is fundamental to both the state and the national science education standards and essential to the development of a standards-led science program. To assist the district team with this principle, the task force offers definitions of science and scientific literacy in Chapter 1.

If the district team chooses to develop their own definitions of science and scientific literacy, they should treat the definitions in Chapter 1 as a

> *It is the task of educators to overlay the nature and discipline of formal science with students' natural curiosities.*
>
> Sue Whitsett (Science Task Force member), 2000

---

[1] Scientific literacy is based on the *WMASS*. Although the statement does not acknowledge that learning is a life long experience, it is implied.

model. It is important to keep in mind that definitions developed by the task force are consistent with the state and national science education standards. By agreeing to this principle, the district team will establish a common understanding of the definitions of science and scientific literacy that will set the stage for all future work.

2. *All students must achieve scientific literacy[2] by the time they complete the K–12 science program.* The importance of this principle is reflected in the following passage from the *NSES* (NRC 1996, 2):

> The intent of the *Standards* can be expressed in a single phrase: science standards for all students. The phrase embodies both excellence and equity. The *Standards* apply to all students, regardless of age, gender, cultural or ethnic background, disabilities, aspirations, or interest and motivation in science. Different students will achieve understanding in different ways, and different students will achieve different degrees of depth and breadth of understanding, depending on interest, ability, and content.

This position is supported by the DPI. In the publication, *Educational Assessment and Accountability for All Students,* former State Superintendent John Benson stated, "*All* children, including children with disabilities deserve the fullest educational experience our schools can provide. This includes the right to be involved in the general curriculum and, to the maximum extent possible, meet the same challenging expectations that have been established for all children" (DPI 2000a, vii).

Although underserved student populations vary from district to district, it is essential that a science program provide the opportunities to meet the needs of all students. In Wisconsin, typical underserved populations in science include students from minority cultural or ethnic backgrounds, students tracked because of abilities and postsecondary interests and aspirations, and students from low-income families (DPI 2001).

A standards-led program must do more than acknowledge that science education is for all students. In addition, the district team must examine the science program to assure that instructional strategies reflective of the needs of individual learners are employed. In the article *Moving Into the Mainstream: From Equity A Separate Concept to High Quality Includes All,* Campbell and Kreinberg (1998; quoted in You 2001, 2) stated that "Equal treatment for all students does not necessarily lead to high-quality instruction in mathematics and science." They further stated that in an equitable school, "differences in achievement will not be based on race, ethnicity, gender, or physical disability. If students' achievement can be predicted by their gender, race, ethnicity, or physical ability, then the system is inequitable and must be changed."

As stated in the *Guide to the Achievement Gap,* "We must close the achievement gap. Only then can we assure that Wisconsin will continue to meet the employment and community needs for a bright future" (DPI 2000b,

---

[2] Scientific literacy is based on the *WMASS*. Although the statement does not acknowledge that learning is a lifelong experience, it is implied.

2). To help educators determine the degree to which their science programs are equitable, the *ENC Focus* issue on *Teaching in the Standards-Based Classroom* cited indicators developed by the New Jersey Statewide Systemic Initiative to examine equity in their science programs. This list can help guide the district team in determining if educational equity in their districts meets national standards (You 2001).

CURRICULUM, INSTRUCTION, AND ASSESSMENT

- Are the teachers implementing standards-led science instructional programs in ALL their classes?
- Do teachers use real-world problems to connect science to students' lives?
- Are the teachers given sufficient resources and equipment to implement inquiry science?
- Are the instructional materials free from bias?
- Does the classroom environment have posters reflecting the contributions of all cultures to science?
- Are all students actively engaged in cooperative learning teams that are heterogeneously mixed? Is there individual accountability for group activities?
- Are alternative assessment strategies used to assess student achievement?
- Do teachers receive professional development in multiple learning styles, teacher/student interaction, and diversity?
- Do guidance counselors receive professional development on expectations, equity, and career development in encouraging all students to consider careers in science?

DISTRICT POLICIES AND PRACTICES

- What are the district policies on tracking and grouping students in science?
- Does the district collect data by gender and equity?
- Are some groups placed in lesser numbers in high-level classes or in greater numbers in low-level classes than their percentages of the total student population would suggest?
- If differentials exist, is the district developing strategies to deal with the differences between over and underrepresented groups in the district?
- Are the requirements in science applicable to all students? Can all students take all types of science classes?
- What criteria are used to enroll students in advanced science classes, and what criteria are used for enrolling students in basic or compensatory classes? Is there representation of ALL students in the classes?
- What are the referral and classification practices for special education? What types of students are enrolled in or classified as special education?
- What are the district practices regarding language-minority students? Are there sufficient support systems in place for English as a second language students?

This chapter maps out the district team's journey toward the standards-led science program.

Science Task Force, May 2000

- Are parents involved in programs at the schools?
- Do parents serve as role models or guest speakers to talk to students about their careers or occupations in science?
- Are there community outreach programs that educate parents about the kinds of science students are taking?

You, A. (2001). High Standards for All—A Key Ingredient of Systemic Reform. ENC Focus 8(2) 4–45. *Reprinted with permission of Eisenhower National Clearinghouse. visit ENC online (http://www.enc.org).*

3. *The science program must focus on the learner.* The concepts students are learning should be consistent with their past experiences and their intellectual development. Meaningful learning occurs when educators use learners' existing concepts and allow new knowledge to enhance and refine those concepts (DPI 1986). In addition, the program must respect and embrace the cultural background of each student. Research findings from learner-focused science are discussed in Chapter 1.

Science faculty must recognize that science pervades all areas of life, and that, in a learner-focused program, many topics will arise in the process of teaching science. Some topics may be controversial, difficult to express, and contrary to individual beliefs. Because of the diverse social, economic, and religious backgrounds among students, a similar diversity in values and opinions should be expected and even welcomed. It is important to encourage an environment where this diversity can be accepted, appreciated, and perhaps even celebrated by other students.

4. *Wisconsin's Model Academic Standards for Science are the cornerstones for the standards-led K–12 science program and provide the fundamental knowledge students need to be science literate.* The innermost circle of Figure 2.2, "Enduring Understandings in Science," represents the *WMASS*. These enduring understandings[3] are the concepts that all students are expected to learn and retain (Wiggins and McTighe 1998, 10). This is contrary to the long list of random concepts often found in textbooks, represented by the outermost circle. The "Important Science Ideas" circle[4] represents concepts that students may learn, as time permits.

Paul Tweed of the task force, in an electronic communication in April 2001, explained the concept of enduring understandings in science in the following manner: "In science the nature of knowledge changes." He went on to say that "Enduring understandings in science represent core understandings and abilities required for lifelong learning and problem solving." He divides enduring understandings into four categories:

- Science as history: the facts, the books, the articles, sometimes even trivia

[3] Wiggins and McTighe use the term "enduring understanding" to mean a concept that is learned and retained throughout a person's life; the task force uses the same meaning for the term.
[4] From *Understanding by Design* by Wiggins, G., & McTighe, J. Alexandria, Va.: Association for Supervision and Curriculum Development. Copyright © (1998) ASCD. Reprinted by permission. All rights reserved.

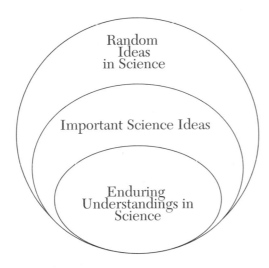

FIGURE 2.2

- Science as "the need to know" information for problem solving, research, social, and environmental citizenship
- Science as knowledge that is gathered, understood, and validated
- Science as a way of knowing, a research activity, or a process.

Tweed views all four knowledge categories as equally important and, therefore, advises that individual attention be given to each one, assuring enduring understanding of the WMASS.

5. *Each of the eight content standards in science must be taught in all science classes and science courses.* All students in Wisconsin are required to take a minimum of two credits of science during high school (grades 9 through 12). The Council of Chief State School Officers (CCSSO) report indicates that almost 70 percent of Wisconsin students take three or more science courses during high school (CCSSO 1999). District teams must carefully consider the implications of these data and determine if all students are receiving equitable instruction in the WMASS. This opportunity to learn issue is a concern where there is disparity among the number of science courses students take in high school. The WMASS were developed under the two science-credits requirement. However, the DPI WMASS Task Force recommended that all students take three or more high school science courses. Also, many universities and colleges require three high school science credits for admission.

Each of the WMASS should be a part of each science course, regardless of the type of course. For instance, an eighth grade physical science or earth science class should include instruction in all of the WMASS Content Standards (DPI 2000c).

The following tables indicate suggested instructional times for each of the WMASS in the K–12 science program and are derived from the previous *Guide to Curriculum Planning in Science* (DPI 1986). Because the current organization and nature of the science curriculum has changed to include the WMASS, these tables represent the *relative emphasis* of each content standard in the K–12 standards-led program. It is important to understand that this section refers to the content standards only. Figures 2.3–2.6 clearly illustrate the importance of addressing all of the content standards, regardless of the type of science course, such as integrated science, biology, or physical science. These tables are designed to assist the district team with planning a K–12 standards-led science program. Figure 2.3 shows the emphasis of science content standards in K–4 classrooms. Figures 2.4 and 2.5 represent the emphasis of science content standards in grades 5 through 8 and grades 9 through 12, respectfully. Figure 2.6 illustrates the relative emphasis of each content standard and how that changes throughout the K–12 standards-led science program.

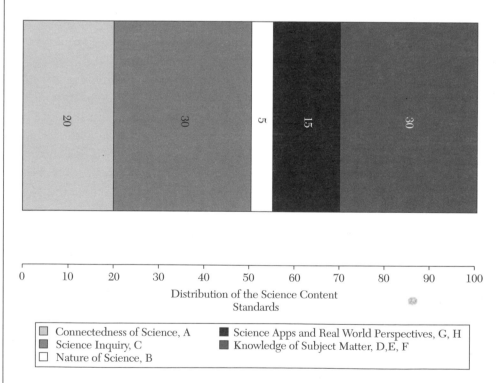

Distribution of the Science Content Standards

☐ Connectedness of Science, A	■ Science Apps and Real World Perspectives, G, H
■ Science Inquiry, C	■ Knowledge of Subject Matter, D,E, F
☐ Nature of Science, B	

FIGURE 2.3 **Science Content Standards and Their Emphasis in K–4 Science Classrooms**

Note: This chart represents the "relative emphasis" of each content standard. Relative emphasis means that for grades K–4 significance is placed on each content standard and that all the standards are connected.

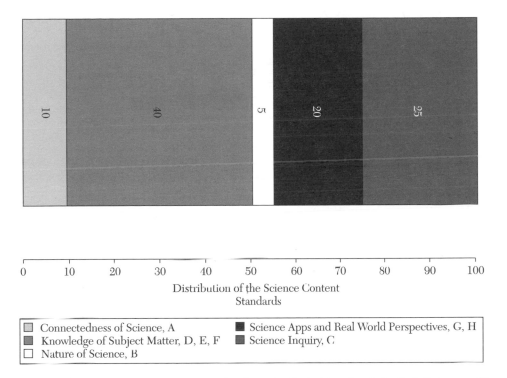

0   10   20   30   40   50   60   70   80   90   100

Distribution of the Science Content
Standards

☐ Connectedness of Science, A   ■ Science Apps and Real World Perspectives, G, H
■ Knowledge of Subject Matter, D, E, F   ■ Science Inquiry, C
☐ Nature of Science, B

FIGURE 2.4 **Science Content Standards and Their Emphasis in 5–8 Science Classrooms**
Note: This chart represents the "relative emphasis" of each content standard. Relative emphasis means that for grades
5–8 significance is placed on each content standard and that all the standards are connected.

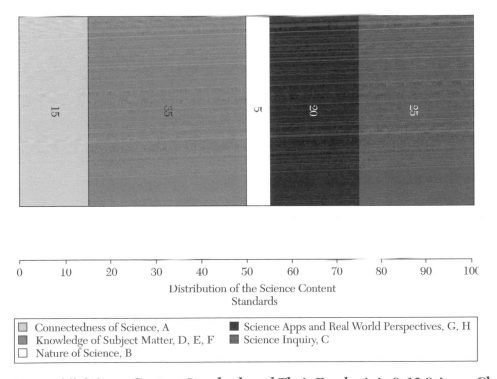

0   10   20   30   40   50   60   70   80   90   100

Distribution of the Science Content
Standards

☐ Connectedness of Science, A   ■ Science Apps and Real World Perspectives, G, H
■ Knowledge of Subject Matter, D, E, F   ■ Science Inquiry, C
☐ Nature of Science, B

FIGURE 2.5 **Science Content Standards and Their Emphasis in 9–12 Science Classrooms**
Note: This chart represents the "relative emphasis" of each content standard. Relative emphasis means that for grades
9–12 significance is placed on each content standard and that all the standards are connected.

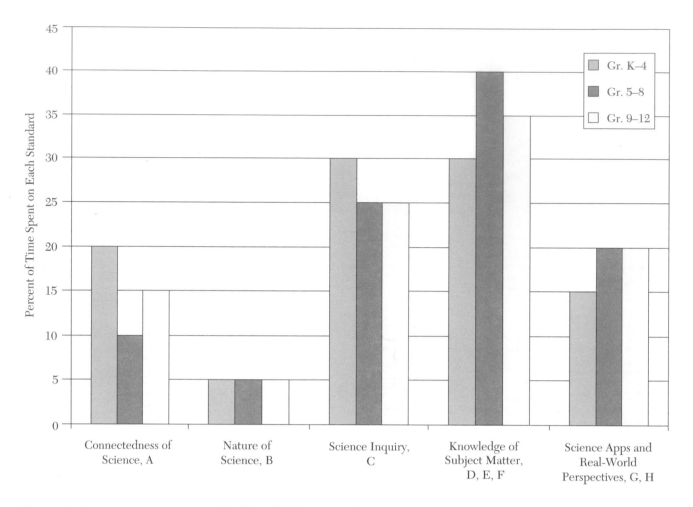

FIGURE 2.6 **Science Content Standards and Their Emphasis in Combined K–12 Science Classrooms**

6. *The science program must provide adequate time for teaching science at all grades.* The previous DPI science curriculum guide, published in 1986, gives recommendations for minimum times for science instruction. These times are shown in Table 2.2. Although individual districts schedule differently, it is essential in planning the standards-led science program that sufficient time be allocated to meet the program's goals. When the task force discussed this principle, they concluded that the recommended time allocations in the table are still applicable to meeting the goals of a standards-led science program.

"Beyond sixth grade, DPI recommends that all required science courses meet for one full class period every school day" (DPI 1993, 27). The task force suggests that the district team make decisions about science courses or science program scheduling recognizing that districts have a variety of scheduling methods.

TABLE 2.2 **Time Allocation for Science Instruction**

Grade	K	1	2	3	4	5	6
Time	10% of total time	100 min/wk	100 min/wk	150 min/wk	150 min/wk	175 min/wk	250 min/wk

How Does a District Team Develop a K–12 Standards-Led Science Program?

A quality K–12 science program builds upon and integrates with other district strategic planning efforts. The flowchart in Figure 2.7 can help the district team organize the development of a K–12 standards-led science program. In the next sections, how each component of the flowchart contributes to the development of a K–12 standards-led science program is discussed in detail.

1. *The district should form the district team.* Ideally, everyone should be involved in developing a K–12 standards-led science program, whether the district team develops an overall program or works with part of the science program. Everyone should include faculty who teach science, parents, students taking science, and representative community members. This ideal situation, however, is unrealistic; consequently, the goal should be a group with a representative balance of teachers, parents, students, and community members.

It is important that the district team reflect the diversity of opinions about school science, including its purpose, how it is taught and evaluated, and what subjects are taught. Sensitivity toward race and gender is also essential when forming the district team. Sometimes, assembling a large, diverse group, such as the one described, can be difficult. As a convenience, it is suggested that a smaller working group be formed, with the larger group providing advisement.

2. The district team should begin by examining the current practices, policies, and programs in and research on science education reform to help guide the thinking of the district team. Science programs developed from current research on how students learn science are standards-led science programs. Chapter 1 is designed to help the district team reflect on the current research and assess how this research affects the science program. As the district team develops the program, the team should examine their current practices, policies, and programs. Several initial questions have been developed to provide glimpses into the existing program.

- Does the program reflect students' needs?
- Does the program define scientific literacy for all students?
- Is the curriculum coherent?
- Is the curriculum focused?
- Is the curriculum a K–12 curriculum?

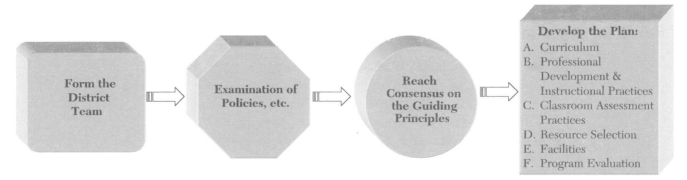

FIGURE 2.7 **Flowchart of Science Program Development**

- Has the program been evaluated?
- Do the instructional materials support students' needs for learning science?
- Is the district philosophy on how students learn consistent with what is being taught and learned in science?
- Are students happy when learning science?
- How closely does the science program align with the NSES program standards?

3. *The district team must reach a consensus on the guiding principles by either adopting the guiding principles provided by the task force or by developing district principles.* Establishing principles is important because they are the foundation for a standards-led science program. As the team moves toward consensus, it must keep in mind that the guiding principles should spell out the district's philosophy about science learning. Team members should keep a copy of the guiding principles and refer to it often, especially when trying to make a difficult decision. A variety of strategies for building consensus among team members exist. The publication *Teacher Change* (ENC 1999), provides several examples.

4. *The district team should develop a plan that includes all aspects of the science program: curriculum, instruction, assessment, professional development, facilities and resources, and evaluation.* A useful district plan is data driven, provides the support and resources needed to accomplish the plan, and includes professional development for all staff involved. It should include a timetable for implementing goals and activities, as well as mechanisms for monitoring progress and making course corrections to complete efficiently the plan's goals and activities. In some Wisconsin districts, success in developing and implementing a K–12 science program has been limited because the plan was too vague, lacked clear direction, or the assignment of responsibility was too diffuse.

The process used in developing the plan must be flexible and ongoing to take advantage of the changes that result from reform in science education. As reform takes hold in the district, new needs and challenges will arise. For example, professional development must grow and change as teachers grow and change. District populations will shift and change over time; therefore, it is important that the science program take into account demographic changes. This is important because demographic changes may cause changes in the overall science program. Another challenge comes with the increasing use of technology. Science programs must be able to take advantage of changes in technology.

The district team should integrate all district K–12 science activities into the overall science program plan, as the plan develops. Successful district science programs are ones in which a district avoids seeing science reform as a collection of projects. Instead, the district team should focus on systemic K–12 science reform. The science program plan must be comprehensive and represent all science being taught and learned at all grades, K–12.

Aspects of the K–12 science program plan are described briefly in the following section. These aspects are discussed in greater detail in the remaining chapters, which are previewed now to help readers better understand the detail they contain.

- *Curriculum.* Using the *WMASS*, the *NSES*, and what the district team has learned about how students learn science, the district team should develop the science curriculum for the standards-led science program. National publications specify a number of methods for developing curriculum, some of which are highlighted and presented below. Each method is provided as a vehicle for the district team to develop the district K–12 science curriculum. The district team must decide which method is most appropriate for their school district.

Several methods are sketched here:

Grade-by-grade benchmark method. Using the *WMASS*, the district team establishes and develops science topics and themes from grade to grade and course to course. As students understand a topic or theme, the emphasis then shifts to a new topic or theme. This method often results in an overall framework for a science curriculum that is benchmarked at each grade and allows for individual interpretation of the benchmarks. Often this method is valuable when a district is larger or where each school building in a district is responsible for curriculum. *Benchmarks for Science Literacy* (American Association for the Advancement of Science 1993) and *Designs for Science Literacy* (American Association for the Advancement of Science 2000b) are excellent resources for the grade-by-grade benchmark method.

Scope and sequence method. The district team determines the information that must be mastered during the student's K–12 science education as reflected in the *WMASS* or whatever other standard used by the district. The scope establishes procedures for teaching each concept. The process for developing a district scope and sequence typically involves making decisions about the scope of the standards and then deciding how the standards will be sequenced in each grade. Greater details of this approach are available from numerous sources, including *A Guide to Curriculum Planning in Science* (DPI 1986).

Relevant science concepts method. This method uses science concepts from sources, such as the *Benchmarks for Science Literacy*, the *NSES*, and the *WMASS*, or uses science concepts as defined by the local school district and articulates them for kindergarten through grade 12. The concepts are then mapped to the science subject matter, resulting in an overall framework for the district science program. Sometimes this method uses concept maps, such as those found in the *Atlas for Science Literacy*, (American Association for the Advancement of Science 2000a). Greater detail is also available in the publication *Resources for Science Literacy* (American Association for the Advancement of Science 1997).

Graphic organizers method. As a clarifying mechanism, the district team can construct graphical representations of key concepts, processes, and sequences for the standards. This method can be used

Wisconsin's Model Academic Standards for Science should be taught to all students at all grades, K–12.

Science Task Force, July 2000

to explain the *WMASS Content Standards* and even the performance statements that accompany each standard. Through the use of such representations, explicit science content is related to key concepts. This method can be used to show relationships between concepts.

Details of this process include a group first deciding on the key ideas, concepts, and processes from the standards. The group then graphically represents those ideas, concepts, and processes. It then looks for overall patterns and organizes the patterns into K–12 sequences. Lastly, the group graphically displays the pattern or patterns from grade to grade. This method provides a valuable visual representation of the curriculum and can show overlaps and gaps in the science program. Commercial software programs are available to help with this process.

A modification of this organizational method is to use Standard A, Science Connections, of the *WMASS* as the organizational overlay. The team first graphically represents each theme: systems, order, organization, and interaction; evidence, models, and explanations; constancy, change, and measurement; evolution, equilibrium, and energy; and form and function for kindergarten through grade 12. Standards B–G are then graphically linked to Standard A. The district team may also establish connections between science and the other disciplines.

- *Professional Development and Instructional Practices.* Through professional development for teachers of science, the district team should ensure that instructional practices are aligned with the K–12 standards-led science program. By providing professional development as described in Chapter 6, the district team will make sure that everyone teaching science has a common understanding of how science is to be taught and how students best learn science. Reaching this type of understanding about teaching and learning science takes time and requires on-going discussion and reflection on the practice of teaching. This common understanding ensures consistency in the practice and presentation of science.
- *Classroom Assessment Practices.* The district team should develop and use assessments that reveal what is being taught and learned from the standards-led science program. Assessment practices must be aligned with the science curriculum and instructional practices. Standards-led science programs require changes in the way that students are assessed, both formally and informally. Assessing students assists teachers in understanding how well or to what extent students are learning the essential science concepts. Assessment practices should reveal to parents, students, and teachers exactly what and how students are learning. Adjustments in what and how science concepts are being taught can be based on feedback from assessments.
- *Resource Selection.* Resources and instructional materials must support the standards-led science program. Five general criteria for resource evaluation were developed by the National Science Foundation and then published in the *Third International Mathematics and Science Study* (NCES 1996). Those criteria are presented in Chapter 7

and include strong scientific content, sound pedagogical design, assessment, equity, and implementation and support for the program. These criteria are summarized in the following paragraph.

Strong scientific content is scientifically accurate and includes information on the history and processes of science. Sound pedagogical design engages students in learning the science content. The pedagogical design should incorporate methods derived from current research on how students learn science. The instructional materials should include assessments that are an integral part of the science materials and are designed to determine how well students are learning the materials. To meet the equity criterion, materials and resources that meet all students' needs should be used. The materials should be unbiased and provide methods for meeting the needs of diverse learning populations. The instructional materials and resources should provide the district with strategies for achieving equitable science education, for implementing the program districtwide, and for appropriate professional training.

- *Facilities.* The district team should recommend facilities that support the effective implementation of a standards-led science program. Science classrooms and laboratories must be equipped to be consistent with the type of science program being implemented by the district. Standards-led science programs call for students to be actively involved in science through inquiry. Inquiry science programs require specialized facilities. For example, if water is needed, a teacher must have easy access to it. First and foremost, classrooms must be safe for students and teachers. Adequate ventilation, appropriate gas and electric fixtures, and proper storage cabinets for chemicals are only a few such requirements.

- *Program Evaluation.* The district team must establish a process for continuous evaluation of the program. The evaluation must be ongoing and provide feedback on the progress of implementing the standards-led science program. Evaluation provides for monitoring and feedback reflective of students' needs and identifies needed adjustments to the program. The district team must plan for, allow for, and value program evaluation.

What If the District Team Wants to Examine One Part of the Science Program, Such as One Grade or One Course?

To examine one grade or one course is not simple, because this type of examination should be done within the context of the overall science program. The first step is to evaluate the course or grade using the evaluation process in Chapter 6. Modifications may be needed to use the process for only one grade or course.

Before beginning a single grade or course examination, considering questions such as the following may be useful:

1. Is the evaluation being done within the context of the overall science program?
2. What is the real issue behind examining a single grade or course?
3. Will the examination lead to changes within the course or grade?
4. Will the examination lead to an appraisal of the overall science program?

Conclusion and Implications

"Planning for the Change" is the theme of this chapter. The chapter provides the district team with a road map toward achieving changes presented in this chapter. The changes are grounded in the *NSES* and the *WMASS* and reinforced by the science task force's guiding principles and essential components for a standards-led science program. Think of these essential components as the road map's guiding points. They are the focus of the remaining chapters.

Chapter 3 focuses on the standards-led science curriculum. It describes, in detail, what is essential for the standards-led science curriculum and attempts to guide the district team through rough spots or bumps in the road that leads to an effective standards-led science curriculum.

References

American Association for the Advancement of Science (AAAS). 1993. Project 2061. *Benchmarks for Science Literacy*. New York: Oxford University Press.

———. 1997. Project 2061. *Resources for Science Literacy*. New York: Oxford University Press.

———. 2000a. Project 2061. *Atlas for Science Literacy*. New York: Oxford University Press.

———. 2000b. Project 2061. *Designs for Science Literacy*. New York: Oxford University Press.

Armstrong, Thomas. 1994. *Multiple Intelligences in the Classroom*. Alexandria, Va.: Association for Supervision and Curriculum Development.

Campbell, Patricia B., and Nancy Kreinberg. 1998. *Moving Into the Mainstream: From Equity as a Separate Concept to High Quality Includes All*. Washington, D.C.: American Association for the Advancement of Science. Quoted in You, Aleta. 2001. "High Standards for All—A Key Ingredient of Systemic Reform." *ENC Focus* 8(2): 43–45.

Council of Chief State School Officers (CCSSO). 1999. *State Indicators of Science and Mathematics Education*. Washington, D.C.: CCSSO.

ENC (Eisenhower National Clearinghouse). 1999. *Teacher Change, Improving K–12 Mathematics*. Columbus, Ohio: Eisenhower National Clearinghouse.

NCES (National Center for Education Statistics). 1996. *Pursuing Excellence: A Study of U.S. Eighth-Grade Mathematics and Science Teaching, Learning, Curriculum, and Achievement in International Context, Initial Findings from the Third International Mathematics and Science Study (TIMSS)*. Washington, D.C.: U.S. Dept. of Education.

NRC (National Research Council). 1996. *National Science Education Standards*. Washington, D.C.: National Academy Press.

———. 1999. *Designing Mathematics or Science Curriculum Programs: A Guide for Using Mathematics and Science Education Standards*. Washington, D.C.: National Academy Press.

Wiggins, Grant, and Jay McTighe. 1998. *Understanding by Design*. Alexandria, Va.: Association for Supervision and Curriculum Development.

Wisconsin Department of Public Instruction. 1993. *A Guide to Curriculum Planning in Science*. Madison, Wis.: Wisconsin Department of Public Instruction. Reprint. 1986. Madison, Wis.: Wisconsin Department of Public Instruction.

———. 1998. *Wisconsin's Model Academic Standards for Science*. Madison, Wis.: Wisconsin Department of Public Instruction.

———. 2000a. *Educational Assessment and Accountability for All Students*. Madison, Wis.: Wisconsin Department of Public Instruction.

———. 2000b. *Guide to the Achievement Gap*. Madison, Wis.: Wisconsin Department of Public Instruction.

———. 2001. *Science Data Retreat Findings*. Madison, Wis.: Wisconsin Department of Public Instruction.

You, Aleta. 2001. "High Standards for All—A Key Ingredient of Systemic Reform." *ENC Focus* 8(2): 43–45.

Additional Readings

American Association for the Advancement of Science (AAAS). 1993. Project 2061. *Benchmarks for Science Literacy*. New York: Oxford University Press.

———. 1997. Project 2061. *Resources for Science Literacy*. New York: Oxford University Press.

———. 2000. Project 2061. *Atlas for Science Literacy*. New York: Oxford University Press.

———. 2000. Project 2061. *Designs for Science Literacy*. New York: Oxford University Press.

Appendix A

Appendix B

Appendix C

Appendix D

Eisenhower National Clearinghouse. 1999. *Teacher Change, Improving K–12 Mathematics*. Columbus, Ohio: Eisenhower National Clearinghouse.

Chapter 3
Essential Components of a K–12 Science Program

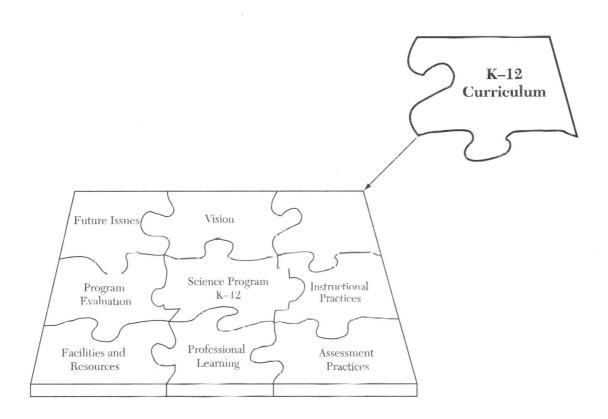

The figure illustrates the interlocking nature of the components of the standards-led science program. The power of the K–12 standards-led science program emerges when all the pieces of the program are present. Chapter 3 provides curricular examples that lead to K–12 scientific literacy.

Science Task Force, May 2000

What Should Students Learn in Science?

The Standards-Led Science Curriculum

The bluffs at Big Bay, Madeline Island, are Precambrian Lake Superior sandstone: Bruce A. Brown of the WGNHS. Wisconsin DNR photo.

Every day our students watch television programs that show sights and sounds from around the world, people who are more and more connected, and countries that are increasingly related. As explained in Chapter 1, students face a world that is changing daily. Those changes are the result of the global interactions and connectivity of people. Chapter 1 revealed the relationship of science to student learning, that students are curious about many things, and that science explains much of our natural and designed world. Chapter 2 discussed the essential components of a standards-led science program that allows all students to understand science leading to scientific literacy. From these chapters, the nature of a district science program is articulated.

Chapter 3 explores *Wisconsin's Model Academic Standards in Science (WMASS)* in detail to provide examples of specificity for the standards and to assist the *district team* in their development of a standards-led science curriculum. By answering key questions, the district team should be able to develop a local standards-led science curriculum.

The key questions to be answered by the district team are the following:

- What is a standards-led science curriculum?
- What are the science curriculum issues that face a district team when developing a standards-led science curriculum?

What Is a Standards-Led Science Curriculum?

The task force has defined a standards-led science curriculum as one that has been developed by the district and includes all science taught and learned from kindergarten through grade 12. The following two essential components of the definition give it greater clarity.

- The *WMASS* serve as the foundation for the science curriculum.
- The K–12 science curriculum must be coherent and focused.

To assist the district team develop the K–12 standards-led science curriculum, a narrative and examples for each component are presented. For the purposes of this discussion, coherence and focus are addressed separately. However, standards-led science curricula must be both coherent and focused. To illustrate how the two components can be addressed in a science curriculum, three district stories with examples of their curricula are available. Each district has chosen to approach the components differently; all three approaches, although different, do provide the district team with valuable guidance. Finally, the task force thought it would be helpful to provide additional examples of science curriculum that show coherence and focus. In these examples, curriculum is organized among three grade ranges: K–4, 5–8, 9–12. If the district team uses these examples, grade-by-grade focus will need to be established.

Wisconsin's Model Academic Standards for Science Serve As the Foundation for the Curriculum

Teaching students science is difficult because educators must prepare them for a world not as understandable as it once was. Even in a changing world, however, there are important science concepts that students must know and understand. Those concepts are developed and defined in the *WMASS* (DPI 1998) and identify *what* Wisconsin students should learn in science. The challenge to the district team is to answer the questions of *when* and *how* the standards are to be implemented. *When* refers to the point or grade where standards must be introduced, and *how* describes the classroom examples, teaching practices, and the instructional materials that encourage students to learn science.

Following is a summary of the *WMASS*. Each content standard has a number of associated performance statements at grades 4, 8, and 12 that are designed to provide detailed performance information for the content standards. The performance statements are not included in this summary, but can be easily obtained from several sources, such as web sites, local libraries, professional associations, district curriculum offices, the Department of Public Instruction (DPI), or the DPI Web site.

A. SCIENCE CONNECTIONS

Content Standard

Students in Wisconsin will understand that, among the science disciplines, there are unifying themes: systems, order, organization, and interactions; evidence, models, and explanations; constancy, change, and measurement; evolution, equilibrium, and energy; and form and function.

These themes relate and interconnect the Wisconsin science standards to one another. Each theme is further defined in the *WMASS* glossary.

Rationale: These unifying themes are ways of thinking rather than theories or discoveries. Students should know about these themes and realize that the more they learn about science the better they will understand how the themes organize and enlarge their knowledge. Science is a system and should be seen as a single discipline rather than a set of separate disciplines. Students will also understand science better when they connect and integrate these unifying themes into what they know about themselves and the world around them.

B. NATURE OF SCIENCE

Content Standard

Students in Wisconsin will understand that science is ongoing and inventive and that scientific understandings have changed over time as new evidence is found

Rationale: Students will realize that scientific knowledge is developed from the activities of scientists and others who work to find the best possible explanations of the natural world. Researchers and those who are involved in science follow a generally accepted set of rules to produce scientific knowledge that others can confirm through experimentation. This knowledge is public, replicable, and is revised and refined based on new experiments and data.

C. SCIENTIFIC INQUIRY

Content Standard

Students in Wisconsin will investigate questions using scientific methods and tools, revise their personal understanding to accommodate new knowledge, and communicate these understandings to others.

Rationale: Students should experience science in a form that engages them in actively constructing ideas and explanations and enhances their opportunities to develop scientific skills. Scientific inquiry should include questioning, forming hypotheses, collecting and analyzing data, evaluating results, reaching conclusions, and communicating procedures and findings to others.

D. PHYSICAL SCIENCE

Content Standard

Students in Wisconsin will demonstrate an understanding of the physical and chemical properties of matter, the forms and properties of energy, and the ways that matter and energy interact.

Rationale: Knowledge of the physical and chemical properties of matter and energy is basic to an understanding of the earth and space, life and environmental, and physical sciences. The properties of matter can be explained in terms of the atomic structure of matter. Natural events result from the interactions of matter and energy. When students understand how matter and energy interact, they can explain and predict chemical and physical changes that occur around them.

E. EARTH AND SPACE SCIENCE

Content Standard

Students in Wisconsin will demonstrate an understanding of Earth's structure and systems and that of other bodies in the universe and their interactions.

Rationale: Students gain a better understanding of Earth by studying its composition, history, and the processes that shape it. Understanding geologic, meteorological, astronomical, and oceanographic processes allows students to make responsible choices and to evaluate the consequences of their choices. In addition, all bodies in space, including Earth, are influenced by forces throughout the solar system and the universe. Studying the universe enhances students' understanding of Earth's origins, its place in the universe, and its future.

F. LIFE AND ENVIRONMENTAL SCIENCE

Content Standard

Students in Wisconsin will demonstrate an understanding of the characteristics and structures of living things, the processes of life, and how living things interact with one another and their environment.

Rationale: Students will enhance their natural curiosity about living things and their environment through study of the structure and function of living things, ecosystems, life cycles, energy movement (transfer), energy change (transformation), and changes in populations of organisms through time. Knowledge of these concepts and processes of life and environmental science will assist students in making informed choices regarding their lifestyles and in understanding their impacts on communities of living things.

G. SCIENCE APPLICATIONS

Content Standard

Students in Wisconsin will demonstrate an understanding of the relationship between science and technology and the ways in which that relationship influences human activities.

Rationale: Science and technology complement each other. Science helps drive technology and technology provides science with tools for investigation, inquiry, and analysis. Together, science and technology applications provide solutions to human problems, needs, and aspirations. Students should understand that advances in science and technology affect Earth's systems.

H. SCIENCE IN SOCIAL AND PERSONAL PERSPECTIVES
Content Standard
Students in Wisconsin will use scientific information and skills to make decisions about themselves, Wisconsin, and the world in which they live.
Rationale: An important purpose of science education is to give students a means to understand and act on personal, economic, social, political, and international issues. Knowledge of the earth and space, life and environmental, and physical sciences facilitate analysis of topics related to personal health, environment, and management of resources, and help evaluate the merits of alternative courses of action.

The district team must assume the responsibility of providing specificity for the standards. Table 3.1, developed by the task force, summarizes the performance standards for the *WMASS Content Standards* and suggests specific verbiage. The district team can use this summary or choose alternative verbiage to summarize the performance standards while the *team* is building the foundation for the K–12 standards-led science curriculum. Other interpretations of the standards are widely available and can be found in publications like *Benchmarks for Science Literacy, Project 2061.*

Coherence within the Science Curriculum

Chapter 2 provides several strategies for developing the curricula of the standards-led science program. Using one of those strategies, the team must now develop a *coherent* and *focused* K–12 curriculum. Coherence refers to the connectedness of the science curriculum, and focus refers to the K–12 enduring understandings in science. To help the district team understand coherence and focus, the concepts are presented separately. The following section explains each concept in detail.

Coherence in a standards-led science program can occur in two ways: sequential and curricular. First, the curriculum is *sequentially* coherent if it builds logically from lesson to lesson, unit to unit, and grade to grade, and begins with students' prior knowledge and refines and extends that knowledge with each new activity (NRC 1999). Second, the curriculum demonstrates coherence if its content standards interconnect as they are presented. This results in students having a unified understanding of science.

Figure 3.1 illustrates the vertical and horizontal articulation of a sequential and curricular coherent science program based on *WMASS*. From year to year, new experiences build logically upon the knowledge gained in previous years, thus establishing the sequential curriculum. At the same time, those experiences, although sometimes seated in a particular subject area, such as biology or earth science, are held together by careful attention to the interconnecting themes, such as science connections, applications, and inquiry. The

TABLE 3.1 **Wisconsin's Model Academic Standards for Science**

Standard	Grades K–4	Grades 5–8	Grades 9–12
Science Connections (A)	Systems, order, organization, and interactions; evidence, models, and explanations; constancy, change, and measurement; evolution, equilibrium, and energy; and form and function (definitions can be found in the *Wisconsin Model Academic Standards for Science*)	Systems, order, organization, and interactions; evidence, models, and explanations; constancy, change, and measurement; evolution, equilibrium, and energy; and form and function (definitions can be found in the *Wisconsin Model Academic Standards for Science*)	Systems, order, organization, and interactions; evidence, models, and explanations; constancy, change, and measurement; evolution, equilibrium, and energy; and form and function (definitions can be found in the *Wisconsin Model Academic Standards for Science*)
Nature of Science (B)	Science as a human endeavor Use of sources to answer questions about science People who have contributed to science	Nature of science and science concepts History of science Science has changed over time	Nature of scientific knowledge Historical perspectives Science assumptions Science research
Scientific Inquiry (C)	Language of science Abilities necessary to do scientific inquiry Understandings about scientific inquiry	Language of science Abilities necessary to do scientific inquiry Understandings about scientific inquiry	Language of science Abilities necessary to do scientific inquiry Understandings about scientific inquiry
Physical Science (D)	Properties of earth materials Position and motion of objects Light, heat, electricity, and magnetism	Properties and changes of properties in matter Motions and forces Transfer of energy	Structures of atoms and matter Chemical reactions Motions and forces Conservation of energy and the increase in disorder Interactions of matter and energy
Earth and Space Science (E)	Properties of earth materials Objects in the sky Changes in the earth and sky	Structure of the earth system Earth's history Earth in the solar system	Energy in the earth system Geochemical cycles The origin and evolution of the earth system The origin and evolution of the universe
Life and Environmental Science (F)	The characteristics of organisms Life cycles of organisms Organisms and their environment	Structure and function in living things Reproduction and heredity Regulation and behavior Populations and ecosystems Diversity and adaptations of organisms	The cell The molecular basis of heredity Biological evolution The interdependence of organisms Matter, energy, and organization in living systems The behavior of organisms
Science Applications (G)	Abilities of technological design Understandings about science and technology Abilities to distinguish between natural and objects made by humans	Skills needed for careers in science Influence of science and technology on society Interdependence of science and technology	Personal interests in science Use of models in science and technology Alternative solutions to a scientific or technological problem

TABLE 3.1 **Wisconsin's Model Academic Standards for Science** (*continued*)

Standard	Grades K–4	Grades 5–8	Grades 9–12
Science in Social and Personal Perspectives (H)	Personal health Characteristics and changes in populations Types of resources Changes in environments Issues that citizens must make decisions about	Populations, resources, and environments Natural hazards Scientific solutions to issues or problems Risks and benefits Science and technology in society	Community health Population growth and resource management Environmental quality Natural and human-induced hazards Science and technology in local, state, national, and global issues and challenges Scientific decision making

Note: Some concepts are not repeated from grades K–4 to grades 9–12. It is assumed that each concept is built from concepts from previous grades.

dotted lines between subject areas intend to convey that traditional approaches to separating knowledge in subject-specific areas are not as defining as they once were. As districts develop a standards-led curriculum, they may discover that integrating subject-specific knowledge results in a stronger sequential and coherent curriculum.

Deep understanding of science concepts in a coherent program is achieved when content is presented to students at intellectually and developmentally appropriate ages. Students must be able to see the relationships between the ideas they are learning now and those previously mastered. Educators must recognize that scientific inquiry, science connections, the nature of science, science applications, real-world perspectives, and knowledge of science subject matter form the essence of a coherent curriculum, fundamental to achieving scientific literacy.

The following explanations serve as interpretations of coherence for the content standards in the *WMASS* as presented in Figure 3.1. This information can assist the district team further their understanding of how the standards can be coherently organized.

Science Connections, Standard A: Connections in science unify the disparate science disciplines and provide students with powerful ideas to help them understand the natural and designed world. The themes of science, as listed in the *WMASS*, are repeated throughout the standards because they show how science is interconnected. They provide students with productive and insightful ways of thinking about and integrating a range of basic ideas (NRC 1996).

Making connections within the sciences and from the sciences to other disciplines allows students to understand science better because they can connect and integrate unifying themes from the standards with their knowledge about themselves and the world around them. The connectedness of science provides the foundation needed to develop a coherent curriculum (DPI 1998).

Nature of Science, Standard B: "Science distinguishes itself from other ways of knowing and from other bodies of knowledge through the use of empirical standards, logical arguments, and skepticism, as scientists strive for the best possible explanations about the natural world" (NRC 1996, 201).

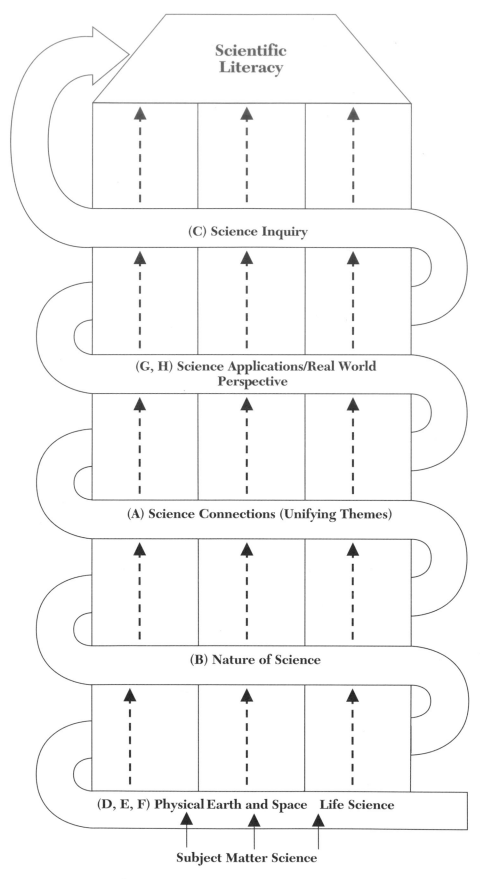

FIGURE 3.1 **Use of Content Standards in a Coherent Science Curriculum**

The nature of science illustrates for students that science has a historical past and is an ongoing, changing enterprise. Students learn through studying the history of science that scientific knowledge changes as new evidence is found. Examples, fundamental ideas, theories, and concepts in science, such as the laws of motion, have been subjected to a wide variety of confirmations, from experimental design to practical applications of the concept. The nature of science provides students with an understanding of the difference between scientific and other questions, as well as the contributions of science to society (DPI 1998). It is the interactions between science and scientists and the study of the history of science that leads students to a coherent understanding of science.

Scientific Inquiry, Standard C: Above all else, science is an endeavor that responds to questions by collecting evidence and analyzing data to offer explanations about the natural world. Classroom inquiry features include engaging in a scientifically oriented question, giving priority to and using evidence in responding to questions, making connections to scientific knowledge, and communicating and justifying students' explanations.

Scientific inquiry today goes beyond the traditional view of science as a process whereby students simply learn science through the "scientific method." Inquiry requires students to combine traditional processes of science with scientific knowledge (content) as they use scientific reasoning and critical thinking to develop their personal understanding of science (NRC 1996). Students must experience science in a way that engages them actively in constructing ideas and explanations by allowing them to ask and answer their own questions about science and communicate those ideas to others (DPI 1998). Student inquiry allows them to develop coherent ideas in science.

Knowledge of Science Subject Matter, Standards D, E, F: Students organize what they learn from scientific inquiry into concepts, generalizations, and unifying principles, which often leads to further questions and interpretations about objects and events in the natural and designed world. The standards for physical science, life and environmental science, and earth and space science, make up the subject-matter knowledge in science. The subject-matter standards were not meant to be an exhaustive list of course content, but rather, they set forth the ideas, principles, models, and theories inherent to all science (DPI 1998). Coherence within the curriculum can be achieved through the lenses of inquiry, connections, applications, and the nature of science. Figure 3.1 provides an example of the relationship of the subject-matter standards to each of the other standards.

Science Applications and Real World Perspectives, Standards G, H: Science and technology complement each other. The science application standard establishes connections between the natural and designed world through science and technology. Students grow to understand that science and the application of science provide solutions to human problems and that science and technology impact Earth's systems. Being scientifically literate also means being able to understand and act upon personal and social issues and make decisions about those issues (DPI 1998). The science in personal and social perspectives is a vehicle for this process and the heart of scientific literacy.

Focus in the Science Curriculum

A *focused* science curriculum presents the essential science skills and concepts previously described as enduring understandings.[1] A focused science curriculum allows students to develop deep and lasting understandings of the essential science concepts throughout their years in science classrooms. In Wisconsin, the *WMASS* serve as the enduring understandings that provide the focus for a standards-led science program. A focused curriculum will not suffer the shortcomings of typical science curricula, which one critic deemed as being "a mile wide and an inch deep." A focused curriculum, like a coherent one, depends upon consistency in choice of materials and assessments.

Table 3.2 is from work by the *WMASS* task force on the development of the science standards. The work is provided to help the district team develop curricular focus. The example is not intended to be exhaustive, but to provide suggestions for major concepts for Standard A, grade by grade. Standard A was chosen because of the extreme difficulty in understanding the standard. The performance statements from the *WMASS* are not repeated here. This interpretation of Standard A represents the concepts students must have to understand Standard A. The district team must assume the responsibility of determining how to provide curricular focus.

Three District Stories

The three district stories provide examples of real Wisconsin curricula that illustrate different treatments of coherence and focus, with presentations of the *WMASS*. These stories exemplify the work taking place in districts throughout Wisconsin.

Kenosha Unified School District

The Kenosha Unified School District began its standards and benchmarking process in 1995. After forming a district team, the administration brought in outside experts to assist the team in developing a set of standards for science. The team developed 17 standards, listed below. The district team, the entire faculty, and the school board agreed that the 17 science standards were consistent with or went beyond the *WMASS*. The 17 standards formed the foundation for the next step and established the focus for the curriculum.

The next step was to determine what expectations would characterize the standards at each grade range: K–2, 3–5, 6–8, and 9–12. The team selected age-appropriate benchmarks at each range for each of the 17 standards. Their goal was to make sure that the benchmarks increased in complexity, even though the 17 standards were identical throughout the ranges. This process ensured a coherent curriculum. Science teachers field tested the benchmarks in their classrooms for practicality, comprehensibility, and scalability. Benchmarks were revised based on field testing. The most significant outcome from this testing was

---

[1] The term "enduring understandings" is a science concept (explained in Chapter 2) a student will retain and remember throughout his or her life, and for Wisconsin is the *WMASS*.

TABLE 3.2 **A Focused Curriculum Using Unifying Themes Found in the WMASS Standard A**

Systems, order, and organization	Evidence, models, and explanation	Constancy, change, and measurement	Form and function
Kindergarten Objects are made of parts. Objects are part of the whole. Objects can be sorted according to their properties. Objects have more than one property.	Many of the toys children play with represent real things in nature. Scientific inquiry starts with careful observation.	Things change in some ways and in some ways they stay the same.	Objects have many characteristics.
First grade Systems may not work if some of their parts are missing. Objects in a group share some characteristics but differ in others.	A model is different from the real thing but can be used to learn about the real thing. Scientists raise questions about the world around them and seek answers to some of the questions by combining observations and trying things out.	Some things can be observed to move from place to place, whereas other things stay in one location.	Pictures can be used to represent features of objects being described.
Second grade When things are put together, they can do things that they couldn't do separately. Some events are more likely to happen than other events. Some events can be predicted more accurately than others. Often, students can find out about a group or groups by studying just a few of the objects in a group or groups.	One way to describe something is to describe it like something else.	Things in nature and things people make have very different characteristics. Estimates of lengths, weights, and time intervals can be confirmed by measurement. Things can change in different ways. Some changes are very slow or very fast, so they are hard to see.	The shape of something is often related to its use.
Third grade Events can be classified as likely or unlikely, possible or impossible. A group of objects may be classified in many ways.	Sketches can be useful in explaining ideas and models.	Some predictions can be made based on the past.	Almost everything has limits on its size and use.
Fourth grade Objects may not work if a part of it is missing, broken, worn out, mismatched, or improperly connected. In something that consists of many parts, the parts interact with each other. Objects can be organized and ordered.	Records need to be kept during investigations.	Finding out the biggest and smallest possible values of something is often as revealing as knowing their average value. Some features of objects may stay the same even when others change. Some patterns look the same when they are shifted, turned, reflected, or seen from a different direction.	

TABLE 3.2 **A Focused Curriculum Using Unifying Themes** (*continued*)

Systems, order, and organization	Evidence, models, and explanation	Constancy, change, and measurement	Evolution and equilibrium
Fifth grade Events in nature often can be measured. It is easier to predict how a group will experience an event than to predict which member will experience the event. It is easier to predict "how often" something will happen than "when" it will happen. Summary predictions are usually more accurate for large collections. Unlikely events may occur fairly often in large populations. Objects and events can be classified as members of a hierarchy.	Seeing how a model works after changes are made to it may suggest how the real object would work. Geometric figures, number sequences, graphs, diagrams, sketches, number lines, maps, and stories can be used to represent objects, events, and processes in the real world. Conclusions must be supported by reasons and explanations.	Measurements can be checked by comparing them to typical values. The best way to describe a change is to make a table or graph representing the change.	Changes occur so sporadically that it is difficult to document the changes. In evolving systems, change can be gradual, steady, repetitive, irregular, or regular.

Systems, order, and organization	Evidence, models, and explanation	Constancy, change, and measurement	Form and function
Grade six A system includes processes and things. Thinking systems means looking at how every part relates to others.	Models often represent processes that happen too slowly, too quickly, on a micro scale, on a grand scale. It is important to keep honest, clear, and accurate records. Predictions can be based on data from similar conditions in the past.	Appropriate units for answers can be determined by examining the units needed for answers. Symmetry or the lack of symmetry may determine properties of many objects.	The function of an object is frequently related to its form; the form of an object frequently limits its function.

Systems, order, and organization	Evidence, models, and explanation	Constancy, change, and measurement	Evolution and equilibrium
Grade seven Output and input of a system are related. Feedback can serve to control what goes on in a system. Objects can be ordered.	Models can be displayed and then modified.	As the complexity of any system increases, gaining an understanding of it depends increasingly on summaries and examples of the system.	Systems may stay the same because nothing is happening or because things are happening but exactly counterbalance one another. Many systems contain feedback mechanisms that serve to keep changes within limits.

TABLE 3.2 **A Focused Curriculum Using Unifying Themes** (*continued*)

Systems, order, and organization	Evidence, models, and explanation	Constancy, change, and measurement	Evolution and equilibrium
Grade eight			
A system can be connected to other systems to form new systems. Complex classification schemes contain multiple criteria for determining membership in the system.	Many types of models can be used to represent the same thing. Different explanations can often be given based on the same evidence. Curiosity, honesty, openness, and skepticism are highly regarded in science.	Properties of systems vary with proportion. In any measurement, the degree of precision needed should be determined prior to measuring.	Systems tend to change until they become stable and then remain that way. Things that change in cycles, such as the seasons or body temperature, can be described.
Grade nine			
Even in some simple systems it may not always be possible to predict the result of changing some part of the system. A system usually has some properties that are different from those of its parts. The larger the sample of a population is, the more accurate the statistics about the population. To avoid bias, samples are usually selected by some random system.	The idea of modeling is to show connections. A model may give insight about how something really works. The way data are displayed can make a big difference in how they are interpreted.	Data for two groups can be compared by representations. Measurement errors may have effects on data. Scale drawings can make larger values more easily understandable. Rate is a measure of change.	A system in equilibrium may return to the same state of equilibrium if the disturbances it experiences are small, but large disturbances may cause it to escape that equilibrium and eventually settle into some other state of equilibrium.
Grade ten			
Understanding how things work and designing solutions to problems can be facilitated by systems analysis. A correlation between two variables doesn't always mean one causes the other; sometimes some other variable causes both to change, or the correlation might be attributable to chance alone.	Computer technology has greatly improved. The usefulness of a model can be tested by comparing its predictions to actual observations in the real world. Answers to problems can be judged as reasonable by reviewing the process used to develop the answers.	Changes in scale typically change the way that things work in various systems. As the number of parts for a system changes, the number of possible interactions changes. Disparities between estimates and calculated answers must be analyzed and explained.	Things can change in detail but remain the same in general. Changes are necessary for a system to retain its constancy in the presence of changing conditions. In evolutionary change, the present arises gradually from the past. The precise future of a system is not completely determined by its present state and circumstances.

the determination that benchmarks be established for each grade rather than for each range. This change was implemented the following year.

After public hearings, the standards and benchmarks were adopted. Each Kenosha faculty member received a curriculum notebook containing the standards and benchmarks, assessment tools, rubrics for assessment, differentiation strategies, and so forth. The final step in the process was to select science materials that were consistent with standards and benchmarks. The end product is a focused and coherent curriculum. The following excerpts are taken from the Kenosha Unified School District (KUSD) No. 1 Curriculum Notebooks (KUSD 1999).

KENOSHA UNIFIED SCHOOL DISTRICT SCIENCE STANDARDS, K–12

Standard: 1. Understands basic features and structure of the Earth

Standard: 2. Understands basic Earth processes

Standard: 3. Understands essential ideas about the composition and structure of the universe and the Earth's place in the universe

Standard: 4. Understands that unity and diversity characterize life

Standard: 5. Understands the genetic basis for the transfer of biological information from one generation to the next

Standard: 6. Understands the relationship between the general structure and function in living systems

Standard: 7. Understands the interrelationship of species and their environment

Standard: 8. Understands the cycling of matter and flow of energy through the environment

Standard: 9. Understands the basic concepts of the evolution of species

Standard: 10. Understands basic concepts about the structure and properties of matter

Standard: 11. Understands energy and its changes from one form to another

Standard: 12. Understands the principles of motion

Standard: 13. Knows the kinds of forces that exist between and/or within particles

Standard: 14. Understands the process by which scientific knowledge is acquired

Standard: 15. Uses scientific inquiry

Standard: 16. Understands the application of science to technological design

Standard: 17. Understands the interactions of science, technology, and society over time

EXCERPTS FROM KENOSHA UNIFIED SCHOOL DISTRICT SCIENCE
    BENCHMARKS
Science—Grade 4
Standard 1. Understands basic features and structure of the Earth
    Benchmarks:
        ■ Understands basic concepts of the water cycle

- Knows the major differences between fresh and ocean waters and that water covers three-fourths of the Earth's surface
- Understands the difference between the rotation and the revolution of the Earth
- Knows that the Sun provides the energy necessary to maintain the temperature of the Earth

Standard 2. Understands basic Earth processes

Benchmarks:

- Understands that smaller rocks come from weathering of larger rocks
- Understands that rock is composed of different combinations of minerals (e.g., quartz, calcium carbonate, mica ...)
- Understands that the surface of the Earth can change slowly (e.g., erosion, weathering) or rapidly (e.g., landslides, earthquakes, volcanoes)

Standard 3. Understands essential ideas about the composition and structure of the universe and the Earth's place in the universe

Benchmarks:

- Knows that the Sun can be seen only in daytime, however, the Moon is visible sometimes at night and sometimes during the day
- Understands that the Earth is one of several planets that orbit the Sun and that the Moon orbits the Earth
- Understands that stars are like the Sun but are so distant they look like points of light

Standard 10. Understands basic concepts about the structure and properties of matter

Benchmarks:

- Knows that some common substances, such as water, can be changed from one state to another by heating or cooling

Standard 11. Understands energy and its changes from one form to another

Benchmarks:

- Knows that electricity in circuits can produce light, heat, sound, and magnetic effects
- Knows that electrical circuits require a complete loop through which the electrical current can pass

Standard 12. Understands the principles of motion

Benchmarks:

- Knows that light travels in a straight line unless it strikes an object
- Knows that when a force is applied to an object, the object either speeds up, slows down, or goes in a different direction
- Knows that the greater the force applied to an object, the greater the change in motion the object will have; the more massive the object, the smaller the effect a given force will have
- Knows that an object's motion can be described by indicating the change in its position over time (e.g., speed = distance divided by time)

Standard 13. Knows the kinds of forces that exist between and/or within particles

Benchmarks:
- Knows that electrically charged materials can attract or repel other objects
- Knows that just as electric currents can produce magnetic forces, magnetic fields can produce electric currents

Standard 14. Understands the process by which scientific knowledge is acquired
Benchmarks:
- Knows that the same scientific investigation may give slightly different results when it is carried out by different persons or at different times or places; however, if the results of repeated experiments are significantly different, this indicates experimental design error or human error
- Knows that in scientific investigation it is necessary to recognize variables and to have controls as standards of comparison
- Knows that scientific investigations revolve around the themes of science (e.g., change, constancy, equilibrium, evidence, evolution, explanation, form and function, measurement, models, order, organization, systems)

Standard 15. Uses scientific inquiry
Benchmarks:
- Knows that scientific investigations involve asking and answering a question and comparing the answer to what scientists already know about the world
- Knows that scientists use different kinds of investigations (e.g., naturalistic observation of things or events, data collection, simulation, controlled experiments) depending on the questions they are trying to answer
- Plans and conducts a simple investigation by using scientific inquiry

Standard 16. Understands the application of science to technological design
Benchmarks:
- Categorizes items into groups of natural objects and those designed by people
- Knows that designing a solution to a simple problem may have constraints (e.g., cost, materials, time, space, and safety)
- Implements proposed solutions using suitable tools, techniques, and quantitative measurements where appropriate (e.g., graphs, charts, drawings, written descriptions)
- Evaluates a product or design based on constraints

Standard 17. Understands the interactions of science, technology, and society over time
Benchmarks:
- Knows that women and men of all ages, backgrounds, and groups participate in the various areas of science and technology as they have for many centuries

- Knows that although men and women doing scientific inquiry have learned much about the objects, events, and phenomena in nature, there is still much more to be understood
- Knows that people have always had questions about their world; science is one way of answering questions and explaining the natural world

Science—Grade 5

Standard 2. Understands basic Earth processes
  Benchmarks:
  - Knows why the Earth's land surface constantly changes (e.g., waves, wind, water, ice)
  - Understands that changes take place through erosion, transportation, and deposition of weathered materials
  - Understands that processes of erosion transport and deposit weathered material
  - Knows that fossils provide evidence about the plants and animals that lived long ago and the nature of the environment at that time

Standard 4. Understands that unity and diversity characterize life
  Benchmarks:
  - Understands that plants and animals have a life cycle, which includes reproduction, growth and development, and death

Standard 5. Understands the genetic basis for the transfer of biological information from one generation to the next
  Benchmarks:
  - Knows that many characteristics of an organism are inherited from the parents of the organism but other characteristics result from an individual's interactions with the environment

Standard 7. Understands the interrelationship of species and their environment
  Benchmarks:
  - Understands that living things are found almost everywhere in the world; different types of plants and animals live in different places
  - Knows that an organism's patterns of behavior are related to the nature of that organism's living and nonliving environment
  - Understands that when an environment changes, some species survive and reproduce and others die or move to new locations

Standard 8. Understands the cycling of matter and flow of energy through the environment
  Benchmarks:
  - Knows that over the whole Earth, organisms are growing, dying, and decaying, and new organisms are being produced by the existing ones

Standard 9. Understands the basic concepts of the evolution of species
Benchmarks:
- Knows that organisms (e.g., bacteria, algae, whales) of the same species vary, and sometimes the differences give organisms an important advantage in surviving and reproducing
- Knows that fossils provide evidence that some organisms which lived long ago may be extinct; fossils can be compared to one another and to living organisms to observe their similarities and differences
- Knows that the relative age of fossils can be determined by their position in rock layers which have not experienced upheaval and shifting

Standard 10. Understands basic concepts about the structure and properties of matter
Benchmarks:
- Knows that matter has properties (e.g., magnetism, conductivity, density, solubility) which can be used to distinguish substances from one another
- Knows that matter is composed of particles too small to be seen (atoms and molecules)
- Knows that substances have both chemicals and physical properties
- Knows that the mass of matter is conserved regardless of the changes it undergoes (e.g., ice melts, water vaporizes ...)

Standard 11. Understands energy and its changes from one form to another
Benchmarks:
- Knows that things that give off light often also give off heat
- Knows that heat moves by conduction, convection, and radiation
- Knows that some materials conduct heat better than others; materials that do not conduct heat well can reduce heat loss (insulators)

Standard 14. Understands the process by which scientific knowledge is acquired
Benchmarks:
- Knows that the same scientific investigation may give slightly different results when it is carried out by different persons or at different times or places; however, if the results of repeated experiments are significantly different, this indicates experimental design error or human error
- Knows that in scientific investigation it is necessary to recognize variables and to have controls as standards of comparison
- Knows that scientific investigations revolve around the themes of science (e.g., change, constancy, equilibrium, evidence, evolution, explanation, form and function, measurement, models, order, organization, systems)

Standard 15. Uses scientific inquiry
Benchmarks:
- Knows that scientific investigations involve asking and answering a question and comparing the answer to what scientists already know about the world
- Knows that scientists use different kinds of investigations (e.g., naturalistic observation of things or events, data collection, simulation, controlled experiments), depending on the questions they are trying to answer
- Plans and conducts a simple investigation by using scientific inquiry

- Uses equipment and tools to gather scientific data and extend the senses (e.g., computers, rulers, thermometers, magnifiers, microscopes, calculators)

Standard 16. Understands the application of science to technological design
Benchmarks:
- Categorizes items into groups of natural objects and those designed by people
- Knows that designing a solution to a simple problem may have constraints (e.g., cost, materials, time, space, and safety)
- Implements proposed solutions using suitable tools, techniques, and quantitative measurements where appropriate (e.g., graphs, charts, drawings, written descriptions)
- Evaluates a product or design based on constraints

Standard 17. Understands the interactions of science, technology, and society over time
Benchmarks:
- Knows that women and men of all ages, backgrounds, and groups participate in the various areas of science and technology as they have for many centuries
- Knows that although men and women doing scientific inquiry have learned much about the objects, events, and phenomena in nature, there is still much more to be understood
- Knows that people have always had questions about their world; science is one way of answering questions and explaining the natural world
- Knows that people have always had problems and invented tools and techniques (ways of doing something) to solve problems; studying the effects of various solutions helps people avoid future problems
- Knows that people continually invent new ways of doing things, solve problems, and accomplish tasks; these new ideas and inventions often affect other people—with beneficial or, at times, detrimental results
- Knows that science and technology have improved transportation, health, sanitation, and communication; however, the benefits of science and technology are not equally available to all people

Reprinted with permission of Kenosha Unified School District No. 1.

Wauwatosa School District

Wauwatosa's story is different from Kenosha's. The district formed a district team responsible for developing science program goals and a science mission statement. The goals strive for curricular coherence by being applicable to any science content knowledge. Furthermore, an attempt is made within each instructional unit to include concepts from each of the three knowledge standards: physical, earth and space, life and environmental.

The district team used the *WMASS* to develop a scope and the *WMASS* sequence matrix for three grade ranges: K–5, 6–8, and 9–12. Focus is achieved by identifying the units in which the Wisconsin performance standards are implemented. The final step was to make science materials deci-

TABLE 3.3 **Wauwatosa School District Middle-Level Science Scope and Sequence Matrix**

Grade 6

	Unit I* **Science and Technology**	Unit III **It's a Small World**	Unit IV **Investigating Matter**	Unit V **Chemical Changes**	Unit VIII **Our Changing Earth**
Concept Focus	The nature of science and what scientists do	Interrelationships among microorganisms, food, and people	Matter and its properties	The chemical nature of substances encountered in everyday life	Long- and short-term changes that shape the surface of the planet Earth
Content Focus	Life, Earth	Life	Physical	Physical	Physical, Life
Supporting Content	Physical	Physical	Life	Life	

Grade 7

	Unit I **Interactions**	Unit III **Solutions**	Unit IV **Force and Motion**	Unit VI **The Restless Earth**	Unit VII **Toward the Stars**
Concept Focus	Interactions that occur among plants, animals, and the environment	The properties of solutions and solutions in the environment and body	The concepts of force and motion and methods of measurement	The earth's processes of geological change	The structure of the universe
Content Focus	Life	Physical	Physical	Earth	Earth
Supporting Content	Physical	Life, Earth	Earth	Life, Physical	Physical

Grade 8

	Unit I **Life Processes**	Unit II **Particles**	Unit IV **Oceans and Climates**	Unit VII **Light**	Unit VIII **Heredity**
Concept Focus	Processes of living things	The particle model of matter	Causes of weather and ocean currents	The characteristics of light and phenomena associated with interactions with other objects	Chromosomes, genes, and heredity
Content Focus	Life	Physical	Life, Earth	Physical	Life
Supporting Content	Physical, Earth	Life	Physical	Life, Earth	Physical

Note: This matrix serves as an example of Wauwatosa's effort to adapt an integrated textbook curriculum and to link that curriculum to the WMASS and illustrates their interpretation of coherence.

*Units adapted by the school district from *Science Plus: Technology and Society*, Level Green, Annotated Teacher's Edition, Copyright © 2002 by Holt, Rinehart, and Winston.

TABLE 3.4 Example of Alignment by Wauwatosa School District Middle-Level Science and the *Wisconsin's Model Academic Standards for Science*

Unit Name/ Standard Number	A.8.1	A.8.2	A.8.3	A.8.4	A.8.5	A.8.6	A.8.7	A.8.8	B.8.1	B.8.2	B.8.3	B.8.4	B.8.5	B.8.6	C.8.1	C.8.2	C.8.3	C.8.4	C.8.5	C.8.6	C.8.7
°°GREEN																					
I. Science and Technology	X	X	X	X	X	X	X	X				X		X	X	X	X	X	X	X	
III. It's A Small World	X	X	X	X	X	X						X		X	X	X	X	X	X	X	X
IV. Investigating Matter							X			X		X		X	X	X	X				X
V. Chemical Changes	X									X				X							X
VIII. Our Changing Earth	X	X	X	X	X	X	X	X		X	X	X	X	X	X			X	X		
°°RED																					
I. Interactions	X								X											X	
II. Solutions	X																				X
IV. Force and Motion	X						X		X						X		X				
VI. The Restless Earth		X	X	X	X	X	X	X			X	X	X		X	X	X		X	X	
VII. Toward the Stars	X			X	X	X	X	X			X		X	X			X		X	X	
°°BLUE																					
I. Life Processes	X			X		X						X			X	X	X	X	X	X	
II. Particles		X	X		X			X		X		X			X	X	X	X	X	X	
IV. Oceans and Climates	X	X	X											X	X	X	X	X	X	X	
VII. Light	X		X	X			X					X			X	X	X	X	X	X	
VIII. Heredity	X		X						X	X	X		X		X	X	X	X	X	X	

X—Point when the WMASS performance statement is met

°°—Instructional materials in the middle grades

sions and integrate those materials with the scope and sequence matrix and the *WMASS* in Tables 3.3 and 3.4. The school district developed documents and brochures to inform the public about the science program. The Wauwatosa goals and the middle school science curriculum outline are included as examples of their work. (WSD, 1999)

Wauwatosa School District Middle School Science Curriculum Guide, Grades 6–8
Mission Statement

The constantly changing scientific and technological environment has a profound impact on people's present and future lives.

Our mission is to enable students to apply scientific knowledge and processes in continuous lifelong learning. Their experiences shall develop their scientific literacy, maximize their individual talents, and enable them to be critical thinkers and problem solvers in the global community.

We believe that an understanding of science is a critical aspect of knowledge, and that teaching science enhances basic skills.

K–12 Science Goals to Achieve Scientific Literacy

The Wauwatosa School District science program will enable all students to:

1. Become aware of the interdependence of the sciences and how they fit together as a part of a larger body of knowledge.
2. Recognize and distinguish between scientific theory, fact, and law.
3. Understand **how** they come to know about science concepts, **why** they believe those concepts, and how they test and revise their thinking about these concepts.
4. Relate their own experiences and interests in science by means of hands-on experiences.
5. Develop skills in data collection, graphing, record keeping, and the use of language in verbal and written assignments.
6. Develop positive attitudes toward science and its relevance of the individual, society, and the environment.
7. Understand the interdependence of all living things and respect the fragility of the Earth's resources.
8. Explore career possibilities in science and technology at all ability levels for all citizens including women, minorities, and special populations.

Middle School Science Program Goals

Students will:

1. Understand the interrelationships among science, technology, and society
2. Understand important science concepts, processes, and ideas
3. Use higher order thinking skills
4. Solve problems and apply scientific principles
5. Have a commitment to environmental protection
6. Show interest in independent study of scientific topics

To accomplish these goals, a wide variety of teaching strategies are employed. Students investigate, experiment, gather data, organize results, and draw conclusions based on their own actions. Individual students' observations are respected and ideas are often incorporated into group decisions.
Reprinted with permission of the Wauwatosa School District.

Madison Metropolitan School District

The Madison Metropolitan School District (MMSD) began its quest for a standards-led science curriculum by first developing a grade-by-grade science curriculum that outlined the content standards and grade-level performance standards concentrating on focus. From this work, the district team recommended the school board adopt the *WMASS*. However, the team recognized that the district developed content standards and grade level performance standards described in the district science document had focus but lacked coherence. Therefore, the team began working toward a science curriculum that was also coherent. The team achieved coherence by deciding what science content and concepts were reasonable for kindergarten through grade 12 students.

The team recognized that science education reform is built upon two main ideas: new understandings about how learning occurs and a view of science as a "way of knowing." The district team used the concepts of consistency, continuity, and spiraling to guide them through the development of a district scope and sequence. Consistency, continuity, and spiraling[2] were achieved by the articulation of developmentally appropriate experiences and a sequenced curriculum throughout each grade from kindergarten to grade 12, which spirals key science concepts. Through this process, the team produced both a coherent and focused science curriculum with a grade level district scope and sequence (MMSD 2000).

The district team knew their work was not complete. The next step was to select and recommend science instructional materials (programs) that were consistent with the district scope and sequence. Programs were selected, piloted, and evaluated extensively. Programs that survived this rigorous process were then recommended for implementation. But the task of the district team was still not complete. Every teacher of science has had and will continue to have the opportunity to participate in professional development that supports the implementation of the district scope and sequence.

Overall Curricular Examples Related to the Standards

Tables 3.5, 3.6, and 3.7 provide additional curricular examples that relate the standards to one another and thus contribute to curricular coherence and focus. Column 1 indicates which standards are being related to one another. Column 2 shows the targeted skill or skills and example activities that contribute to the skill or skills. For example, the first block in K–4 shows a relationship between the nature of science standard and the inquiry standard. The targeted skill that establishes that relationship is for the student to ask answerable questions (inquiry) about the nature of science.

---

[2] Spiraling curriculum is illustrated in Figure 3.2.

TABLE 3.5 **Examples of Standards-Led Curricula from** *Wisconsin's Model Academic Standards for Science*, **Grades K–4**

Science Standards	Curricula Examples
Nature of Science (B) with Inquiry (C)	**Ask questions:** The student will ask answerable questions about the nature of science: *Note patterns,* • Relationships among objects and events by noting similarities or differences in sets of objects; ~ similarities or differences in events. *Note discrepant events,* • Exceptions to patterns by using pictures and books ~ to verify patterns, ~ to manipulate objects, or ~ to verify personal experiences. *Seek information,* • Use a variety of resources when seeking information about objects and events and discuss objects and events with others. *Formulate questions,* • Use identical information to ask questions that are structured so they can be answered by investigation.
Inquiry (C) with *all* the other Standards	**Collect data:** The student will collect pertinent data: *Observe,* • Make accurate observations of objects and events ~ using the senses, or ~ using instruments to aid the senses. *Measure and quantify,* • Order by magnitude of measurable characteristics ~ using the senses, or ~ using standard measuring devices to collect data. **Analyze data:** The student shall analyze data: *Predict,* • Use observations and known information to predict events, such as ~ time, or ~ weather. *Infer,* • Use observations to make inferences, ~ know the difference between observation and inference, or ~ infer a reason for a behavior. *Classify,* • Use characteristics of objects or events to group them noting similarities and differences. **Explain:** The student shall use results of analysis to explain natural phenomena: *Describe,* • Use the observed characteristics of objects or events to develop verbal and written descriptions of them. *Define,* • Use the common characteristics of sets of objects or events to develop definitions that include members of those sets, ~ For example, using the case of a ball rolling on a flat, level surface, develop the definition of the concept "speed."

Science Standards	Curricula Examples

Science Connections (A) with Physical Science (D), Earth and Space Science (E), Life and Environmental Science (F)	**Interactions:** Through inquiry activities, the student shall understand that natural phenomena display a wide variety of similarities and differences:
	Life and environmental science,
	• Organisms can be grouped by specific structures,
	  ~ hair color, eye color, or size of hands or feet.
	  ~ distinguish between types of plants through comparisons.
	  ~ plants and animals are different in different environments.
	  ~ organisms can be grouped by specific structures or by the habitats in which they live.
	  ~ much of the diversity that exists in the living world is because of adaptations to the environment.
	  ~ organisms can be grouped according to criteria and placed in predetermined categories.
	Physical science,
	• Objects have properties that can be detected with the senses, such as the sense of touch, to describe objects as rough/smooth,
	  ~ hard/soft, or to compare sounds by pitch, loudness.
	• Materials can be grouped by their properties, such as float or sink or dissolve in water,
	  ~ objects can be described by their measurable properties such as length, capacity, or weight.
	  ~ matter is described in terms of properties that can be detected with the senses.
	• When energy is added or taken away from matter, some of the properties are changed.
	• Matter may be classified according to exhibited properties under a given set of conditions.
	  ~ most matter can be classified as solid, liquid, or gas.
	  ~ energy can be classified as kinetic or potential.
	Earth and space science,
	• There are many types of rocks that can be grouped by properties.
	• There are objects in the sky that can be identified.
	• The relationship of objects causes changes.
	Change: Through inquiry activities, the student shall understand that our environment is constantly undergoing change:
	Life and environmental science,
	• Organisms can be grouped by specific structures.
	  ~ Plants and animals are different in different environments.
	  ~ The appearance of living things varies with the seasons.
	  ~ Living things grow, age, and change in form and activity.
	  ~ Changes in specific environments can cause change in the kinds of organisms that can live in the environment.
	Physical science,
	• The direction or speed of moving objects will change when a force is applied.
	  ~ A moving object will change its speed or direction only when a force is applied.
	  ~ When the forces applied to matter are changed, some of the properties of the matter may be changed.
	• As time passes, cold or hot objects change in temperature.
	  ~ The temperature of matter changes when energy is exchanged between the matter and its environment.

Science Standards	Curricula Examples

	Earth and space science,
	• Objects in the sky change positions throughout the day.
	• Rocks change over time due to weathering.
	  ~ The rate of weathering depends on the characteristics of the material being weathered and the cause of the weathering.
	  ~ Fossil records indicate that there has been a change in the form and complexity of life over time.
	Constancy: Through inquiry activities, the student shall understand that that there is continuity in cause-and-effect relationships which make change explainable:
	Life and environmental science,
	• Living things reproduce their own kind.
	Physical science,
	• Matter can be changed in position,
	  ~ motion, shape, and other conditions and shall retain its identifying characteristics.
	• There are special properties of kinds of matter that are always the same, such as the boiling point of water.
	Earth and space science,
	• Fossils found in rocks suggest that life processes have continued the same way for a long time.
	• The length of day and night always varies in predictable ways.
	Organization/Systems: Through inquiry activities, the student shall understand that related systems within systems comprise the universe:
	Life and environmental science,
	• Living things within ecosystems in which each organism is adapted to its living and nonliving environment.
	Physical science,
	• The properties of an object depend on the properties and function of its physical parts.
	Earth and space science,
	• Objects in the sky move together as a system.

Science Applications (G) with Science in Social and Personal Perspectives (H)	**Personal needs:** Through inquiry activities, the student shall understand that science and technology impact life-styles, such as work environments: • Technological development and medical science improve chances of good health and longer life. • Lifestyles have changed over time due to science and technology. **Decision making:** Through inquiry activities the student will understand that citizens must make decisions based on science.

[3] Tables 3.5–3.7 are not intended to be a complete curriculum, some enduring understandings are not captured in these examples. Much of the information is from *Guide to Curriculum Planning in Science*, 1986; reprinted 1993.

TABLE 3.6 Examples of Standards-Led Curricula from *Wisconsin's Model Academic Standards for Science*, Grades 5–8

Science Standards	Curricula Examples

Nature of Science (B) with Scientific Inquiry (C)	**Ask questions:** The student will ask answerable questions about the nature of science: · *Note patterns,*
	 • Relationships exist among objects and events by noting similarities or differences in sets of objects,
	    ~ Similarities or differences in events,
	    ~ Perceive reoccurring events, or
	    ~ Perceive persistent behaviors.
	 Note discrepant events,
	 • Compare single events to related patterns and note differences,
	    ~ use prior knowledge to identify unusual objects, organisms, or events.
	 Seek information,
	 • Study objects or events to ask informed questions, such as verification of personal experiences,
	    ~ Location of reliable sources of information for inferences about nature, or
	    ~ ask meaningful questions about the nature of science.
	 Formulate questions,
	 • Use initial information to ask questions that are structured so they can be answered by investigation, such as separating theoretical questions from questions that can be answered by experience,
	    ~ or, to distinguish between guessing and predicting.
	 Generate hypothesis,
	 • Use information and questions to generate statements that describe expected results of an investigation.

Inquiry (C) with *all* the other Standards	**Collect data:** The student shall collect pertinent data:
	 Observe,
	 • Make accurate observations of objects and events using the senses,
	    ~ or instruments to aid the senses,
	    ~ choose appropriate instruments to aid the senses when making observations,
	    ~ make observations both with and without inferences,
	    ~ repeat observations to verify them or to establish consistency,
	    ~ refine the observations,
	    ~ separate observations from those that are extraneous, or
	    ~ identify sources of error.
	 Measure and quantify,
	 • Use standard measuring devices to collect data.
	 Identify significance,
	 • Select data that are relevant and accurate.
	    ~ use fundamental units of the metric system to measure,
	    ~ measure rates of change,
	    ~ choose appropriate instruments,
	    ~ limit observations to those that are relevant to the question, or
	    ~ recognize situations where estimated data can be used.
	 Estimate,
	 • Use experience to estimate the values of qualitative data.
	 Analyze data: The student shall analyze data.
	 Predict,
	 • Use observations and known information to predict events.
	    ~ describe the differences between prediction and estimation, or
	    ~ predict a new event from repeated observations.

Science Standards	Curricula Examples

	Infer,
	• Use evaluations and judgment to make inferences based on observation.
	Tabulate,
	• Increase the value of data by organization and systematic display.
	Use numbers,
	• Use applied mathematics as a means of analyzing data.
	Correlate,
	• Note related changes in variables.
	Classify,
	• Use the characteristics of objects or events to group them,
	  ~ describe the difference between one-stage and two-stage classification schemes, or
	  ~ classify a set of plants or a set of objects using multiple schemes.
	Explain: The student shall use the results of analysis to explain natural phenomena:
	Describe,
	• Use words,
	  ~ symbols, and diagrams to explain an investigation,
	  ~ use a written narrative,
	  ~ draw a diagram or diagrams, or
	  ~ use numbers or mathematics to show how data is collected and explained.
	Define,
	• Use the common characteristics of sets of objects or events to develop definitions that include the members of the sets.
	  ~ For example, use data to develop operational definitions.
	Interpret,
	• Use the results of analyzing an investigation to interpret the meaning and significance of the investigation.

Science Connections (A) with Physical Science (D), Earth and Space Science (E), Life and Environmental Science (F)	**Interactions:** Through inquiry activities, the student shall understand that natural phenomena display a wide variety of similarities and differences. Through inquiry activities, the student shall understand that the interaction of matter and energy determines the nature of the environment:
	Life and environmental science,
	• Understand that green plants use energy from the sun, water, and carbon dioxide from the environment to produce food,
	  ~ Example, test the leaves of plants for starch before and after exposure to sunlight, or
	  ~ Set up a pond water culture to show the changing balance as organisms interact.
	• Biological communities tend toward a balanced condition.
	• Balanced conditions can shift over time as resources or conditions change.
	Physical science,
	• Understand that a force is necessary to change the speed or direction of moving objects, i.e., use a variable incline to study the effect of gravity on a rolling ball.
	• Chemical and physical changes depend on the special properties of the substances that interact.
	Earth and space science,
	• Tides result from the interaction of the earth, moon, and sun as their relative positions change.
	• Weather is the result of the interaction of masses of air at different temperatures and pressures. For example, chart the weather over an extended period of time.

Science Standards	Curricula Examples
	Change: Through inquiry activities, the student shall understand that our environment is constantly undergoing change: *Life and environmental science,* • Living things have changed in form, complexity, and appearance over time, ~ For example, examine fossil records and compare them to present-day related species. • Inherited characteristics that may result in greater survival values of the species, ~ For example, study recorded evidence of species that have existed in Wisconsin. • Changing earth conditions cause changes in biotic communities; for example, note migration patterns. *Physical science,* • When the forces applied to matter are changed, some of the properties may be changed, ~ For example, study the effects of force on changing the position or speed of objects. • Classify a group of elements according to their characteristics, i.e., solid, liquid, gas. ~ observe a variety of reactions. • Changes that involve matter and energy are either physical or chemical changes. *Earth and space science,* • Different earth materials are weathered at different rates. ~ For example, compare the ability of sandstone, limestone, and quartzite to withstand abrasion. • Changes in solar radiation cause changes in seasons. **Constancy:** Through inquiry activities, the student shall understand that there is continuity in cause-and-effect relationships that make change explainable: *Life and environmental science,* • Cells contain genetic materials that carry inherited traits, i.e., the work of Gregory Mendel. • Characteristics are inherited by offspring from the parent generation in definite patterns; for example, use fruit flies to show patterns of inheritance. *Physical science,* • In a chemical change, matter and energy are conserved. ~ The numbers of atoms of each element remain the same. • Energy is conserved in a moving system, i.e., changes from kinetic to potential. *Earth and space science,* • Earth has a magnetic field that remains constant for long periods of time, use of a compass. ~ The moon's appearance and position change in regular and predictable ways; for example, cause for the phases of the moon, or ~ calculate the number of degrees the moon moves in orbit in one day. **Organization/Systems:** Through inquiry activities, the student will understand that related systems within systems comprise the universe: *Life and environmental science,* • Survival of living organisms is dependent on the complementary functioning of their organs; for example, kidney failure in humans. • Specialized cells within living things perform special functions; for example, contrast the shape and function of cells within the human body. • Complexity in organisms is a matter of degree of specialization and interaction of the organs of an organism.

Science Standards	Curricula Examples
	Physical science, • Mechanisms made of subsystems control the interaction of matter and energy. • Electrical properties of matter are related to the distribution of electrical charges; for example, static electricity. *Earth and space science,* • Earth's crust is made up of a few basic materials that are organized in many ways; for example, identification of the elements that make up the Earth's crust. • The planets in the solar system move in the same direction around the sun in roughly the same plane, model of the solar system. • Earth's crust is divided into several rigid plates that are slowly moving.

Science Applications (G) with Science in Social and Personal Perspectives (H)	**Personal needs:** Through inquiry activities, the student will understand that science and technology are related:
	• The products of science and technology often become controls on individual lifestyles; for example, use case studies to accept or reject ideas about science and technology.
	• Scientific knowledge makes it possible to make wise decisions about lifestyles.
	• Science and technology affects career choice and the kind of work people do.
	• Science and technology impact leisure time.
	Decision making: Through inquiry activities, the student will understand that citizens must make decisions based on scientific evidence:
	• Decisions/scientific solutions have both risks and benefits,
	  ~ consequences, or
	  ~ trade-offs.

TABLE 3.7 **Examples of Standards-Led Curricula from *Wisconsin's Model Academic Standards for Science*, Grades 9–12**

Science Standards	Curricula Examples

Nature of Science (B) with Scientific inquiry (C)	**Ask questions:** The student will ask answerable questions about the nature of science: *Formulate questions,*
	 • Use initial information to ask questions that are structured so they can be answered by investigation,
	   ~ such as separating questions that can be answered by empirical investigations from all other questions, or
	   ~ distinguish between guessing and predicting.
	 Generate hypothesis,
	 • Use information and questions to generate statements that describe expected results of an investigation,
	   ~ design tests for a given hypothesis.

Inquiry (C) with *all* the other Standards	**Collect data:** The student shall collect pertinent data from nature:
	 Measure and quantify,
	 • Use standard measuring devices to collect data.
	   ~ use indirect means to measure quantities,
	   ~ use approved techniques, and
	   ~ recognize the limitations of measurements.
	 Identify significance,
	 • Select data that are relevant and accurate.
	   ~ define relative error allowable for data.
	 Select variables,
	 • Identify the variables acting on a phenomenon and select those to be observed.
	   ~ Control of variables,
	   ~ dependent variable and independent variable, and
	   ~ eliminate extraneous observations and effects during investigations.
	 Estimate,
	 • Use experience to estimate values of quantitative data.
	 Analyze data: The student shall analyze data:
	 Graph,
	 • Use a variety of graphing techniques to expose data.
	 Tabulate,
	 • Use tables, charts, and matrixes to systematize data.
	 Use numbers,
	 • Use mathematics to analyze data.
	 Correlate,
	 • Note related changes in variable.
	 Classify,
	 • Use the characteristics of objects or events to group them by noting patterns.
	 Explain: The student shall use the results of analysis to explain natural phenomena:
	 Interpret,
	 • Use the results of data to interpret the meaning and significance of an investigation; for example, use predicted sources or errors to predict anomalies in data.
	 Develop mental models,
	 • Use information from resources or evidence obtained from investigations to develop mental models that explain natural events; for example, reaction of chemical elements.
	 Develop physical models,
	 • Build or describe physical systems that are analogous in structure or function to natural phenomena.

Science Standards	Curricula Examples

	Communicate:
	• Use a variety of techniques to communicate the results of investigations to others.
	  ~ Defend a conclusion to others that is based on evidence.
	  ~ Present results in a systematic and logical manner so others can follow the investigation.
	  ~ Develop a completed investigation.

Science Connections (A) with Physical Science (D), Earth and Space Science (E), Life and Environmental Science (F)	**Interactions:** Through inquiry activities, the student shall understand that natural phenomena display a wide variety of similarities and differences. Through inquiry activities, the student shall understand that the interaction of matter and energy determine the nature of the environment:
	Life and environmental science,
	• Interactions of matter and energy determine the nature of the environment.
	• Diversity in organisms is due to differences in the chemical composition of the genetic material of cells.
	  ~ Describe the concept of genes as areas on chromosomes.
	  ~ Identify the chemical nature of the proteins that make the structure of DNA possible.
	  ~ Discuss variations that can occur in DNA molecules.
	• Variation among species is passed on from generation to generation within the same species.
	  ~ Determine the difference between species and races.
	• Genetic differences in species allow them to adapt to different environments. Some species have very specific environmental requirements.
	  ~ Ascertain why Kirtland's warbler is so rare.
	  ~ List reasons why so many species are on the endangered list at the present time.
	• Interaction of living organisms in a community results in the flow of energy and cycling of matter.
	  ~ Identify several important predators, and construct the food chains which make their existence possible.
	• There is a continuous chemical interaction among the cells and organs of organisms.
	  ~ Investigate the role of enzymes in providing energy to the cells of humans.
	• Photosynthesis is the basic process that provides energy for life.
	  ~ Investigate the effect on the starch content of an area of a geranium leaf that is kept from light.
	Physical science,
	• Kinetic potential and radiant energy appear in a variety of forms.
	  ~ Compare radio waves, infrared radiation, visible light, and ultraviolet radiation. List similarities and differences in the effects they cause.
	  ~ Investigate the energy transfer that occurs when a light bulb lights, a piece of paper burns, a rock falls, or a pendulum clock ticks.
	• Most of the physical properties of matter result from forces acting on the basic particles of matter and the relative energy of the particles.
	  ~ Explain change of phase in terms of kinetic molecular motion.
	• The chemical elements show systematic similarities and differences that are the basis for the periodic chart of the elements.
	  ~ Develop alternative charts of the elements that are different from the standard periodic charts. (Use alternate systems of classification.)
	• Force is the result of an interaction of matter.
	  ~ Show that the result of the Earth's attraction for any mass produces a constant acceleration (the acceleration of gravity).

Science Standards	Curricula Examples
	• The interaction of atoms to form molecules or ionic crystals is due to forces between electric charges.
	~ Use diagrams or physical models to show the mechanics of ionic and covalent bonds.
	• Force fields are the areas of influence around masses, electrical charges, or magnetic poles.
	~ Describe an electromagnetic wave in terms of energy and force fields.

Earth and space science,

- Landscapes reflect the diversity of climate, rock type and structure, and past history.
  - ~ Discover evidence of dramatic change in the landscape of Wisconsin. (glacial effects, mountain remnants, monadnocks.)
  - ~ Using written resources, develop a geologic history of Wisconsin that explains the driftless area, central golden sands area, and granite of the northern highlands.
- The diversity of rock-forming minerals is the result of the unique chemical properties of silicon.
  - ~ Conjecture on what the Earth would be like if it were not for the fact that silicon and oxygen combine to form silica.
- The diverse role of water on the planet due to its abundance and its chemical-physical properties.
  - ~ Evaluate the fact that water expands as it freezes and the effect this has on the Earth's surface.
  - ~ Determine the approximate percentage of the Earth's surface that has been altered by water in the form of glaciers.
- Variations in air temperature, density, and relative humidity, combined with effects of the Earth's rotation, produce weather systems.
  - ~ Use the principle of conservation of angular momentum to explain the high velocity of winds in a tornado. Develop a three-dimensional model to describe the direction of winds and sources of energy in a tornado.
- Angular velocity and gravitational force interact to produce the stable orbits of the moons and planets in the solar system.
  - ~ Speculate on the possibility of a large mass from outer space being captured in an orbit around the sun.
- Interactions between the Earth's crustal plates are constantly changing the Earth's surface.
  - ~ Develop a model to show the effects of plate subduction.

Change: The student shall understand that our environment is constantly undergoing change:

Life and environmental science,

- Evolution is the major theory that explains the changes over time in living species.
  - ~ Find examples of the principle of the survival of the fittest.
  - ~ Compare the Lamarkian theory of evolution with the Darwinian theory.
- Mutations occur when the genetic material of an offspring is different from that of parent organisms.
  - ~ List known as well as possible causes of mutation.
  - ~ Investigate genetic diseases that are actually mutations.
- Changes in biological systems correspond to changes in their environments.
  - ~ Develop models to show how environmental changes can lead to species extinction.
  - ~ Use one-celled animals to investigate ways that chemical changes in a cell's environment affect the activity of the cell.

Science Standards	Curricula Examples
	• Changes occur at all levels of biological organization.
	~ Find examples of predictable change in biotic communities.
	Physical science,
	• Normally neutral aggregates of matter demonstrate electrical properties when exposed to an electric potential.
	~ Investigate the electrical properties of solutions and emulsions (saltwater solution, an alcohol-milk emulsion).
	• The wavelength of radiant energy can be changed by changing the density of the medium through which it passes.
	~ Develop a model lens to demonstrate chromatic aberration.
	• Chemical changes always involve energy changes.
	~ Demonstrate both exothermic and endothermic reactions.
	Earth and space science,
	• Erosion opposes volcanism and mountain building to constantly change the surface of the earth.
	~ Find local evidence of uplifting and stress on rock formations.
	~ Find local short-term and long-term evidence of water, wind, and ice erosion.
	• Climates in areas of the earth change with time.
	~ Describe conditions that must have existed in southwestern Wisconsin (the driftless area) during the last ice age.
	• The seas of the earth are dynamic and constantly changing.
	~ Find information on what is happening to the mineral content of the oceans.
	Constancy: The student shall understand that there is continuity in cause-and-effect relationships which makes change explainable:
	Life and environmental science,
	• Life forms closely resemble the parental forms from which they are reproduced.
	~ Describe the mechanism by which DNA is replicated in reproductive cells.
	• Organisms pass traits to their offspring through transmission of genetic material.
	~ Describe the structure of chromosomes, genes, and related chemical systems that result in specialized cells.
	~ Compare the events of mitosis and meiosis. Explain the formation of chromosome pairs and the significance of dominant and recessive genes in determining the traits of offspring.

What Are the Science Curriculum Issues a District Team Faces When Developing a Standards-Led Science Curriculum?

As the district team begins creating or evaluating a standards-led science curriculum, they will occasionally have to make decisions about the organization, approach, or inclusion of materials in the science program. In this section, those concerns will be called issues. Identifying common issues and providing additional information regarding that issue is intended to assist the district team with their decisions. This information is not intended to be exhaustive, but rather to highlight the important concepts associated with the issue.

Issue: Traditional Vs. Standards-Led Approaches to Science

Traditional science, which classifies the subject matter of science into life science, earth science, and physical science, typically does not encourage students to make the connections in science. This results in disjointed content. The traditional approach results in students not grasping the big ideas in science or the unifying concepts that are so important for understanding. Project 2061 in *2061 Today* (AAAS 2000, 1) states, "Much of the typical curriculum is obsolete, fostering little of what is needed for literacy." It further states that the science curriculum "is usually assembled from unrelated fragments, without reference to a conceptual whole and with no *coherence* across grade levels or subject matter" (ibid 1).

Standards-led science curriculum means that the curriculum allows teachers and students to work together as active learners of science. A reformed curriculum fosters an atmosphere where students are allowed to make connections to what they already know about science.

Issue: Science Integration Vs. Subject-Matter Science

Wisconsin's Model Academic Standards for Science advocate interconnectedness in science. The standards illustrate the importance of content in earth and space science, life and environmental science, and physical science, but also reflect the interconnectedness of science through inquiry, connections, and applications. When planning a science curriculum, it is important for the district team to seek ways where the students are able to understand how the sciences are connected and integrated. Integration is not an issue as long as all content standards are accounted for in the required K–12 curriculum.

Issue: Technology Use in the Curriculum

The incorporation of technology into the curriculum begins with asking the right questions. According to Lynne Schrum, President of the International Society for Technology in Education, the key questions include "What do we know about appropriate ways to enhance student learning with technology?" and "How can technology change the nature of teaching and learning?"

(Schrum 1999, 16) To use technology effectively in the curriculum, the district team must develop methods that encourage students and teachers to think about why they are using the technology.

Jamie McKenzie provides answers to these questions. The appropriate use of technology leads to powerful questions, developed both for and by students (McKenzie 2000). In *Beyond Technology, Questioning, Research and the Information Literate School*, McKenzie wrote that "powerful questioning leads to 'Information Power'—the ability to fashion solutions, decisions, and plans that are original, cogent, and effective" (McKenzie 2000, 3).

The use of technology to ask good questions is important for the local district team to remember when developing a science curriculum. Technology use in the science classroom must support the overall science curriculum and program and the outcome of achieving scientific literacy. Technology, for the sake of using technology, does not lead to this outcome.

Issue: Including Inquiry in the Curriculum

Wisconsin's Model Academic Standards for Science support inquiry as an integral part of the curriculum. Inquiry can take many forms. Teachers can structure investigations so that students proceed toward known outcomes, or inquiry can be free-ranging explorations of unexplained phenomena. There can also be partial inquiries where the students investigate a question through activities, such as library research or a technology search. In partial inquiry, students may or may not be engaged in a laboratory experience. In each inquiry or partial inquiry there must be activities that ask and answer scientific or other relevant questions.

The form of inquiry in the curriculum depends largely on the educational goals of the K–12 standards-led science program. Because these goals are diverse, all forms of inquiry have their place in the science program. It is important for the district team to recognize that inquiry is fundamental to students learning science and fundamental to the standards-led science program.

Issue: Unifying Themes of Science, Science Connections, and Standard A in the Curriculum

The decision to divide the *WMASS* into eight content standards follows the presentation of the *National Science Education Standards (NSES)*. Creating eight content standards for the *NSES* was not done arbitrarily (NRC 1996); the *NSES* do encourage cross-disciplinary approaches to science. The task force feels strongly that students and learners must be able to make connections among the standards, and the unifying themes of Standard A are designed to accomplish this. Further, the unifying themes of Standard A are considered basic to all science.

Issue: Evolution in the Curriculum

In the *WMASS*, evolution is defined as "a series of changes, some sporadic some gradual, that accounts for the present form and function of objects."

(DPI 1998, 34) The task force believes evolution must be an integral part of the science curriculum. Evolution is one of the unifying or connecting themes in Standard A that students must comprehend to better understand science.

As the district team develops the curriculum, it is important to keep the following in mind:

1. According to the National Science Teachers Association (NSTA) position statement, "Science curricula should emphasize evolution in a manner commensurate with its importance as a unifying theme in science, and its overall explanatory power." (NSTA 1999)
2. The overall science program should emphasize evolution as a concept that is present in the curriculum from kindergarten through grade 12.

Issue: Meeting all Eight Content Standards in Specialized Classes

Every science class must be standards-led, whether the class is biology, earth science, an integrated science class, or even chemistry. A student's exposure to science must include all of the *WMASS*. This means that discrete subjects, such as biology or physics, must draw from material from all subject matter standards, as well as from connections, nature of science, inquiry and science applications, and real world perspectives.

According to Bonnie J. Brunkhorst, to accomplish a standards-led science program, we need to identify the many areas of content that overlap in the standards (Brunkhorst 1997, 53). As an example, earth and space science can help add context to chemistry classes by allowing teachers to address components of both the physical science and earth and space science standards. She supports this position with the following example: Many science concepts are actually built on each other. For instance, rocks are made of minerals, and the minerals have definite chemical compositions. The crystal structures of those chemical compositions provide scientists with valuable clues to the Earth's past.

The task force stated that science is about connections. The connections allow students to see patterns, understand clues about the past, and predict future events. The connections answer questions about science and allow all students to better know, understand, and do science. It is the responsibility of the district team to ensure that all eight of the *WMASS* content standards are integral parts of the science curriculum and of each science class.

Issue: Animals in the Science Classroom

According to the National Science Teachers Association (NSTA), "Observation and experimentation with living organisms give students unique perspectives of life processes that are not provided by other modes of instruction. Studying animals in the classroom enables students to develop skills of observation and comparison, a sense of stewardship, and an appreciation for the unity, interrelationships, and complexity of life. This study, however, requires appropriate, humane care of the organism. Teachers are expected to be knowledgeable about the proper care of organisms under study and the safety of their students" (NSTA 1991, 191).

Included in the issue of animals in the science classroom is the issue of animal dissection. The National Science Teachers Association again recommends that dissection is appropriate in the science classroom provided that the following considerations are taken into account:

- Laboratory and dissection activities must be conducted with consideration and appreciation for the organism.
- Laboratory and dissection activities must be conducted in a clean and organized work space with care and laboratory precision.
- Laboratory and dissection activities must be based on carefully planned objectives.
- Laboratory and dissection objectives must be appropriate to the maturity level of the student.
- Student views or beliefs sensitive to dissection must be considered; the teacher will respond appropriately.

The task force concurs with the NSTA guidelines for dissection. However, the district team may wish to consider alternatives to the actual dissection of an organism, such as a computer simulation, multimedia presentations, or realistic models as examples.

Issue: Service Learning in Science

The DPI defines service learning as a method by which students learn and develop through active participation in thoughtfully organized service experiences that fulfill the following:

- Meet actual community needs
- Are coordinated in collaboration with the school community
- Are integrated into each young person's academic curriculum
- Provide structured time for people to think, talk, and write about what they did and said during the service project
- Provide young people with opportunities to use newly acquired academic skills and knowledge in real-life situations in their own communities
- Enhance what is taught in the school by extending student learning beyond the classroom
- Help to foster the development of a sense of caring for others. (DPI 2000a)

Wisconsin's Model Academic Standards for Science support service learning as an active part of the science curriculum. Standard G, *Science in Social and Personal Perspectives*, indicates that students should be actively engaged in science issues that are local in nature and that potentially have a global impact. When the district team develops the local curriculum, service learning should be an integral part of the curriculum.

An example of a Wisconsin school district using service learning within their curriculum comes from the New Auburn School District. In this service learning example, science knowledge and concepts from the *WMASS* are foundational to the project entitled *Lake Awareness—Vandalism at Parks and Lakes*. (DPI 2000, 17–18)

New Auburn High School Service Learning Project: *Lake Awareness—Vandalism at Parks and Lakes*

Project Profile

The Lake Awareness project was developed in response to a community request and need. A local lake management organization asked the students at New Auburn High School to help curb vandalism at a nearby lake and park. The students met with Round Lake District members, town and county representatives, the police, and park and forest officials. During the course of the project, students hosted a conference and wrote a brochure that focused on curbing vandalism. Students also conducted research and reported the results in the school newsletter and at the Wisconsin Lakes Convention. The research findings were delivered to most schools and parks in Wisconsin.

Making Curriculum Connections

Students realized that they could play an important part in solving a problem. They understood that their opinions were important. Students also gained insight about their position in society. Students developed skills in the areas of desktop publishing, sociology, art, writing, speaking, and math.

The Lake Awareness project met several of the *Wisconsin's Model Academic Standards for performance in Environmental Education and Social Studies*. Those standards are highlighted in *The Curriculum Connections* column.

Prepping for the Project

"With the help of student leaders, one teacher organized ninety percent of the activities."

The Lake Awareness project involved multiple grades and multiple disciplines. Seven to twelve art students and eight sociology and history students assisted the teacher. Project planning time took place after school hours. Financial resources included funds from the art club, a Service Learning grant, and donations from lake-related business groups. The donations allowed for the printing and distribution of a brochure.

Initially, local leaders informed students about a number of concerns and issues regarding the lakes. Students chose to work on vandalism. Perhaps vandalism had directly affected them at their lake, beach, or park. This group of student-leaders organized a convention; invited guests, which included fifteen seventh and eighth grade students; introduced and informed speakers; and compiled the results of their research.

Designing a Meaningful Service

The Round Lake District encouraged the group to work on reducing vandalism. Students were very aware of vandalism and wanted to focus on it. Therefore, the group did not identify other project ideas. The students decided to research the vandalism problem. They compiled data and reported the findings at the Wisconsin Lakes Convention and in their newsletter. Because the students already had written the results for their newsletter, the teacher suggested that they create a brochure using the same information. Students developed the brochure while their teacher-advisor facilitated the work by arranging for a meeting space and brochure printing.

Many individuals and organizations have benefited from the Service-Learning project. The primary beneficiaries included local community members, Round Lake District, Chippewa County Parks Department, Chippewa County Sheriff Department, fifty other students in the school and other communities, plus Wisconsin parks and lakes. The partners in the Lake Awareness project were the New Auburn High School Art Club, Round Lake District, Town of Sampson, Chippewa County Parks and Forest Department, Chippewa County Sheriff Department, and several local businesses.

Structuring Reflection Opportunities

The project became part of the high school art club's activities. The group reflected on the project and discussed their thoughts during art club meetings. Students often discussed the project on their own in the halls between classes and after school. To spark discussion, the group used one Cooperative Education Service Agency 2 questionnaire that touched on this subject; however, the manner of their reflection was primarily casual conversation. Everyone involved in this project was able to offer their own evaluation of the project.

Creating Assessment Criteria

> "When the Wisconsin Department of Natural Resources (WDNR) featured us and our vandalism abatement work on the WDNR web page, the entire community thought about our success."

The students generated information about other lakes for different organizations. When others demonstrated support for their work, the students and teacher interpreted that support as positive assessment. The group measured its success through the positive response they had received *and* by the Lake Stewardship Award, which was presented to them because of their vandalism abatement project and other related work.

Learning from Experience

The Lake Awareness program is working well. Students know that if they get involved, they will have fun, do good things for lakes, meet other students, plus earn prizes, awards, and perks. They may even attend a convention. Since the service-learning project is not tied to any particular grade level, students can participate anytime they choose to do so.

A few challenges did arise. One problem was that teachers were usually stretched for time. The project also was difficult to coordinate with other disciplines.

In addition, it was difficult to focus on just one lake issue because there are many that demand attention.

> "The students' experiences often caused me to want to guide them rather than let them discover."

Conclusion and Implications

The first step toward a district standards-led science program was for the *district team* to make decisions about the science program and to build the district's vision for scientific literacy. This chapter built upon that work and asks the *district team* to put together a curriculum that supported the district's vision of scientific literacy. The task force introduced the concepts of coherence and focus as the vehicle the team was to use to develop the curriculum that achieved scientific literacy for *ALL* students. As the *district team* completes the curriculum work, it is important for the *team* to step back and ask the fundamental question, does the curriculum really advocate scientific literacy for *ALL* students?

Once the question is answered satisfactorily, the team should concentrate on curriculum implementation. The first priority of implementation is to examine *how* the curriculum will be implemented. Thus, the next chapter is about teachers and teaching and about the classroom environment needed to support the curriculum that is part of the overall standards-led science program.

References

AAAS (American Association for the Advancement of Science). 2000. Project 2061. Designs for Science Literacy Guiding K–12 Curriculum Reform. *2061 Today* 10 (1) Washington, D.C.: AAAS.

Brunkhorst, Bonnie J. 1997. Grounding Chemistry with Earth and Space Science. In *Chemistry in the National Science Education Standards: A Reader and Resource Manual for High School Teachers*. Edited by American Chemical Society. Washington, D.C.: American Chemical Society.

Bybee, Rodger W., and Patrice L. Legro. 1996. *On Teaching Biological Evolution and the Nature of Science: the Role of the National Science Education Standards*. Washington, D.C.: National Academy Press. Quoted in National Resource Council. *National Science Education Standards*. 1996. Washington, D.C.: National Academy Press. p. 201.

Kenosha Unified School District No. 1. 1999. *Curriculum Notebook Including Academic and Lifelong Learning Standards and Benchmarks*.

Lee, Shelley A. 2000. *Model Academic Standards for Science: Defined.* (Discussion Paper, March 2, 2000), Madison, Wis.: Wisconsin Department of Public Instruction.

Madison Metropolitan School District (MMSD). K–5 Scope and Sequence Task Force. 2000. *Elementary Science Curricula Scope & Sequence and Alignment to Standards*. Working Draft.

McKenzie, Jamie. 2000. *Beyond Technology: Questioning, Research and the Information Literate School*. Bellingham, Wash.: FNO Press.

NRC (National Research Council). 1996. *National Science Education Standards*. Washington, D.C.: National Academy Press.

———.1999. *Designing Mathematics of Science Curriculum Programs: A Guide for Using Mathematics and Science Education Standards*. Washington, D.C.: National Academy Press.

National Science Teachers Association (NSTA). 2000. *NSTA Handbook 2000–2001*. Arlington, Va.: NSTA Press.

Schrum, Lynne. "Technology in the Classroom: Asking the Right Questions." *ENC Focus* 6(3): 16.

Wauwatosa School District. 1999. *Middle School Science, Grades 6–8 Curriculum Guide*.

Wisconsin Department of Public Instruction. 1993. *A Guide to Curriculum Planning in Science*. 1986. Reprint. Madison, Wis.: Wisconsin Department of Public Instruction.

———. 1998. *Wisconsin's Model Academic Standards for Science*. Madison, Wis.: Wisconsin Department of Public Instruction.

———. 2000a. *Learning From Experience: A Collection of Service-Learning Projects Linking Academic Standards to Curriculum*. Madison, Wis.: Wisconsin Department of Public Instruction.

Yager, Robert, and Charles McFadden. 2002. *Science Plus Technology and Society, Level Green*. Austin, Tex.: Holt, Rinehart and Winston.

Additional Reading

AAAS (American Association for the Advancement of Science 2000). *Project 2061. Benchmarks for Science Literacy*. Washington, D.C.: American Association for the Advancement of Science.

———. 2000. *Project 2061. Designs for Science Literacy*. Washington, D.C.: American Association for the Advancement of Science.

National Research Council. 1999. *Designing Mathematics of Science Curriculum Programs: A Guide for Using Mathematics and Science Education Standards*. Washington, D.C.: National Academy Press.

Chapter 4
Essential Components of a K–12 Science Program

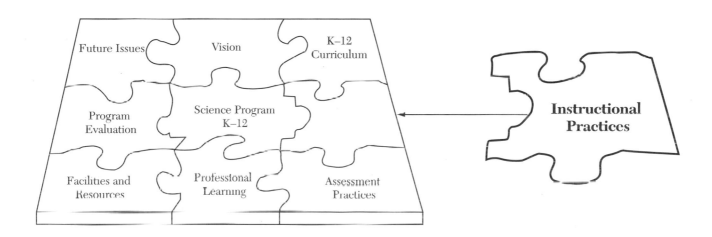

The figure illustrates the interlocking nature of the components
of the standards-led science program. The power of the K–12
standards-led science program emerges when all the pieces
of the program are present. Chapter 4 characterizes the instructional strategies that assist teachers in achieving scientific
literacy.
Science Task Force, May 2000

How do Teachers Teach Science and Students Learn Science in a K–12 Standards-Led Science Classroom?

Instructional Practices

An outcrop of dolomite along the Niagara Escarpment East of Lake Winnebago: Bruce A. Brown, WGNHS. Wisconsin DNR Photo.

Essential to any K–12 science program are teachers and teaching and learners and learning. When making standards-led science program decisions, all aspects of teaching and learning must be considered. Typically, when curriculum committees develop science programs, discussion is limited to the content to be taught, paying little attention to how students learn science. This approach results in science programs that are inconsistent with the intellectual development of students (DPI 1986). Ultimately, the success of any K–12 standards-led science program lies in the teachers' abilities to teach science and students to learn, understand, and use the content and concepts in science. This excerpt from the *Wisconsin Fast Plants* vignette captures the essence of a standards-led science program that focuses on both teaching and learning.

The first science class after winter break is unusually full of energy. Mr. L.'s students are informally surveying their classmates to see what research project they are interested in doing. Mr. L.'s class topics are not unlike other introductory biology class topic where genetics, protein synthesis, evolution, taxonomy, and the like assume major curricular importance. In the past, Mr. L. has presented these topics from a classic biological perspective.

However, Mr. L. wants to go further. He wants to design an educational setting, in the confines of a freshman introductory biology curriculum, where his students can demonstrate their ability to apply the information and experiences they gained from their experience of growing *Wisconsin Fast Plants* to model the actions and thought processes of a scientific researcher.

Building upon the research presented in Chapter 1, this chapter will provide information on how standards-led instructional practices influence student learning. Included in this discussion is information on the *National Science Education Standards (NSES) Teaching Standards* and the *Wisconsin Standards for Teacher Development and Licensure*. Using additional vignettes illustrating the teaching standards, exemplary classroom practices are highlighted for kindergarten through grade 4, grades 5–8, and grades 9–12. The chapter provides a summary of unique characteristics of the learner at each level. Through the vignettes, the chapter illustrates how standards-led teaching practices impact students learning science.

Specifically, the chapter answers the following questions:

- How do the *Wisconsin Standards for Teacher Development and Licensure* and the *NSES Teaching Standards* support teaching in a standards-led science classroom environment?
- What does a standards-led science classroom environment "look like"?
- What is the relationship between the student and teacher in creating standards-led classroom environments?
- What does K–4 science "look like" in the classroom?
- What does science "look like" in grades 5–8?
- What does high school science "look like" in grades 9–12?

How do the *Wisconsin Standards for Teacher Development and Licensure* and the National Science Education Standards Teaching Standards Support Teaching in a Standards-Led Classroom Environment?

Standards-led science teaching is a complex activity that lies at the heart and vision of science education presented in *Wisconsin's Model Academic Standards for Science* (WMASS), *PI 34*, and the *National Science Education Standards (NSES)* (NRC 1996). This shift in science teaching reflects the broader changes that have occurred both nationally and across Wisconsin in education. Two major events in science education support standards-led science teaching. They are the development of *Wisconsin Standards for Teacher Development and Li-*

censure *PI 34* and the development of the *NSES Teaching Standards*. Each is presented separately, then the relationship between *PI 34* and the *NSES Teaching Standards* is explored as the foundation for the remainder of this chapter.

In 1994, the Wisconsin Department of Public Instruction (DPI) commissioned a task force to create state standards for teaching. These standards, in addition to new rules on teacher licensure, were incorporated into a new administrative code now known as *PI 34*. The rules under *PI 34* encompass a broad range of issues that apply to all teachers, from their preparation through professional practice. The *PI 34* standards are presented below.

Wisconsin Standards for Teacher Development and Licensure (DPI 2000)

Standard 1	Teachers know the subjects they are teaching.
Standard 2	Teachers know how children grow.
Standard 3	Teachers understand that children learn differently.
Standard 4	Teachers know how to teach.
Standard 5	Teachers know how to manage a classroom.
Standard 6	Teachers communicate well.
Standard 7	Teachers are able to plan different kinds of lessons.
Standard 8	Teachers know how to test for student progress.
Standard 9	Teachers are able to evaluate themselves.
Standard 10	Teachers are connected with other teachers and the community.

The *National Science Education Standards Teaching Standards* (NRC 1996, 27) "provide criteria for making judgments about progress toward the vision" of standards-led science teaching presented in this chapter. The teaching standards provide the framework and set the stage for effective instructional practices which better allow students to learn science. These teaching standards define the context for exemplary science teaching focused on student achievement within a standards-led science classroom. The *NSES Teaching Standards* are endorsed by the Wisconsin Society of Science Teachers and the National Science Teachers Association.

The following section provides a brief overview of these standards. More detailed information about the *NSES Teaching Standards* can be found in the *NSES* document (NRC 1996, 30–51).

Effective instructional practices, which are at the heart of the teaching standards and PI 34, allow students to construct an accurate model of the natural and designed world and to reject their misconceptions

Frank Zuerner (Science Task Force member), 2000

Teaching Standard A

Teachers of science plan an inquiry-based science program for their students. In doing this, teachers

- develop a framework of year-long and short-term goals for students.
- select science content and adapt and design curricula to meet the interests, knowledge, understanding, abilities, and experiences of students.
- select teaching and assessment strategies that support the development of student understanding and nurture a community of science learners.
- work together as colleagues within and across disciplines and grade levels.

Teaching Standard B

Teachers of science guide and facilitate learning. In doing this, teachers

- focus and support inquiries while interacting with students.
- orchestrate discourse among students about scientific ideas.
- challenge students to accept and share responsibility for their own learning.
- recognize and respond to student diversity and encourage all students to participate fully in science learning.
- encourage and model the skills of scientific inquiry, as well as the curiosity, openness to new ideas and data, and skepticism that characterize science.

Teaching Standard C

Teachers of science engage in ongoing assessment of their teaching and of student learning. In doing this, teachers

- use multiple methods and systematically gather data about student understanding and ability.
- analyze assessment data to guide teaching.
- guide students in self-assessment.
- use student data, observations of teaching, and interactions with colleagues to reflect on and improve teaching practice.
- use student data, observations of teaching, and interactions with colleagues to report student achievement and opportunities to learn to students, teachers, parents, policymakers, and the general public.

Teaching Standard D

Teachers of science design and manage learning environments that provide students with the time, space, and resources needed for learning science. In doing this, teachers

- structure the time available so that students are able to engage in extended investigations.
- create a setting for student work that is flexible and supportive of science inquiry.
- ensure a safe working environment.
- make available science tools.
- identify and use resources outside the school.
- engage students in designing the learning environment.

Teaching Standard E

Teachers of science develop communities of science learners that reflect the intellectual rigor of scientific inquiry and the attitudes and social values conducive to science learning. In doing this, teachers

- display and demand respect for the diverse ideas, skills, and experiences of all students.
- enable students to have a significant voice in decisions about the content and context of their work and require students to take responsibility for the learning of all members of the community.

- nurture collaboration among students.
- structure and facilitate ongoing formal and informal discussion based on a shared understanding of rules of scientific discourse.
- model and emphasize the skills, attitudes, and values of scientific inquiry.

Teaching Standard F

Teachers of science actively participate in the ongoing planning and development of the school science program. In doing this, teachers

- plan and develop the school science program.
- participate in decisions concerning the allocation of time and other resources to the science program.
- participate fully in planning and implementing professional growth and development strategies for themselves and their colleagues.

Reprinted with permission of National Research Council.

This method of providing instruction as called for in the teaching standards, may be a paradigm shift for some— from "sage on the stage" to "guide on the side."

Wayne LeMahieu (Science Task Force member), 2000

Table 4.1 (NRC 1996, 51) compares teaching strategies often found in typical science teaching with those teaching strategies that lead to standards-led science teaching. After implementing the modified strategies presented here, the teacher's role becomes that of a facilitator of student learning, as well as an active participant in the learning process.

TABLE 4.1 **Changing Emphases in K–12 Science Programs**

Traditional Science: Less Emphasis On	Standards-Led Science: More Emphasis On
Treating all students alike and responding to the group as a whole	Understanding and responding to individual student's interests, strengths, experiences, and needs
Rigidly following curriculum	Selecting and adapting curriculum
Focusing on student acquisition of information	Focusing on student understanding and use of scientific knowledge, ideas, and inquiry processes
Presenting scientific knowledge through lecture, text, and demonstration	Guiding students in active and extended scientific inquiry
Asking for recitation of acquired knowledge	Providing opportunities for scientific discussion and debate among students
Testing students for factual information at the end of the unit or chapter	Continuously assessing student understanding
Maintaining responsibility and authority	Sharing responsibility for learning with students
Supporting competition	Supporting a classroom community with cooperation, shared responsibility, and respect
Working alone	Working with other teachers to enhance the science program

Reprinted with permission of National Research Council.

Building from the chart, the *NSES Teaching Standards*, and the *PI 34 Standards for Teacher Development and Licensure*, the task force developed content guidelines for *PI 34* in science. The science content guidelines presented here provide the specificity and interpretive detail needed for the more general *PI 34* standards.

PI 34 Content Guidelines for Science

It is important to note that the *PI 34* content guidelines presented are designed for practicing teachers of science. Detailed content guidelines for the preparation of teachers of science (preservice teachers) are available from the Department of Public Instruction, and provide specificity for obtaining a *PI 34* license in science.

PI 34 Standard 1. Teachers know the subjects they are teaching.

The teacher understands the central concepts, tools of inquiry, and structures of the disciplines he/she teaches and can create learning experiences that make these aspects of subject matter meaningful for students.

Teachers of science shall demonstrate knowledge and understandings sufficient to teach subject matter or grade level science in the following areas:

1. Science classroom safety standards, practices, and procedures
2. The interconnectedness of science and science connections
3. Science as inquiry
4. Physical science, including physics and chemistry
5. Life science, including biology and environmental science
6. Earth and space science
7. Science and technology
8. Science in personal and social perspectives
9. History and nature of science

Teachers of science shall demonstrate the ability to

1. understand the central concepts, tool of inquiry, and structures of the discipline he/she teaches.
2. create learning experiences that make the subject matter meaningful for students.
3. select science content consistent with *Wisconsin's Model Academic Standards in Science* and adapt and design curricula to meet the interests, knowledge, understandings, abilities, and experiences of students.
4. encourage and model the skills of scientific inquiry, as well as curiosity, openness to new ideas and data, and skepticism.
5. plan inquiry based science programs.

Note: For more specific content details, see the *WMASS* and the *NSES*.

PI 34 Standard 2. Teachers know how children grow.

The teacher understands how children learn and develop and can provide learning opportunities that support their intellectual, social, and personal development.

Teachers of science shall demonstrate the ability to

1. understand how students learn and develop.
2. provide learning opportunities that support student intellectual, social, and personal development.

PI 34 Standard 3. Teachers understand that children learn differently.

The teacher understands how students differ in their approaches to learning and creates instructional opportunities that are adapted to diverse learners, including students with disabilities.

Teachers of science shall demonstrate the ability to

1. understand how students differ in their approaches to learning.
2. creates instructional opportunities that are adapted to diverse learners, including students with disabilities.
3. recognize and respond to student diversity and encourage all students to participate fully in science learning.

PI 34 Standard 4. Teachers know how to teach.

The teacher understands and uses a variety of instructional strategies, including the use of technology, to encourage students' development of critical thinking, problem solving, and performance skills.

Teachers of science shall demonstrate the ability to

1. understand and use a variety of instructional strategies, including the use of technology, to encourage students' development of critical thinking, problem solving, and performance skills.
2. orchestrate discourse among students about scientific ideas.
3. challenge students to accept and share responsibility for their own learning in science.
4. create a setting for student work that is flexible and supportive of science inquiry.
5. nurture collaboration among students.
6. structure and facilitate ongoing formal and informal discussions based on shared understanding of rules of scientific discourse.
7. model and emphasize the skill, attitudes, and values of scientific inquiry.
8. focus and support inquiry while interacting with students.

PI 34 Standard 5. Teachers know how to manage a classroom.

The teacher uses an understanding of individual and group motivation and behavior to create a learning environment that encourages positive social interaction, active engagement in learning, and self-motivation.

Teachers of science shall demonstrate the ability to

1. understand individual and group motivation and behavior to create a learning environment that encourages positive social interaction, active engagement in learning and self-motivation.
2. develop a framework of year-long and short-term science-learning goals for students.
3. plan a school science program.
4. ensure a safe science classroom.
5. structure the time available so students can engage in extended investigations.
6. create a setting for student work that is flexible and supportive of science inquiry.
7. manage science tools, materials, media, and technological resources.
8. identify and use resources outside the school.
9. engage students in designing a learning environment.

PI 34 Standard 6. Teachers communicate well.

The teacher uses knowledge of effective verbal and nonverbal communication techniques as well as instructional media and technology to foster active inquiry, collaboration, and supportive interaction in the classroom.

Teachers of science shall demonstrate the ability to

1. use knowledge of effective verbal and nonverbal communication techniques as well as instructional media and technology to foster active inquiry, collaboration, and supportive interaction in the classroom.

PI 34 Standard 7. Teachers are able to plan different kinds of lessons.

The teacher plans instruction based upon knowledge of subject matter, students, the community, and curriculum goals.

Teachers of science shall demonstrate the ability to

1. plan instruction based on knowledge of subject matter, students, the community, and curriculum goals.
2. use *Wisconsin Model Academic Standards in Science* in the development of lessons.
3. engage students in designing the learning environment.

PI 34 Standard 8. Teachers know how to test for student progress.

The teacher understands and uses formal and informal assessment strategies to evaluate and ensure the continuous intellectual, social, and physical development of the learner.

Teachers of science shall demonstrate the ability to

1. understand and use formal and informal assessment strategies to evaluate and ensure the continuous intellectual, social, and physical development of the learner.

2. select assessment strategies that support development of student understanding.
3. use multiple methods to assess student understanding and ability.
4. systematically gather and analyze assessment data to guide teaching.
5. guide students in self-assessment.

PI 34 Standard 9. Teachers are able to evaluate themselves.

The teacher is a reflective practitioner who continually evaluates the effects of his/her choices and actions on others (students, parents, and other professionals in the learning community) and who actively seeks out opportunities to grow professionally.

Teachers of science shall demonstrate the ability to

1. be a reflective practitioner who continually evaluates the effectiveness of his/her choices and actions on others (students, parents, and other professionals in the learning community) and who actively seeks out opportunities to grow professionally.
2. use student data, observations of teaching, and interactions with colleagues to reflect on and improve teaching practice.
3. plan and implement professional growth and development strategies.

PI 34 Standard 10. Teachers are connected with other teachers and the community.

The teacher fosters relationships with school colleagues, parents, and agencies in the larger community to support students' learning and well-being.

Teachers of science shall demonstrate the ability to

1. foster relationships with school colleagues, parents, and agencies in the larger community to support students' learning and well being.
2. use student data, observations of teaching, and interactions with colleagues to report student achievement and opportunities to learn to students, teachers, parents, policymakers, and the general public.
3. work with colleagues within and across disciplines and grade levels.

Student centered classroom environments are environments where teachers pay "close attention to the knowledge, skills, and attitudes that students bring into the classroom" (NRC 1999, 19).

Lisa Wachtel (Science Task Force member), 2000

What Does a Standards-Led Science Classroom Environment Look Like?

A standards-led science classroom environment is an environment established in a science classroom that is student-centered, knowledge-centered, and assessment-centered. This concept is based on the *PI 34 Standards for Teacher Development and Licensure*, the *NSES Teaching Standards*, and from the research previously presented on how students learn science.

The task force found that the answers to three basic questions serve as the foundation for any standards-led science classroom environment. Together, the three questions and their respective answers serve to assist the district team with understanding what is meant by a standards-led science classroom environment.

1. *What is a student centered classroom environment?* "Learning is influenced in fundamental ways by the context in which it takes place" (NRC

1999, 22). The classroom environment must first be student centered. This means simply that the student is the focus. Teachers must use students' pre-cognitions, or prior knowledge, to design the classroom environment. Teachers must pay close attention to the cultural differences among students, their comfort levels in working collectively versus working alone, and the backgrounds that the students bring to the learning environment. The teacher must also pay close attention to the individual progress of each student and devise tasks that are developmentally and intellectually appropriate.

2. *What is a knowledge-centered classroom environment?* Knowledge-centered classroom environments emphasize learning for understanding and application rather than learning solely with memory. Teachers instructing in knowledge-centered classroom environments must pay close attention to what is taught as defined by the *WMASS* and the district curriculum. Knowledge-centered classroom environments imply that knowledge is gained through the depth rather than the breadth of content coverage, which is contrary to many typical classrooms. Learning for understanding is considered more difficult to accomplish but is at the heart of the standards. Learning for understanding takes time.

3. *What is an assessment-centered classroom environment?* In a classroom environment that is assessment-centered, teachers must inform students on how well they are learning science. Assessment-centered classroom environments incorporate a variety of methods and do not rely solely on the typical quiz at the end of the week or the multiple-choice, fill in the blank test, where students are given only a ranking and grade relative to other students. Teachers in assessment-centered classroom environments provide students with opportunities to monitor their own progress and to revise their thinking over weeks, months, or even years. Teachers in assessment-centered classroom environments collect and use evidence of what and how students are learning in science to gauge their instructional practices.

In summary, it is the role of the teacher to create a standards-led classroom environment sensitive to the needs of each student. The route to accomplishing a standards-led classroom environment is by incorporating the characteristics of student-centered, knowledge-centered, and assessment-centered classroom environments as represented in Figure 4.1.

The next section describes in detail the nature of the student and the role of a teacher and provides vignettes that portray standards-led science classroom environments in three grade ranges—elementary, middle, and high school. With each vignette, is a description of how the teacher developed the student-centered, knowledge-centered, and assessment-centered classroom environment.

What Does K–4 Science Look Like in the Classroom?

The Nature of the K–4 Student

The task force found the best description of the nature of the elementary learner in the National Science Teachers Association publication (NSTA) *Pathways to the Science Standards*. (NSTA Press 1997, 31–32)

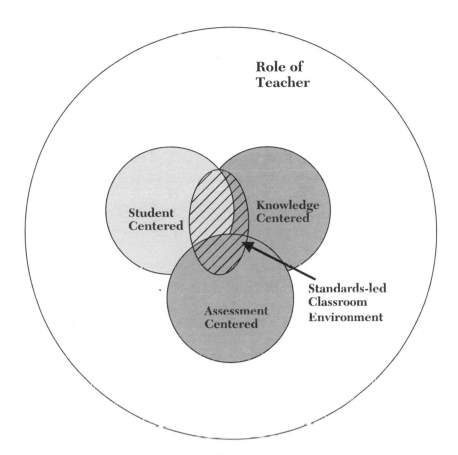

FIGURE 4.1 **Standards-led Science Classroom**

Most primary level students [in kindergarten through second grade] have a natural interest in almost everything around them. They explore the world using all of their senses. They push, pull, and transform objects by acting upon them. They explore their world by watching what others do, mimicking them exactly. These children often make inquiries by guessing about how things work and behave. They tend to believe whatever adults tell them.

Young children's natural capacities for inquiry can be seen when they observe, sort, group, and order objects. . . . Even without being taught, primary level students pair objects in one-to-one correspondences. Pairings are made on the basis of single attributes inherent in objects. . . . By pairing, students learn basic concepts about how things are alike or different. . . . Primary students learn best by building understanding from their own actions upon objects and by telling stories about what they did and what they found out.

Middle elementary grade students [in grades 3 and 4] retain the learning capabilities that they developed at the primary level and begin to experience a broad view of the world. The mental construct of the middle elementary grade student is comprehensive, and has a rationale or logic to it. Instead of being satisfied with matching objects, they tend to want to create large, complex organizations. If a student puts leaves together on the basis of their shapes, then a logical arrangement has been made by imposing a singular rule on the objects. Students are able to discover and understand singular rules if they are given the opportunity. They are now able to think back through a story to find the cause of an event. Because they understand antecedents, they begin to make simple predictions about outcomes ... and see a continuous chain of sequences that has no beginning and no end.

Reprinted with permission of National Science Teachers Association Press

Table 4.2 summarizes the nature of a typical learner in kindergarten through grade 4. The chart shows the relationship of the learner to the teaching license required in *PI 34*. The chart was developed by the task force (DPI 2000) and adapted from the *Biological Basis of Thinking and Learning* (Lowery 1998), *Pathways to the National Science Education Standards* (NSTA 1998), and the *Guide to Curriculum Planning in Science* (DPI 1993).

The Role of the K–4 Teacher

Teachers must help young students build accurate concepts, use process skills, and foster scientific curiosity through a standards-led classroom environment. Teachers can engage students, structure time, create a setting, make tools available, identify resources, assess students' progress, and guide students' self-assessments.

To accomplish the previous tasks, teachers must employ effective practices specified by the teaching standards (NRC 1996). The contemporary teacher understands the unique needs of each child in the classroom and meets their diverse needs. Constructivist techniques of assessing students' preconceptions, building on their past experiences, taking sufficient time to teach, and fostering continuing inquiry, are the hallmarks of these effective practices.

Research strongly supports the idea that children learn best by building their own knowledge through appropriate experiences. Because students acquire knowledge at different rates and through different learning styles, teachers need to provide instruction that is flexible and sensitive to these individual differences.

It is important that teachers make thoughtful choices about what they want their students to learn. They should engage students in ideas that are relevant and likely to serve them well over their lifetimes. It is also important to recognize that not all hands-on experiences reflect constructivist approaches to teaching. Recipe-type experiences, in which students follow directions to replicate an experiment or build a model, are not considered constructivist experiences. Even though students' needs vary from district to district, teachers must base their instruction on the *WMASS* and prepare students for a lifetime of scientific literacy (NSTA 1997).

Standards-Led Science Classroom in Action

The following vignette is an example of an exemplary elementary classroom in action. The science knowledge (content) the students learn illustrates the

TABLE 4.2 **The Nature of the Elementary Student in Science**

PI 34 Wisconsin Teacher License	Approximate Grade Level of Student	Nature of the Learner
Early Childhood	**K–2**	**Most students** • learn from their observations, using as many of their senses as they can. • can follow the sequence of a science story. • have a natural interest in almost everything around them. • begin grouping objects on the basis of similarities and differences, physical properties. • can make direct measurements • begin connecting actions and outcomes in activities. • think only about what is being acted upon. • exhibit irreversible thinking. • show egocentric behavior. • center attention on only one detail of an event in an inquiry activity. • have linear thinking. • reasoning is not based on accepted adult logic. **Students may find it difficult to** • classify objects by multiple characteristics. • transfer abstract ideas to objects and events outside their direct experience. • use observations to draw simple conclusions. • use trial and error to solve problems. • compare the past with the present.
Early Childhood through Middle Childhood	**3–4**	**Students continue to** • make observations using their senses. • make simple comparisons of objects. • improve their ability to communicate in spoken and written form. • sequence events to tell a science story logically. • can classify if given a classification system. • produce new knowledge by reorganizing existing concepts in an activity. • operate logically on real objects but not on ideas. • behave in less egocentric ways resulting in ability to perform more effectively in-group work. • use their observations to draw simple conclusions. • use trial and error to solve problems. • predict results based on experiences. • compare the past with the present. • are able to communicate in various ways. **Students continue to improve their ability to** • describe changes. • communicate their ideas in variety of ways. • collect and share data. • work collaboratively. **They begin** • making simple predictions. • designing simple comparative tests. • gathering information to answer their own questions. **Students may find it difficult to** • draw inferences from data and identify large patterns in data taken over time. • predict unknown data from data that are known. • understand a thought sequence based on simple logic. • discover cause-and-effect relationships.

WMASS Content Standards Science Inquiry (B) and the Science Connections (A) with Physical Science (D) unfolding through the teacher's actions. Following the vignette are examples of representative practices of the standards-led science classroom environment. (NRC 1996, 124–125)

Willie the Hamster

Ms. W. encourages students to engage in an investigation initiated by a question that signals student interest. The context for the investigation is one familiar to the students—a pet in the classroom. She teaches some of the important aspects of inquiry by asking the students to consider alternative explanations, to look at the evidence, and to design a simple investigation to test a hypothesis. Ms. W. has planned the science classes carefully, but changes her plans to respond to student interests, knowing the goals for the school science program and shaping the activities to be consistent with those goals. She understands what is developmentally appropriate for students of this age—she chooses not to launch into an abstract explanation of evaporation. She has a classroom with the resources she needs for the students to engage in an inquiry activity.

George is annoyed. There was plenty of water in the watering can when he left it on the windowsill on Friday. Now the can is almost empty, and he won't have time to go to the restroom and fill it so that he can water the plants before science class starts. As soon as Ms. W. begins science class, George raises his hand to complain about the disappearance of the water. "Who used the water?" he asks. "Did someone drink it? Did someone spill it?" None of the students in the class touched the watering can, and Ms. W. asks what the students think happened to the water.

Marie has an idea. If none of the children took the water, then it must be that Willie, their pet hamster, is leaving his cage at night and drinking the water. The class decides to test Marie's idea by covering the watering can so that Willie cannot drink the water. The children implement their investigation, and the next morning observe that the water level has not dropped. The children now have proof that their explanation is correct. Ms. W. asks the class to consider alternative explanations consistent with their observations. Are they sure that Willie is getting out of his cage at night? The children are quite certain that he is.

"How can you be sure?" asks Ms. W. The children devise an ingenious plan to convince her that Willie is getting out of the cage. They place his cage in the middle of the sand table and smooth the sand. After several days and nights, the children observe that no footprints have appeared in the sand, and the water level has not changed. The children now conclude that Willie is not getting out of his cage at night.

"But wait," says Kahena, "Why should Willie get out of his cage? Willie can see that the watering can is covered." So the class decides to leave the cage in the middle of the sand table and take the cover off the watering can. The water level begins to drop again, yet there are no footprints in the sand. Now the children dismiss the original idea about the disappearance of the water, and Ms. W. takes the opportunity to give the class more experiences with the disappearance of water.

At Ms. W.'s suggestion, a container of water with a wide top is placed on the windowsill and the class measures and records changes in the water level each day using strips of paper to represent the height of the water. These strips are dated and pasted on a large sheet of paper to create a bar graph. After a few days, the students discern a pattern: The level of water fell steadily but did not decrease the same amount each day. After considerable discussion about the differences, Patrick observes that when his mother dries the family's clothes, she puts them in the dryer. Patrick notes that the clothes are heated inside the dryer and that when his mother does not set the dial on the dryer to heat, the clothes just spin around and do not dry as quickly. Patrick suggests that water might disappear faster when it is warmer.

Based on their experience using strips of paper to measure changes in the level of water and in identifying patterns of change, the students and Ms. W. plan an investigation to learn whether water disappears faster when it is warmer.

The children's experiences with the disappearance of water continue with an investigation about how the size (area) of the uncovered portion of the container influences how fast the water disappears and another where the children investigate whether using a fan to blow air over the surface of a container of water makes the water disappear faster.

Ms. W. understands what is developmentally appropriate for her students.

NRC, 1996, 124.

Reprinted with permission of National Research Council.

Ms. W. used the following teaching strategies to develop a student-centered science classroom environment:

- Ms. W. encouraged students to propose explanations about the disappearance of the water.
- Ms. W. used the "teachable moment" of a student discovery of the disappearing water and connected it to an important concept of evaporation appropriate to student-development level.
- Ms. W. asked students thought-provoking questions such as, "How can you be sure?"
- Ms. W. provided additional experiences to further and extend students' questions and inquiry.
- Ms. W. allocated the necessary time, tools, skills, and resources to investigate the disappearance of the water.
- Ms. W. encouraged the involvement of all students.

Ms. W. planned what performance statements from the *WMASS* students would learn in *Willie the Hamster*. The following list represents the knowledge-centered classroom environment:

- Science Connections: A. 4.3. When investigating a science-related problem, decide what data can be collected to determine the most useful explanations. A. 4.4. When studying science-related problems, decide which of the science themes are important.

- Physical Science: D. 4.3. Understand that substances can exist in different states–solid, liquid, gas. D. 4.4. Observe and describe changes in form, temperature, color, speed, and direction of objects and construct explanations for the changes.
- Science Inquiry: C. 4.1. Use the vocabulary of the unifying themes to ask questions about objects, organisms, and events being studied. C. 4.5. Use data they have collected to develop explanations and answer questions generated by investigations.

Assessment strategies Ms. W. could use in an assessment-centered classroom environment:

- Assess students' precognition by discussing pets at home and their knowledge about water.
- Assess to reveal the important aspects of inquiry by asking students for verbal and written evidence for alternative explanations for the disappearing water.
- Assess important science content, from the standards, needed to explain the students' work.
- Assess the students' abilities to transfer the science content (evaporation) to other examples.

What Does Science Look Like in Grades 5–8?

The Nature of the Middle-Level Learner

Middle-level learners have unique characteristics as they transition from elementary- to middle-level education. This transition can be challenging to educators. Teachers must understand the diverse natures of middle-level students; although some behave predictably and maturely, others exhibit erratic and inconsistent behavior that is more childlike.

Students at the middle level should become accustomed to working in a laboratory situation. However, many middle-level students lack coordination, which may impact laboratory design. Cognitively, they should be competent in recognizing patterns in events, which leads to questions that can be answered by investigation. The students should be able to make observations carefully and to use measuring devices. They should be able to organize data and analyze measurements. Students at this level can manage a much greater array of intellectual tasks than they could in earlier years. Because middle-level students are very self-conscious, they should have ample opportunities to identify and discuss issues among themselves (NSTA 1998).

Table 4.3 summarizes the nature of a typical learner in middle-level science. The chart shows the relationship of the learner to the teaching license required in *PI 34*. The task force developed this chart in March 2000 by turning to the *Biological Basis of Thinking and Learning* (Lowery 1998), *Pathways to the National Science Education Standards* (NSTA 1998), and the *Guide to Curriculum Planning in Science* (DPI 1986) for guidance.

TABLE 4.3 **Nature of the Typical Middle-Level Student in Science**

PI 34 Wisconsin Teacher License	Approximate Grade Level of Student	Characteristics of the Learner
Middle Childhood through Early Adolescence	5–8	**Students continue to** • make observations and comparisons. • ask questions. **Most students are able to** • interpret and record data. • view situations from different perspectives. • determine the relationship between cause and effect. • measure size, weight (mass), temperature, capacity, and time accurately. • observe and describe the use of science and technology in everyday life. • determine relationships between organisms and their environments. • predict unknown data from data that is known. • apply knowledge to solve complex problems • visualize simple models prepared by self or others. • intuitively deal with proportions. **Students begin** • identifying variables. • designing detailed experiments. • designing fair tests in which variables are changed. • creating and interpreting graphs. • analyzing sets of data for patterns. **Some students may find it difficult to** • make a formal hypothesis that includes a possible cause and predicts an outcome. • devise their own controlled experiment. • predict possible sources or error in an inquiry activity. • build and understand their own models. • solve problems with proportional relationships.

The Role of the Middle-Level Teacher

How can teachers support diverse learners in their middle-level classrooms and work to build a real community of learners? The first step is to model acceptance and tolerance for all members of the classroom. Secondly, teachers must consciously choose methods and assessments that support the diverse nature and learning styles of the students. Teachers need to practice sensitivity when critiquing and evaluating student work. Middle-level science should be grounded in inquiry and provide a multisensory approach to instruction. The science should be personally relevant to students, as well as provide a window into the inner workings of the natural and designed worlds.

Standards-Led Science Classroom in Action

The following vignette is an example of an exemplary middle-level classroom in Wisconsin. In the vignette, the science knowledge (content) students learn illustrates the *WMASS Content Standards Science Inquiry (B)* and the *Science Connections (A)* with *Life and Environmental Science (F)* unfolding through the teachers' actions. Following the vignette are examples of representative practices of standards-led science classroom environment.

Wisconsin Fast Plants Vignette: Mr. B., Seventh Grade

"OK! Let's *rapa* it up!"

"Arrrgh! Mr. B.! That is soooo weak!!!"

"You have ten minutes! Get with it! Remember to put the forceps back in the green bottle on the cart. Make sure you have labeled the front of your film cans with the date, hour, and initials."

Mr. B.'s seventh grade science class will be using *Wisconsin Fast Plants*, a variety of *Brassica rapa*, to learn about plant growth and development. But first he will use the three-day-old seedlings to introduce the kids to the world of science inquiry. He uses the inquiry process to help students sharpen the critical thinking skills that he emphasizes throughout the course. This will be the first of several student research experiences in the year.

A group of three students approaches Mr. B. with their film cans in hand. "Mr. B., we have the seedlings stuck to the sides of the film can by their hypocotyls . . ." Scott glances at the drawing on the board,—their cotyledons. "Do we need to cover the open end with a lid?"

Avoiding giving an answer, Mr. B. coaxes the students to think further. "Well, what do you think?"

"If we don't cover it, it could dry out?"

"That's a thought. . . . Katie, what do you think?"

"Wouldn't we also want a cover on the film can to eliminate light?"

"Oh yeah!" The light bulb goes off in Scott's head. "We want to remove light as a variable!"

Jackie joins in, "But I thought plants needed light to grow!? Won't they die without light?"

"That's a good question!" Mr. B. adds with a grin.

It seems simple enough. The students are setting up one of Mr. B.'s favorite activities: The Crucifer Cross. In this experiment, students cut four, three-day-old Fast Plant seedlings at the soil line leaving the stem (hypocotyl) and seedling leaves (cotyledons) intact. A gravitropism chamber is then constructed by placing four moist paper towel strip wicks along the inner side of a film can so that there is one wick each along the length of the top, bottom, and both sides of the can when it is placed on its side. The cotyledons of each seedling are then stuck to each wick so that the water on the wick holds the seedling in place. A cross section of the final chamber set up is below.

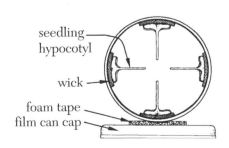

seedling

hypocotyl

wick

foam tape

film can cap

He turns to the class and addresses them as a whole. "Remember! When you are done, you need to make a prediction. Copy the frontal view into your lab notebooks. Then draw what you expect the hypocotyls to look like by tomorrow. Stick your necks out! Make a prediction!"

Joann raises her hand "What do you mean? Like, what will the stems do?"

"Yes. What do you think the four hypocotyls will look like when you open this tomorrow?"

Bobby interjects, "You mean like all limp and dead?" His friends snicker.

"If that's what you think, then write that down. But it won't be an easy way out because you must back up your prediction with some solid reasoning."

"No! I'm not slackin'. Seriously! We killed them! They are dead, so—"

Mr. B. cuts in, "Is that an observation, or an inference?"

A sprinkling of kids chimed in, "Inference!!!"

"Why?" He scans the horizon for an arm. "Jaime?"

"Because he's saying they are dead, but doesn't KNOW they are dead. He doesn't have any data … observations to support that."

"But," Bobby protests, "we cut them down. Slashed them above their roots! They are dead!"

"OK! OK! Hold on to that thought. Journal on it if it helps you sleep tonight. So, maybe we might want to clarify. Assuming they are still alive, I'd expect … "

Jason blurts out, "OH! That maybe they'd bend toward the back?"

Mr. B. continues, "OK, let's run with that. How else could these 'stems' respond? Don't tell me why you say it, just give me some ideas."

Sarah's hand shoots up, "They could bend downward?"

"OK," Mr. B. draws dotted lines down, representing hypocotyls that are bent down.

"What else? Billy?"

"Well, they could all stay straight, or maybe bend up?"

"OK. So we have some options here, bend up, bend down, stay straight, toward front or back."

He announces one last time, "Make sure you draw your predictions for tomorrow. Then write a brief passage telling why you think they will do this! You cannot open your canister unless you've made a prediction. No peeking and no talking to other classes!"

Day 2

Seventh hour seems to come more quickly today. Students stream in a few at a time. The students are pumped to open their canisters. Some fidget in anticipation. Others feign disinterest.

"OK, everyone has made a prediction! When you open your film can, you should draw the Fast Plants the way you see them. Go do it!"

Things get quite loud on days like today. Geoff, seated near the front, has some interesting results. His Fast Plants have managed to stay adhered to the side. That is crucial! Mr. B. asks Geoff to make a chart on the board, as his peers provide categories for grouping their data.

"Start with yours, Geoff." Geoff approaches the front and draws a picture of what is inside his canister. The two horizontal hypocotyls have curved upwards. The one pointing down has arched 180 degrees, bending it into a U shape. Only the hypocotyl originally pointing up has remained unchanged.

Geoff asks each of his peers what they got for results. As the numbers are tallied up, it is clear that a trend can be seen in the data with 19 students reporting 'up', 1 reporting 'down', 2 reporting 'same', and 6 as inconclusive. Now they need to draw some conclusions.

"So! What do you think? What should we do with these?"

Lynn starts things rolling, "Trina, how did you get 'down'?"

Trina looks inside her canister and replies, "Well, the one on the left is kinda, a little bit, tipped down." A few kids snicker.

Mr. B. interrupts, "Hey! Watch it! It's not her fault if we didn't develop some better criteria! . . . What do we mean if a canister is recorded as 'up' or 'down'?"

An outburst ensues, as kids clarify with neighbors just what they had meant by 'up' or 'down'. As things quiet down, a self-appointed spokesperson blurts out, "To call it an 'up', all hypocotyls had to be pointing up or at least three of them!"

Mr. B. asks for clarification. "At least three? So if one was pointing down—"

John cuts to the chase. "No, if the three, besides the bottom one, were pointed up, then we called it 'up'. So, like, Katie's bottom one tipped over, but we can still count hers as 'up' because the other three bent up."

Mr. B. attempts to summarize: "So, you all agree that to score yours as 'up', you should have all except the bottom one curved up?"

"YES!"

Steve still isn't satisfied. "If some fell off I think we should ignore them. We should count the can as 'up' if the ones that stayed stuck curved up."

Cindi nods in agreement. "Mine was 'inconclusive' because three had fallen off but the one that stayed stuck definitely curved upwards."

"So what's our criteria?" Mr. B. pushes.

Steve is on to it. "If any one curves upwards, it counts as an 'up'. And it has to **curve** so the one that started out pointing up doesn't count." Most people nod, satisfied.

"So with those criteria, there are 21 'up'. We can at least say that there's a consistent 'tendency' toward bending up. Right? OK . . . is that what you predicted?"

The noise level rises again.

"Given our class data—and I'll add that we've basically seen the same thing throughout the day—what do you think is going on?"

A hand flies up.

"Wait, I want you to write! Assume now, that we are seeing a tendency toward curving up. How would you account for this? What's causing this? Write it in your journal for tomorrow."

Day 3

Mr. B. knows that a challenging discussion faces the class today. Developing hypotheses to account for unexpected results—a challenge in any research lab, but precisely the kind of stick-your-neck-out creative thinking that middle school students are generally not encouraged to do academically or socially.

"OK! Ideas? What's going on here? Why would these stems bend up?" Even he isn't sure why the plants did this. Mr. B. has some ideas, but he is after something else. He has seen this before; kids have a hunch, a feeling—call it a hypothesis if that makes you feel good. But they will reserve comments until someone breaks the ice. Looks like he'll need to push them today.

"Carlos?"

"Huh?"

"C'mon, give me some idea, a guess, about why these plants are bending up."

"You mean a hypothesis?"

"Sure, if you want to call it that. Give me a hypothesis."

Ashley adds, "Ummm ... isn't that an educated guess?"

A number of students burst out laughing. Carlos laughs and goes on, "Yeah, that's my point! I don't really know much about plants, so I don't think I'll give the right answer."

Mr. B. smiles. "Is that what experimentation is about? Getting the right answer? Carlos has said something that I am certain many of you were thinking—'what's the right answer?' or 'I'm gonna say something stupid!' And that is the difference between traditional cookbook labs and real science. In cookbook labs everything has been done a thousand times and, if done correctly, there is a right answer. But this, . . . this is science. The plants bent correctly—what happened, happened. Now we need to think about that, and in order to really come up with a good idea, we are going to need to think creatively—take chances, engage your brains, be messy, make mistakes, and make lots and lots of observations. It's not about answers so much as it is about questions." He goes on, "So, again, why do these plants curve up? Jamie?"

"Maybe they are looking for water?"

"OK ... " Mr. B. writes this on the board . . . , "Water ... any others? Carlos?"

"Maybe gases? Like oxygen or carbon dioxide?"

"OK ... " The dance continues as the students generate a half dozen possible variables that could be causing the plants to curl. The tension in the room decreases as kids begin to realize that this was a safe environment to share.

After reviewing the potential causal factors with his students, Mr. B. takes it a step further. "OK, now I want you to think about which of these factors you feel is most likely to cause the curving of the hypocotyls. Write this down in your lab notebooks. Then, I want you to write a brief statement telling how you would test to see if this is indeed the factor that causes the plants to curl. You've got two minutes—no talking."

Mr. B. gives them a few minutes to jot down some thoughts. As the students begin reaching some closure, he announces: "Now! Go to your lab stations and talk amongst yourselves. What variable would your group like to experiment with and why? This should be something that we could do with the resources we have here—the film can set-ups. First-come, first-served, no repeats. You've got seven to ten minutes, and then we've got to share ideas."

After ten minutes, Mr. B. announces that the students will need to finalize things within their groups, then give an informal explanation of what they were thinking about doing. As students share their experimental designs, their peers, within and between groups, offer advice and criticism. By the time they hit the last group, there is just enough time to assign a journal entry: "Explain, in your own words, what your group would like to do for an experiment. Use the terms 'control' and "experimental variable'. Predict what will happen and explain what kind of data you will collect to help support your claims."

Inquiry is the foundation of Mr. B.'s class.

Science Task Force, 2000

Overall, the discussions have been broad ranging, the experimental results are messy and the conclusions ambiguous. But Mr. B. feels that the students are gaining a more realistic understanding of and appreciation for the inquiry process of science. And scientists or not, this will serve them well later in life.

This vignette was developed by Professor Emeritus Paul Williams, Wisconsin Fast Plants, under a contract with the Department of Public Instruction.

Mr. B. used the following teaching strategies to develop a student-centered science classroom environment:

- Mr. B. asked students thought-provoking questions, such as, "Well if we don't cover it, will it dry out?" or, "What do you think?"
- Mr. B. provided opportunities to expand the learning experience.
- Mr. B. encouraged students to develop scientific curiosity.
- Mr. B. allowed students to explore their own questions about the activity.
- Mr. B. orchestrated discourse among students.
- Mr. B. was able to determine if students understood the science concepts through questioning techniques.

Mr. B. planned what performance statements from *WMASS* students would learn in the fast plants activity. The following standards represent the knowledge-centered classroom environment:

- Science Connections: A. 8.2. Describe the limitations of science systems and give reasons why specific science themes are included or excluded from those systems. A. 8.5. Show how models and explanations, based on systems, were changed as new evidence accumulated.
- Life and Environmental Science: F. 8.5. Show how different structures both reproduce and pass on characteristics of their group. F. 8.6. Understand that an organism is regulated internally and externally.

- Science Inquiry: C. 8.3. Design and safely conduct investigations that provide reliable quantitative or qualitative data to answer their questions. C. 8.5. Use accepted scientific knowledge, models, and theories to explain their results and to raise further questions about their investigations. C. 8.7. Explain their data and conclusions in ways that allow an audience to understand the questions they selected for investigations and answers they have developed.

The following are assessment strategies Mr. B. could use in an assessment-centered classroom environment:

- Assess students' precognitions, including misconceptions
- Assess critical-thinking skills through inquiry activities during the fast plant activity
- Monitor journal entries
- Assess science content from the standards needed to understand the activity
- Assess students' abilities to apply learning in a different context
- Assess students' abilities to use research methods to answer questions
- Assess students' abilities to translate the knowledge and skills gained in this experience to new lab situations.

What Does High School Science Look Like in Grades 9–12?

The Nature of the High School Student

Many students in high school have developed the capacity to solve a problem in science. However, not all high school students can use formal reasoning, think abstractly, and form theories and explanations to solve these problems. High school students can simultaneously manipulate more than one variable. A typical high school student can begin to solve problems by suggesting probable hypotheses. Some high school students are fully able to understand someone else's mental model but have not developed the capacity to construct their own mental model. For example, some students can classify if given a classification system but cannot develop their own classification system. High school students must have the opportunity to experience science beyond a textbook. Activities must be designed to allow students to maximize their learning through inquiry-based instruction. This would include allowing students to design a controlled experiment and to collect and analyze the data. They should be provided opportunities to practice and refine their problem-solving skills and communication of the findings (NSTA 1996).

Table 4.4 summarizes the nature of a typical learner in high school science. The chart shows the relationship of the learner to the teaching license

TABLE 4.4. **Nature of the Typical High School Student in Science**

PI 34 Wisconsin Teacher License	Approximate Grade Level of Student	Nature of the Learner
Early Adolescence through Adolescence	9–12	**Students continue to** • make observations and comparisons. • ask questions. • design multiple experiments. • identify multiple variables in an experiment or experiments. • analyze sets of data for multiple patterns. **Most students are able to** • use logical thought processes as part of their normal thinking. • make formal hypotheses that include probable causes and predictions on the possible outcome. • design controlled experiments. • determine all possible combinations of variables in an experiment. • include mathematical relationships in analysis and conclusions. • express proportional relationships. • practice and refine their abstract problem-solving skills.

required in *PI 34*. It was developed by the task force (DPI 2000), and adapted from the *Biological Basis of Thinking and Learning* (Lowery 1998), *Pathways to the National Science Education Standards* (NSTA 1998), and the *Guide to Curriculum Planning in Science* (DPI 1986).

The Role of the High School Teacher

The high school teacher today can no longer be a one-subject encyclopedia of knowledge. Teachers must facilitate learning, as opposed to disseminating facts. Teachers must provide students opportunities to explore their own understandings about science. High school students bring to the classroom environment a wide range of educational experiences, both formal and informal. The teacher's role is to provide an opportunity for those experiences to be used in the classroom, culminating in scientific understandings of the natural and designed world.

Connections to students' postsecondary goals and plans must be incorporated into lessons. High school science curricula provides more opportunities for teachers to introduce issue-based discussions, respecting differing opinions of maturing high school students. Finally, high school teachers must transmit the importance of lifelong learning in science. As science and technology rapidly expand in our world, students need to appreciate the need for continuously learning (NSTA 1996).

Standards-Led Science Classroom in Action

The following vignette is an example of an exemplary high school classroom (NRC 1996). The featured Wisconsin teacher was developing strategies for students to learn science content found in the *WMASS* Content Standards *Science Connections (A)* with *Life and Environmental Science (F)* and the classroom environment unfolds through the teacher's actions. Following the vignette are examples of representative practices of the standards-led science classroom environment. (NRC 1996, 63–66)

Genetics

Ms. J. recently attended a workshop with other teachers at the university where she learned equally from the instructors and the other attendees. She also reads research regularly, reviews resources, and makes judgments about their value for her teaching. Ms. J. engages in an iterative planning process, moving from a broad semester plan to daily details. The students in her high school class have opportunities to develop mental models, work with instructional technology, use multiple materials, teach one another, and consider the personal, social, and ethical aspects of science. She has the support of the school and district and has the resources she needs. She also relies on resources in the community.

Ms. J. is eager to begin the school year, and is particularly looking forward to teaching a semester course on transmission genetics—how traits are inherited from one generation to the next. She taught the course before and read extensively about the difficulties students have with transmission genetics conceptually and as a means of developing problem-solving skills. She also has been learning about new approaches to teaching genetics. From her reading and from a workshop she attended for high school teachers at the local university, she knows that many people have been experimenting with ways to improve genetics instruction. She also knows that several computer programs are available that simulate genetics events.

Ms. J. is convinced that many important learning goals of the school's science program can be met in this course. She wants to provide the students with opportunities to understand the basic principles of transmission genetics. She also wants them to appreciate how using a mental model is useful to understanding. She wants her students to engage in and learn the processes of inquiry as they develop their mental models. Ms. J. also wants students to understand the effect of transmission genetics on their lives and on society; here she wants them to address an issue that includes science and ethics.

Selecting an appropriate computer program is important, because simulation will be key to much of the first quarter of the course. Ms. J. has reviewed several and noted common features. Each simulation allows students to select parental phenotypes and make crosses. Offspring were produced quickly by all the programs; genotypes and phenotypes are distributed stochastically according to the inheritance pattern. With such programs, students will be able to simulate many generations of crosses in a single class period. All the programs are open-ended—no answer books are provided to check answers. All the programs allow students to begin with data and construct a model of the elements and processes of an inheritance pattern. Students will be able to use the model to predict the phenotypes and genotypes of future offspring and check predictions by making the crosses. Ms. J. chooses one of the simulations after reviewing it carefully and considering the budget she has for supplies. Enough computers are available to permit students to work in teams of four.

Students will work in their teams to develop models of inheritance patterns during the first quarter. Ms. J. plans to obtain reprints of Mendel's original article for students to read early in the quarter. It has a nice model for an inheritance pattern, and students will examine it as they identify elements of a mental model. In addition to using the simulations, Ms. J. wants students to work with living organisms. She will need to order the proper yeast strains, fruit flies, and Fast Plants. She has commercially prepared units in genetics using each of these organisms and has adapted the units to meet the needs of the students. Each organism has advantages and limitations when used to study transmission genetics; students will be working in teams and will share with other teams what they learn from the different organisms.

During the second quarter, students will focus on human genetics. Ms. J. intends to contact the local university to arrange for a particular speaker from the clinical genetics department. The speaker and Ms. J. have worked together before, and she knows how well the speaker presents information on classes of inherited human disorders, human pedigree analysis, new research in genetic susceptibility to common illnesses, and the many careers associated with human genetics. Someone from the state laboratory also will come and demonstrate karyotyping and leave some photographs so students can try sorting chromosomes to get a feel for the skill required to do this. Having students perform a karyotype will give new meaning to a phrase in the text: "the chromosome images are sorted by type."

Each student will become an "expert" in one inherited human disorder, learning about the mode of inheritance, symptoms, frequency, effect on individuals and family, care, and such. Students will present their reports to the class. They will also work in pairs to solve an ethical case study associated with an inherited disorder. Drawing on several articles about teaching ethical issues to children, Ms. J. has created one of her own, and with the help of colleagues and the staff at the clinical genetics center, she has developed several case studies from which the students will develop their ethical issue papers. Part of the case study will require students to draw a pedigree. Ms. J. is gathering print matter: fliers from the March of Dimes, textbooks on clinical genetics, some novels and short stories about people with inherited disorders, and articles from popular magazines. This is an ongoing effort—she has been collecting material for some years now. She also has posters and pictures from service organizations she will put up around the room, but some wall space needs to be saved for student data charts.

Having reviewed the goals and structure of the course, Ms. J.'s next planning step is to map tasks by week. She has a good idea of how long different activities will take from her previous experience teaching this course. Planning for each week helps ensure that the live materials and the speakers are coordinated for the right time. But Ms. J. knows that it is likely that she will need to adjust scheduling. Ms. J. and the students will set routines and procedures during the first week; then students will do much of the class work in their teams.

Finally, Ms. J. begins to map out the days of the first week. On the first day of class, the students will share why they chose this course and what their hopes and expectations are. They might also describe what they already know about genetics and what questions they bring to class.

Reprinted with permission of National Research Council

Ms. J. used the following teaching strategies to develop a student centered classroom environment:

- Ms. J. planned opportunities for students to be actively engaged by acting like scientists and becoming experts on inherited human disorder.
- Ms. J.'s teaching plans ensured that students were responsible for their own learning.
- Ms. J. developed instruction to meet students' needs by planning to constantly gather data on her students.
- Ms J. planned guided instruction with specific questions on the subject matter and science standards.
- Ms. J. encouraged student self-assessment throughout her planning strategies.
- Ms. J. planned to change the physical environment as the structure of the class changed.

Ms. J. planned what performance statements from the *WMASS* students would learn. This represents the knowledge centered classroom environment:

- Science Connections: A. 12.5. Show how the ideas and themes of science can be used to make real-life decisions about careers, work places, lifestyles, and use of resources. A. 12.7. Reexamine the evidence and reasoning that led to conclusions drawn from investigations, using the science themes.
- Life and Environmental Science: F. 12.3. Explain current scientific ideas and information about the molecular and genetic basis of heredity. F. 12.4. State the relationships between functions of the cell and the functions of the organism as related to genetics and heredity. F. 12.6. Using concepts of evolution and heredity, account for changes in species and the diversity of species, include the influence of those changes in science, such as breeding of plants or animals.

Ms. J. could use the following assessment strategies in an assessment-centered classroom environment:

> *Ms. J. reads research regularly, reviews resources, and makes judgments about their value for her teaching.*
> NRC, 1996, 63

- Assess students' precognitions, including misconceptions
- Assess critical thinking skills during the inquiry experience
- Assess how students' development of the mental models helped them understand the process of inquiry
- Assess the use of mental models to explain science knowledge
- Assess students' abilities to translate science knowledge and processes to real-world settings.
- Assess students' abilities for verbal and written communication
- Assess students' abilities to make informed decisions from issue papers derived from the synthesis of scientific knowledge and applications.

Conclusion and Implications

The chapter has led the district team on a path of exploration and discovery. The district team explored teaching and learning through the lens of the standards. The team discovered how *PI 34* and the *NSES Teaching Standards* shape and change the classroom environment from a traditional to a standards-led classroom environment, and the team has discovered how students' natures influence instructional practices.

At this point in the process, the district team needs to consider that the road map may lead them to several destinations simultaneously. The team may decide to consider professional development for the staff and selection of the instructional materials together, or they may wish to consider assessment. The choice must be made based on district needs.

References

Lowery, Lawrence F. 1998. *The Biological Basis of Thinking and Learning*. Berkeley, Calif.: Full Option Science System.

NRC (National Research Council). 1996. *National Science Education Standards*. Washington, D.C.: National Academy Press.

———. 1999. *How People Learn: Bridging Research and Practice*. Washington, D.C.: National Academy Press.

NSTA (National Science Teachers Association). 1996. *Pathways to the Science Standards: Guidelines for Moving the Vision into Practice (High School Edition)*. Arlington, Va.: NSTA Press.

———. 1997. *Pathways to the Science Standards: Guidelines for Moving the Vision into Practice (Elementary School Edition)*. Arlington, Va.: NSTA Press.

———. 1998. *Pathways to the Science Standards: Guidelines for Moving the Vision into Practice (Middle School Edition)*. Arlington, Va.: NSTA Press.

Teacher Education Program Approval and Licenses under Chapter PI 34, Wis. Admin. Code. Madison, Wis.: Wisconsin Department of Public Instruction.

Wisconsin Department of Public Instruction. 1993. *A Guide to Curriculum Planning in Science*. 1986. Reprint. Madison, Wis.: Wisconsin Department of Public Instruction.

———. 1998. *Wisconsin's Model Academic Standards for Science*. Madison, Wis.: Wisconsin Department of Public Instruction.

Additional Reading

Appendix A

Appendix E

Rutherford, James F, and Andrew Ahlgren (for the American Association for the Advancement of Science). 1990. *Science for All Americans*. New York: Oxford University Press.

Zemelman, Steven, Harvey Daniels, and Arthur Hyde. 1998. *Best Practice New Standards for Teaching and Learning in America's Schools* 2nd ed. Portsmouth, NH: Heinemann.

Chapter 5
Essential Components of a K–12 Science Program

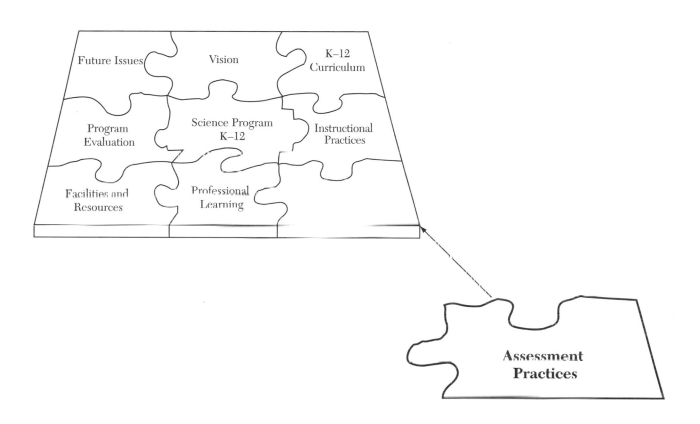

The figure illustrates the interlocking nature of the components of the standards-led science program. The power of the K–12 standards-led science program emerges when all the pieces of the program are present. Chapter 5 outlines the assessment practices in the standards-led science program.
Science Task Force, May 2000

How Are Students' Understandings about Science Revealed?

Assessment Practices

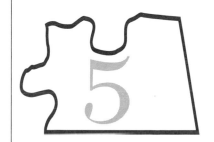

An erosional remnant of Cambrian sandstone at Mill Bluff State Park. The remnant was shaped by a glacial lake; Bruce A. Brown of the WGNHS. Wisconsin DNR photo.

In *Who Moved My Cheese* (Johnson 1999), mice were able to find new sources of cheese only after they let go of old beliefs and practices and explored new avenues for finding their cheese. This simple parable, "old beliefs do not lead to new cheese" holds similar truths when considering classroom assessment practices and beliefs. Part of the job of the *district team* is to confront old beliefs and misconceptions and replace them with current, accurate information about the role and importance of classroom assessment in the teaching-learning-assessment triad.

As national and state science standards evolved, there has been a paradigm shift around the delivery of science education. This paradigm shift reflects a movement toward the identification of fundamental science concepts that connect scientific knowledge with the integration of scientific processes, such as inquiry, to expand students' science understandings. This view contrasts with traditional approaches to science education, where facts are disconnected and the scientific process is separated from science knowledge (NRC 1996). As described in the previous chapters, *Wisconsin's Model Academic Standards for Science (WMASS)* (DPI 1998e) identified fundamental science concepts and processes for students, written both as content and performance standards.

As districts develop, implement, and evaluate new curricula that provide students opportunities to learn these standards, attention must also be directed toward how teachers and school districts will identify *if* and *when* students meet the targeted goals. This chapter covers assessment programs and practices that provide feedback for the district team in determining student achievement in science. The importance of science assessment practices that science teachers can use in their classrooms is discussed. In addition, the Wisconsin Student Assessment System (WSAS) is discussed in detail. The WSAS includes the *Wisconsin Knowledge and Concepts Examination (WKCE)* and the *High School Graduation Test (HSGT)*. With a solid understanding of the state assessment programs and effective classroom assessment practices, the district team will be able to develop a quality K–12 standards-led science program that recognizes and incorporates good assessment practices.

This chapter provides answers to the following questions:

- What is the difference between testing and assessment?
- Why is assessment an integral part of a K–12 standards-led science program?
- What state-level assessment practices should be considered when developing the district K–12 standards-led science program?
- What district-level assessment practices should be considered when developing the district K–12 standards-led science program?
- What does classroom assessment look like in a K–12 standards-led science program?

What Is the Difference Between Testing and Assessment?

The ability to distinguish differences among definitions of familiar assessment terms is essential to understanding assessment practices. Often in conversation, assessment terms, such as tests and assessments, are used interchangeably. However, this misuse of terms leads to confusion and misunderstanding among educators, as well as people outside the field of education.

Standards for Educational and Psychological Testing (AERA 1999), published in cooperation with the American Educational Research Association, American Psychological Association, and the National Council on Measurement in Education, established testing standards, which include standard definitions and legal requirements for test developers. To assure a clear understanding of the terms in this chapter, the following definitions from *Standards for Educational and Psychological Testing* are provided for reference.

Assessment: Any systematic method of obtaining information from tests and other sources, used to draw inferences about characteristics of people, objects or programs (AERA 1999, 172).

Test: An evaluative device or procedure in which a sample of an examinee's behavior in a specific domain is obtained and subsequently evaluated and scored using a standardized process (AERA 1999, 183).

Table 5.1 shows the three levels of assessment practices discussed throughout this chapter. Accompanying the three assessment levels are their purposes and examples for each purpose. This chart is not an exhaustive list of assessment practices but is rather intended to provide the district team with

TABLE 5.1 **Levels of Assessment for K–12 Science**

Level of Assessment	Purposes	Examples
State Assessments	Assessments that are conducted on an annual basis to measure the overall achievement levels of all students and to provide program-level information about schools, districts, and the state. Participation is usually mandatory and the results may be used for policy, curriculum, and program effectiveness decisions.	
	• Program Evaluation • Accountability • Summative Results • Longitudinal Comparisons • Policy Development	• WSAS
District, School or Program Assessments	Assessments that are conducted on a periodic basis throughout the school year to measure student learning. Districts, schools or programs are encouraged to develop local assessments to complement state tests, resulting in richer, broader assessment picture in science.	
	• Program Quality • Evaluate Student Proficiencies • Allocate Resources • Instructional Placement • Identify Intervention Strategies	• Science Concepts and Skills Tests • Periodic Skills Tests • Performance Tasks • Student Portfolios • Standardized Tests
Classroom Assessments	Assessments that are conducted as a process embedded within day-to-day teaching and learning with students involved as partners. Assessments that reveal to everyone what is being learned in science. Classroom data are primarily used to evaluate instruction and communicate progress to students, parents, and other teachers.	
	• Identify Students' Needs • Monitor Progress • Plan and Evaluate Instruction • Assign Grades • Communicate Results	• Projects • Quizzes • Assigned Problems • Performance Tasks • Observations • Checklists • Student Journals

guidance. This table was adapted with permission from work done by the Co-operative Educational Service Agency (CESA) 4. (CESA 4 1999)

Why Is Assessment an Integral Part of a K–12 Standards-Led Science Program?

All types of assessment are an integral part of all educational systems. Through use of various levels of assessment, as described in Table 5.1, information can be collected to provide feedback on science programs, K–12 science curricula, and instructional practices in addition to determining students' levels of understanding. All assessment instruments, whether administered as large-scale standardized tests, classroom tests, or informal monitoring during class discussions, have the same purpose—to reveal what is being learned and to provide feedback. Feedback from assessment allows teachers, parents, and administrators to determine if levels of understanding and performance are sufficient and to take corrective measures, as necessary, to ensure greater future success in meeting targeted goals. For assessments to be an integral part of a K–12 standards-led science program, assessments should be consistent with how students learn science by

- mirroring good instruction,
- occurring continuously, but not intrusively, as a part of instruction; and
- providing information (to teachers, students, and parents) about the levels of understanding that students are reaching (DPI 2000b, 154; adapted from NRC 2001).

Inferences, drawn from assessment data, must be an integral part of the standards-led science program, because the district team can use the inferences to modify the science program.

Inferences from assessment data will vary in the specificity with which they can be applied. Assessment programs from outside the classroom, such as state-level programs, the SAT and ACT, and off-grade district testing, provide data that allow inferences on a sample of knowledge from a content area. Although the data can be used in conjunction with other evidence to indicate student learning, feedback is general and not immediate. Because student performance reports can take a month or more to receive, the lag-time hinders prompt classroom response. This type of assessment becomes a powerful tool to evaluate the overall district K–12 science program rather than as the sole indicator of students' progress. Data from these tests should not be used to evaluate teacher effectiveness for teacher-evaluation purposes.

Classroom assessments, in addition to being more specific and providing more immediate feedback than large-scale standardized tests, allow for more formats to be used, thus, the assessments more clearly reveal individual student strengths. Also, classroom assessments can be more closely aligned to what is actually taught in the classroom, as well as allow for the creation of more in-depth assessments. Lastly, classroom assessments, unlike large-scale standardized tests, can provide more immediate, detailed information about students' levels of understanding and areas of misconceptions.

Whether the data is derived from large-scale standardized tests, classroom assessments, or informal monitoring during class discussion, teachers need to know how to use this information to make informed decisions about classroom activities and student achievement. The next section describes the WSAS, a required State of Wisconsin assessment program, and provides some guidance on good classroom assessment practices.

What State-Level Assessment Practices Should be Considered When Developing the District K–12 Standards-Led Science Program?

This section provides information about the WSAS, specifically, the *Wisconsin Knowledge and Concepts Examinations (WKCE)* and the *High School Graduation Test (HSGT)* and their classroom and curricular implications. Effective in the 1993–94 school year, Wisconsin law, under 1991 Act 269, required all school districts to administer a state-provided test at Grade 8 and Grade 10. A few years later, under the 1995 Act 27, an additional requirement was added to include fourth grade testing, beginning with the 1996–97 school year.

These required tests, administered at grades 4, 8 and 10, are collectively known as the *WKCE*. These are large-scale, standardized tests designed to measure the level of student understanding in six academic areas—reading, language arts, mathematics, social studies, science, and writing. The developers of these tests, commercial test companies, design and write items based on national standards in the core areas. Within science, the *National Science Education Standards (NSES)* serve as the framework for test design. Because these are commercial tests based on national standards, the Wisconsin Department of Public Instruction (DPI) did a study to determine the alignment of the items to *WMASS*.

The *WKCE* is administered once annually during the spring semester. Typically, school districts set up special assessment schedules, resulting in a testing environment that ensures the best test results possible. Table 5.2 provides information about effective testing environments. In conjunction with the *WKCE*, school districts will often purchase or develop other standardized tests to administer to students in grades other than 4, 8, and 10. This practice, known as "off-grade testing," is used to collect additional data about student achievement.

In addition to the *WKCE*, the State of Wisconsin enacted the *HSGT*. Similar to the design of the *WKCE*, the test assesses students' understandings of concepts in English and language arts, mathematics, social studies, and science. As a customized test, the *HSGT* is created by content-area specialists in the state and aligned specifically to the *WMASS*. In science, the *WMASS* for Grade 12 serve as the benchmarks for levels of student understanding.

Today, the *HSGT* is not considered a "high-stakes" test; rather, it is frequently referred to as a "medium-stakes" test. This is because local school-

TABLE 5.2 **Testing Environments That Promote the Best Performances**

- Testing conditions should be comfortable and similar for all students.
- To the extent possible, conditions should reflect the school's instructional environment.
- Ensure that announcements are not made on the public address system during the testing sessions.
- Provide good lighting, comfortable chairs and desks, and post "QUIET" signs to inform visitors of the testing.
- Conduct testing in small groups, rather than in large group or auditorium-type settings.
- Have visible to all students a clock for monitoring their time.
- Provide a short break with a snack or refreshment if the session is long.

WDPI, Office of Educational Accountability, p. 1–11.

boards base their decision to grant high school diplomas on multiple measures rather than a single measure derived from the *HSGT* scores. Although the *HSGT* is not a high-stakes test, the district team must consider the test, as well as *WKCE,* as they develop the district K–12 standards-led science program. Teachers responsible for science program instruction should understand the design and purpose of both the *WKCE* and *HSGT.*

In developing the K–12 standards-led science program, the district team, as well as the teachers implementing the program, have the responsibility of providing students with opportunities to learn the material tested at the state level. Equally important, students should have sufficient opportunities to become familiar with the style and format of the *WKCE* and the *HSGT.* This opportunity-to-learn principle, often referred to as "OTL," has legal implications. If students are held accountable to the *WMASS* through the *HSGT* as a requirement for graduating from high school, districts are responsible for providing students opportunities to learn *WMASS.*

A 1979 Florida court case, *Debra P. v. Turlington,* set a legal precedent for school districts to establish OTL. In brief, the outcome of this case requires school districts to demonstrate that students have had sufficient opportunity to learn the concepts and knowledge tested on state tests. The district team must be aware of two essential elements of OTL, as defined in the Debra P. case: curricular and instructional validity. Susan Phillips in *Legal Implications of High-Stakes Assessment: What States Should Know* defines these terms as follows:

- Curricular validity – the match between test content and the required curriculum.
- Instructional validity – the match between test content and what is actually taught in the classroom (NCREL 1993, 12).

Using the *WMASS* to guide the district's K–12 science curriculum within the standards-led science program will assure the team that they are meeting the requirement of curricular validity. This is because, as mentioned previously, the *WMASS* serves as the foundation for the *HSGT* content and is closely aligned to the *WKCE.* Establishing curricular validity will often parallel instructional validity, but the district team should not assume those two elements automatically go hand in hand. From lessons learned in *Debra P. v. Turlington,* the school district is responsible for ensuring that what is written as the standards-led science curriculum is what is being taught as the standards-led science curriculum.

Understanding the format and style of the *WKCE* and the *HSGT* will help teachers design classroom assessments that support the state tests, provide students with opportunities to become familiar with test-question format, and provide immediate information on their students' levels of understanding. Science items take two formats on the *WKCE* and the *HSGT*. One format is identified as selected response, more commonly known as multiple choice, and the other is identified as constructed response, also known as short answer. Questions for the two tests are based on a range of thinking abilities, shown in Figure 5.1. Simple recall and recognition questions no longer make up the tests. Instead, the tests' questions require in-depth thinking and synthesis of concepts.

To emphasize the change in thinking required of students, examples in Table 5.3 illustrate the shift in test-question design. Comparing the sample questions makes it clear that there is a movement toward higher level thinking, which not only encompasses basic science knowledge, but also requires students to understand science process and connecting concepts. Teachers who understand and incorporate these changes into their classroom assessments will not only raise the level of understanding expected for their students, but will also better prepare them for the state assessment system.

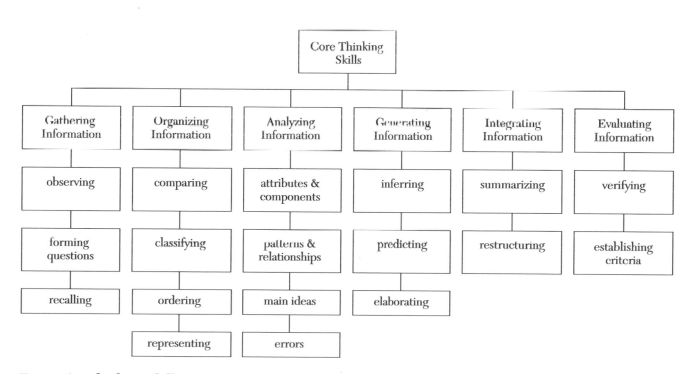

FIGURE 5.1 **Thinking Skills Associated with the WKCE and the HSGT**
Wisconsin High School Graduation Test Educator's Guide, DPI 2000.

TABLE 5.3 **Thinking Skills Required for Example Questions**

Traditional-Based Science Questions	Reformed-Based Science Questions
Grade 4 Which of these is *not* a state of matter? A. solid B. liquid C. gas D. air	**Grade 4** What is the state of matter for water *below* 0° Celsius? A. Gas B. Liquid C. Solid D. Soft
Grade 8 Mass divided by volume defines A. weight B. speed C. density D. area	**Grade 8** Students are given an unknown sample of metal and a chart showing the density of various metals. They are instructed that their unknown metals are one of the metals on the chart that needs to be identified. Explain what the students would do to determine the density of the metal.
Grade 12 A physical state of matter that has both definite shape and definite volume is A. gas B. liquid C. solid D. plasma	**Grade 12** How can the Kinetic-Molecular Theory be used to describe the differences between solids, liquids, and gas?

What District-Level Assessment Practices Should be Considered when Developing the District K–12 Standards-Led Science Program?

One of the first tasks for the district team is to develop a K–12 science assessment plan that spells out the purposes and practices for the identification, collection, and use of data for decision making that improves science teaching and learning. The assessments included in this plan are the devices that provide data for a systemic, comprehensive picture of performance and achievement in science for a student, school, or district. This K–12 science assessment plan must be consistent with the overall district assessment plan. The task force sees the K–12 science assessment plan as one that is consistent with the *National Science Education Standards* assessment criteria, the research presented on student learning, and state-level tests, previously presented.

A balanced approach to assessment is crucial. The K–12 science assessment plan should include multiple measures of student performance. Table 5.4 (CESA #4 1999) shows a skeleton chart the district team can use in organizing the K–12 science assessment plan. On the chart, the district team should indicate the various standardized tests and local assessment practices used in the science program. These should include

- The *HSGT*
- The *WKCE*
- Progressive student portfolios
- Commercially designed off-grade tests for science
- District-developed tests for science
- Map of individual student progress in science, K–12
- Student projects

Once the K–12 science-assessment plan has been established, the district team must develop classroom assessment criteria. The criteria must be consistent from kindergarten to grade 12 and used to show how students understand science concept skills. The classroom assessment criteria for the K–12 assessment plan might include:

- Students' understandings about inquiry
- Students' communication skills
- Students' understandings about science subject matter (science content and science concepts)
- Students' abilities to work well with others
- Students' understandings about issues in science

TABLE 5.4 **District Assessment Chart**

Grade	Standardized Assessments	When Administered	Local Assessment Practices in Science
K			
1			
2			
3	WRCT		
4	WKCE		
5			
6			
7			
8	WKCE		
9			
10	WKCE		
11	HSGT		
12	HSGT		

Reprinted with permission of CESA #4.

TABLE 5.5 Grades K–12 Inquiry Rubric

Grades K–4

Indicators	District-Developed Proficiency Levels
The students ask good questions about objects, organisms, or events.	X 1 2 3 4
The students plan and conduct simple investigations.	X 1 2 3 4
The students use simple tools of science.	X 1 2 3 4
The students connect explanations to scientific knowledge.	X 1 2 3 4
The students communicate explanations.	X 1 2 3 4

Grades 5–8

Indicators	District-Developed Proficiency Levels
The students identify questions that can be answered through scientific investigations.	X 1 2 3 4
The students design and conduct scientific investigations.	X 1 2 3 4
The students use appropriate tools and techniques of science for data.	X 1 2 3 4
The students develop descriptions, explanations, and models using evidence.	X 1 2 3 4
The students think critically and logically to make the relationships between evidence and explanations.	X 1 2 3 4
The students communicate scientific procedures and explanations.	X 1 2 3 4
The students use mathematics in all aspects of inquiry.	X 1 2 3 4

Grades 9–12

Indicators	District-Developed Proficiency Levels
The students identify questions and concepts that guide scientific investigations.	X 1 2 3 4
The students design and conduct scientific investigations.	X 1 2 3 4
The students use technology and mathematics to improve investigations and communications.	X 1 2 3 4
The students formulate and revise scientific models and explanations using logic and evidence.	X 1 2 3 4
The students recognize and analyze alternative explanations and models.	X 1 2 3 4

TABLE 5.6 **Proficiency Levels for Inquiry Rubric**

Score	Description of Scoring Criteria
4 – Advanced	Complete and correct labeled drawing and explanation, that goes beyond in some important way, such as discussing the limitations of the example provided, or giving several correct examples.
3 – Complete and correct	Complete and relevant labeled drawing and explanation with only minor errors.
2 – Partially complete and correct	Complete and relevant drawing or explanation with only minor errors; or incomplete but relevant drawing with an incomplete explanation.
1 – Incomplete and incorrect	Incomplete drawing and/or explanation related to concept of threshold but with major errors or omissions.
0 – Off task	Does not relate to the concept of threshold.
X	No opportunity to respond.

Table 5.5 is an example of one specific criterion, student understandings about inquiry, that begins at kindergarten and is carried through Grade 12 in a standards-led science program. This example is not intended to be exclusive; it is merely provided here for guidance. The table demonstrates the progression of inquiry from one grade grouping to the next and provides proficiency levels through descriptions of scoring criteria. These descriptions serve as guidance only. The descriptions can be found in Table 5.6 (SEPUP 1995, B.7 Section C). The district team must decide the detail for the criteria, the grade-by-grade specificity, and the proficiency levels needed for the criteria.

What Does Classroom Assessment Look Like in a K–12 Standards-Led Science Program?

Teachers of science should use multiple types of assessments to improve classroom practice, plan curricula, guide self-directed learners, report student progress, and conduct research on their classroom practices. Classroom assessment provides teachers with continuous monitoring of students' progress toward the goals established by the district, the building, parents, and teachers. Through continuous monitoring and evaluation of students, teachers can provide complete pictures of students' achievements, as well as modify instruction based on student feedback. In contrast, teachers who only use a single assessment practice at the end of a unit typically cannot adjust instructional practices based on student needs.

Classroom assessments must support the K–12 assessment plan for science and the overall district criteria for assessing students in science. In conjunction with these plans, classroom teachers develop individual, year-long assessment plans that show clear evidence of students' classroom science learning. Keep in mind when preparing the classroom assessment plan that the *National Science Education Standards Assessment Standards* (NRC 1996, 5) provide detailed guidance for quality assessment practices, such as the following:

- The content and form of an assessment task must be congruent with what is supposed to be measured.
- Assessment tasks must be developmentally appropriate, must be set in contexts that are familiar to students, must not require reading skills or vocabulary inappropriate to students' grade levels, and must be as unbiased as possible.
- The choice of assessment form should be consistent with what one wants to measure and infer.

Along with the *NSES*, the task force recommends considering the following questions:

- What content is being addressed?
- Is the content being assessed the content being taught?
- Is there a range of thinking skills, from gathering information to evaluating information, required from students in the assessment plan?
- Is the assessment connected throughout the year?
- Does the assessment plan provide useful data?
- How does the assessment plan provide information for the modification of instruction?
- Can all students demonstrate what they know, understand, and are able to do, free from bias?
- Are there alternative formats and a variety of contexts or situations that are familiar to students from many backgrounds and to both genders?

Essential for the successful implementation of this assessment plan is that students understand the purpose of the assessment. Students need to understand the knowledge and skills they will be assessed on and any and all directions that accompany the assessment task. Students must be allowed to rely on and use prior knowledge when completing a classroom task and assessment for the task.

There are a wide variety of classroom assessment strategies available to teachers. A few of these strategies are summarized in Table 5.7. Several available publications provide more detailed information on these and other types of classroom assessment strategies.

Example of a Middle Level Classroom Assessment

One example of classroom assessment has been taken from the *Science Education for Public Understanding Program's* (SEPUP) publication *Issues, Evi-*

Classroom assessments must have clean purposes.

Science Task Force, March 2000

TABLE 5.7 **Assessment Strategies for Science Classrooms**

Classroom Assessment Strategies	Description
Portfolios	A collection of student work, whether over a year or several years, that shows the progression of students' understanding and development of skills in science. Elements that need to be considered when using this type of assessment strategy: • What is the purpose of the portfolio? • What and how much data/products will be collected? • Who selects the pieces to include? (teacher/student/parent) • Will it contain only work that is done individually? • How will the portfolio be used?
Performance-Based	Through-related classroom activities that allow students to demonstrate their understanding of science knowledge and skills. Elements that need to be considered when using this type of assessment strategy: • Students understand the purpose of the activity. • Performance activity aligns with instruction. • Rubrics are developed and shared with the student prior to the performance.
Extended Projects or Experiments	Where students use principles of research to obtain solutions, assessment strategies will take many days or even weeks to complete. Team skills as well as the science knowledge and process skills are emphasized.
Pre-unit and Post-unit Questions	The postunit question lends itself toward more traditional approaches of classroom assessment. However, if teachers incorporate preunit assessment, more information and better planning can occur that takes into consideration students' prior knowledge and misconceptions.
Teacher Observation	One of the most direct ways of collecting information about student performance is through direct observation. This assessment strategy can provide detailed information about students' science knowledge and understanding and proficiency of skills. Teachers have many ways to organize their observations—through simple checklists to more extensive rubrics. The organizing system a teacher decides upon must be easy enough to use, provide useful information, and not overload the time required from the teacher.
Science Journals	Use of journals in the classroom enables the teacher to see the concepts and skills presented through the eyes of students. Students can use journals to communicate their ideas and findings as they relate to science activities. Sometimes journals contain students' reflections on what they are learning, thus allowing teachers to better understand the unique needs of their students.

dence, and You (SEPUP 1995, section C). This example illustrates how classroom assessment can be an integral part of the science program and how assessment can provide continuous feedback about students' progress. The program, designed for eighth-grade science, clearly defines the criteria used for student assessment throughout the year. The criteria provide teachers, students, and parents with data that allows for monitoring and adjustment during the school year. This program uses multiple methods of assessment, ranging from extensive scoring rubrics to simple classroom check-off procedures.

The program includes assessment-scoring rubrics for each of the five criteria. The criteria are the following:

- Use of scientific evidence to make decisions and tradeoffs ("Evidence and Tradeoffs")
- Understandings of inquiry ("Designing and Conducting Investigations")
- Student communication skills ("Communication of Scientific Information")
- Student group interactions ("Group Interactions")
- Shows understanding of the essential science concepts and standards being covered ("Understanding Concepts")

TABLE 5.8 **Understanding Concepts (UC) Variable: Elements of the Variable**

Score	**Recognizing Relevant Content** Response identifies and describes scientific information relevant to a particular problem or issue.	**Applying Relevant Content** Response uses relevant scientific information in new situations, such as solving problems or resolving issues.
4	Accomplishes Level 3 AND extends beyond in some significant way.	Accomplishes Level 3 AND extends beyond in some significant way.
3	Accurately and completely identifies AND describes relevant scientific information.	Accurately and completely uses scientific information to solve problem or resolve issue.
2	Identifies and/or describes scientific information BUT has some omissions.	Shows an attempt to use scientific information BUT the explanation is incomplete; also may have minor errors.
1	Incorrectly identifies and/or describes scientific information.	Uses scientific information incorrectly and/or provides incorrect scientific information; OR provides correct scientific information BUT does not use it.
0	Missing, illegible, or is irrelevant or off topic.	Missing, illegible, or is irrelevant or off topic.
X	Student had no opportunity to respond.	

An example of one of the assessment-scoring rubrics is in Table 5.8 (SEPUP 1995, B.7) and has been reprinted with permission from SEPUP (1995 B.7) The rubric is called "Understanding Concepts" and is designed to measure how well students are understanding the essential science concepts presented throughout the year. The rubric is used in the classroom and has a student scale score ranging from 0 to 4. There are two essential elements of the Understanding Concepts rubric: recognizing relevant content and applying relevant content. The purpose of the two elements is to provide a more detailed picture of what—recognizing relevant content—and how—applying the relevant content—the students are learning science. During the school year, teachers in this program use various parts of the rubric and keep a log of each student's progress.

Table 5.9 (SEPUP 1995, C.2 Sections A and B) shows a timeline illustrating how the five assessment criteria are used throughout the year. Activities within the program are listed, and an explanation is provided for how the activity is assessed. Sometimes the activity uses only one type of rubric, and sometimes multiple assessments are used within an activity.

Conclusion and Implications

The purpose for having a district K–12 assessment plan and teacher-developed classroom assessment plans is to provide an overall picture of how students are assessed in science. Each of the three assessment levels presented in this chapter contributes important data of varying specificity to this overall picture. As the task force indicated, a balance in assessment is necessary, and all of the information provided is useful to understanding student achievement.

To better understand how each assessment type impacts student learning, Figure 5.2 is provided. As the graph indicates, each assessment type provides student data; however, the greatest amount of data indicating how well students understand science is found at the classroom level.

This chapter further provides information about the state assessment system, types of district assessments, and classroom assessments. The chapter suggests that the district team should develop assessment criteria for the K–12 science program that each teacher in the district who teaches science can use. The chapter maps out strategies that the team can use to develop an overall picture of how K–12 students are learning science. The chapter even illustrates how all types of assessments can be used to develop a progress chart for each student and for the district as students complete their science programs.

TABLE 5.9 **Part 1: Water Usage and Safety**

		Designing and Conducting Investigations • Designing Investigation • Selecting and Recording Procedures • Organizing Data • Analyzing and Interpreting Data	Evidence and Tradeoffs • Using Evidence • Using Evidence to Make Tradeoffs
1	**Drinking-Water Quality**		
2	**Exploring Sensory Thresholds**		
3	**Concentration**		
4	**Mapping Death**		
5	**John Snow**		**A:** Using Evidence (p. 52)
6	**Contaminated Water**	√: Designing Investigation (p. 61)	
7	**Chlorination**	**A:** All elements (p. 66)	
8	**Chicken Little, Chicken Big**		
9	**Lethal Toxicity**	√: Organizing Data (p. 94)	
10	**Risk Comparison**	√: Analyzing and Interpreting Data (p. 109)	
11	**Injection Problem**		√: Both elements (p. 120)
12	**Peru Story**	**A:** Organizing Data **and** Analyzing and Interpreting Data (p. 130)	**A:** Both elements (p. 132)

TABLE 5.9 Part 1: Water Usage and Safety (*continued*)

		Designing and Conducting Investigations • Designing Investigation • Selecting and Recording Procedures • Organizing Data • Analyzing and Interpreting Data	Evidence and Tradeoffs • Using Evidence • Using Evidence to Make Tradeoffs
13	Chemical Detective	√: Analyzing and Interpreting Data (p. 140)	
14	Acids, Bases and Indicators	√: Organizing Data (p.151)	
15	Serial Dilutions of Acids and Bases		
16	Acid-Base Neutralization		
17	Quantitative Analysis of Acid	√: Analyzing and Interpreting Data (p. 182)	
18	The "Used" Water Problem	A: All elements (p. 192)	
19	Is Neutralization the Solution to Pollution?		A: Both elements (p. 200)
20	Water Quality	A: All elements (p. 206)	

TABLE 5.9 **Part 1: Water Usage and Safety** (*continued*)

		Designing and Conducting Investigations • Designing Investigation • Selecting and Recording Procedures • Organizing Data • Analyzing and Interpreting Data	Evidence and Tradeoffs • Using Evidence • Using Evidence to Make Tradeoffs
21	Trouble in Silver Oaks		
22	Water Movement Through Earth Materials		
23	"Ins and Outs" of Groundwater		
24	Investigating Contamination Plumes		
25	Testing the Waters	**A:** All elements (p. 260)	
26	Mapping It Out		
27	Presentation Skills		
28	Cleaning It Up		**A:** Both elements (p. 305)
	Link I	**A:** All elements (Item 3) **except** Organizing Data	**A:** All elements (Items 4 and 5) **and** Using Evidence to Make Tradeoffs (Item 1)

TABLE 5.9 **Sections A and B**

	Understanding Concepts • Recognizing Relevant Content • Applying Relevant Content	Communicating Scientific Information • Organization • Technical Aspects	Group Interaction • Time Management • Role Performance/ Participation • Shared Opportunity
1			
2	√: Both elements (p. 16) *Measurement and Scale**		
3	√: Applying Relevant Content (p. 28) *Measurement and Scale**		
4			√: Time Management; Shared Opportunity (p. 38)
5		A: Both elements (p.52)	
6			
7			
8			√: Shared Opportunity (p. 76)
9	A: Applying Relevant Content (p. 97) *Measurement and Scale**		
10	√: Applying Relevant Content (p. 111) *Measurement and Scale**		
11			
12		A: Both elements (p.132)	

*Indicates content concepts assessed.

TABLE 5.9 **Section C**

	Understanding Concepts • Recognizing Relevant Content • Applying Relevant Content	Communicating Scientific Information • Organization • Technical Aspects	Group Interaction • Time Management • Role Performance/ Participation • Shared Opportunity
13			√: Time Management (p. 137)
14			
15			
16	**A:** Applying Relevant Content (p. 172) *Measurement and Scale*★		
17			
18	**A:** Applying Relevant Content (p. 192) *Measurement and Scale*★		**A:** Time Management (p. 189)
19			
20			

°Indicates content concepts assessed.

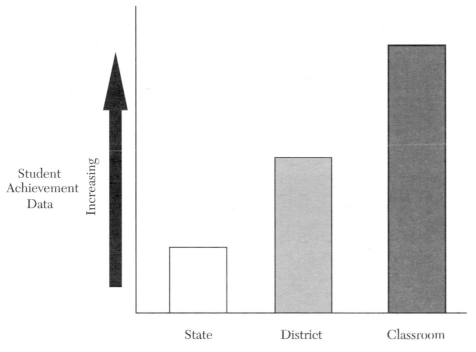

Student Achievement Data

Increasing

State   District   Classroom

Three Assessment Types Found throughout the Chapter

FIGURE 5.2 **Relationship between the Type of Assessment and the Information about Student Achievement Data the Assessment Provides for Science**

References

AERA (American Educational Research Association). 1999. *American Psychological Association, National Council on Measurement in Education. Standards for Educational Psychological Testing*. Washington, D.C.: American Educational Research Association.

Cooperative Educational Service Agency (CESA) #4, West Salem, Wis. 1999. Standards and Assessment Center. Assessment Plan.

CTB/McGraw-Hill. 1997. *The Teacher's Guide to the Terra Nova Knowledge and Concepts Tests*. Monterey, Calif.: CTB/McGraw-Hill.

Johnson, Spencer. 1999. *Who Moved My Cheese?* New York: G.P. Putnam and Sons.

NRC (National Research Council). 1996. *National Science Education Standards*. Washington, D.C.: National Academy Press.

Phillips, S.E. 1993. *Legal Implications of High-Stakes Assessment: What States Should Know*. Oak Brook, Ill.: North Central Regional Educational Laboratory.

Rankin, Stuart C., and Carolyn S. Hughes. 1987. *The Rankin-Hughes Framework, Developing Thinking Skills Across the Curriculum*. Westland, Mich.: Michigan Association for Computer Users in Learning. Quoted in CTB/McGraw-Hill: *Teacher's Guide to Terra Nova*. Monterey, Calif.: CTB/McGraw-Hill.

SEPUP (Science Education for Public Understanding Program, Lawrence Hall of Science, University of California at Berkeley). 1995. *Issues, Evidence and You (Teacher's Guide)*. Ronkonkoma, NY: LAB-AIDS®, Inc. Publishing Division.

NRC (National Research Council). 2001. *Classroom Assessment and the National Science Education Standards: A Guide for Teaching and Learning*. Washington, D.C.: National Academy Press.

Wisconsin Department of Public Instruction. 1993. *A Guide to Curriculum Planning in Science*. Reprint. 1986. Madison, Wis.: Wisconsin Department of Public Instruction.

———. 1998a. *DPI Guidelines for Appropriate Testing Procedures*. Madison, Wis.: Wisconsin Department of Public Instruction. p. 1–11.

———. 1998b. *Wisconsin Knowledge and Concepts Examinations: An Alignment Study at Grade 4*. Madison, Wis.: Wisconsin Department of Public Instruction.

———. 1998c. *Wisconsin Knowledge and Concepts Examinations: An Alignment Study at Grade 8*. Madison, Wis.: Wisconsin Department of Public Instruction.

———. 1998d. *Wisconsin Knowledge and Concepts Examinations: An Alignment Study at Grade 10*. Madison, Wis.: Wisconsin Department of Public Instruction.

———. 1998e. *Wisconsin's Model Academic Standards for Science*. Madison, Wis.: Wisconsin Department of Public Instruction.

———. 2000b. *The Wisconsin High School Graduation Test Educator's Guide*. Madison, Wis.: Wisconsin Department of Public Instruction.

Wisconsin Statutes, 1999–2000, 118.30, Pupil Assessment. Madison, Wis.: General School Operations, State of Wisconsin.

Additional Reading

DuFour, Richard, and Robert Eaker. 1998. *Professional Learning Communities at Work: Best Practices for Enriching Student Achievement*. Reston, Va.: Association for Supervision and Curriculum Development.

Elliott, Stephen N., Jeffery P. Braeden. 2000. *Educational Assessment and Accountability for All Students. Facilitating the Meaningful Participation of Students with Disabilities in District and Statewide Assessment Programs*. Madison, Wis.: Wisconsin Department of Public Instruction.

Love, Nancy, 2002. *Using Data/Getting Results: A Practical Guide for School Improvement in Mathematics and Science*. Norwood, Massachusetts: Christopher-Gordon Publishers, Inc.

NRC (National Research Council). 2001. *Classroom Assessment and the National Science Education Standards: A Guide for Teaching and Learning*. Washington, D.C.: National Academy Press.

SEPUP (Science Education for Public Understanding Program, Lawrence Hall of Science, University of California at Berkeley). 1995. *Issues, Evidence and You (Teacher's Guide)*. Ronkonkoma, NY: LAB-AIDS®, Inc. Publishing Division.

Strong, Richard W., Harvey F. Silver, and Matthew J. Perini. 2001. *Teaching What Matters Most: Standards and Strategies for Raising Student Achievement*. Reston, Va.: Association for Supervision and Curriculum Development.

Chapter 6
Essential Components of a K–12 Science Program

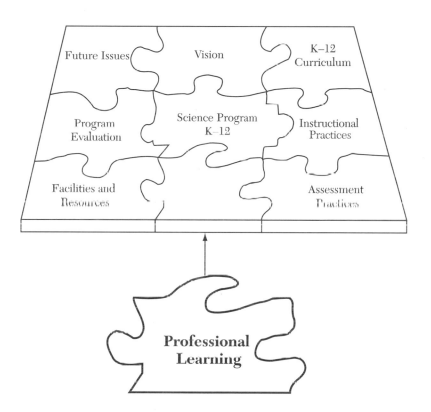

The figure illustrates the interlocking nature of the components of the standards-led science program. The power of the K–12 standards-led science program emerges when all the pieces of the program are present. Chapter 6 summarizes the professional learning for teachers.
Science Task Force, May 2000

What Is Professional Learning in Science Education?

Staff Professional Development and Professional Development for Teachers of Science

Sand dunes near the Blue River in Grant County: Bruce A. Brown of the WGNHS. Wisconsin DNR photo.

Within the vision of all students learning science is the vision that all teachers of science should receive professional development. The knowledge base for doctors, lawyers, and other professionals has increased dramatically with changes in technology and advances in science. As an example, physicians have innumerable ongoing personal and professional growth and development opportunities supported throughout their careers. The public even demands this degree of personal growth.

The knowledge base for teachers of science has dramatically increased as well, suggesting that they also need continuous professional growth and development to maintain their professional relevancy. As an example, increased emphasis on standards and assessment, along with a better understanding of how students learn science, requires ongoing, teacher professional development that is analogous to growth experiences for other professionals (NRC 1996). Hence, lifelong professional learning is a necessary part of a standards-led science program. Indeed, according to the National Research Council (1996, 54), "Becoming an effective science teacher is a continuous process that stretches across the life of a teacher, from his or her undergraduate years to the end of a professional career."

This chapter is designed to provide information about both staff professional development and personal professional development for teachers of science that supports their lifelong professional learning. The chapter also will assist the *district team* build understandings about professional learning for teachers and the staff professional development needed to teach science in a K–12 standards-led science program.

Specifically, the chapter sets the context for professional learning that supports the K–12 standards-led science program. Further, the chapter divides professional development into two separate types of experiences; staff professional development and personal professional development. In this guide, the task force uses the term "staff professional development" to mean "everyone who is involved with the teaching of science" and "personal professional development" to mean "the unique professional development needs and experiences of individual science teachers." The task force recognizes that, ideally, the two development plans should overlap—but may not. The chapter addresses the following questions:

- What is the context for professional development?
- What staff professional development experiences support a K–12 standards-led science program?
- What is lifelong professional learning?

What Is the Context for Professional Development?

The *National Science Education Standards (NSES) Professional Development Standards* (NRC 1996, 72) and the *Wisconsin Standards for Teacher Development and Licensure, PI 34* specify the standards for professional development and provide the context for both staff professional development and personal professional development. Although *PI 34*[1] is not being restated, it should clearly be a part of the context. This context should serve as the guide for the district team when planning any type of professional development experience. Teachers of science should also seek out professional experiences that are guided by the *NSES Professional Development Standards*. The following are the *NSES Professional Development Standards*:

Standard A

Professional development for teachers of science requires learning essential science content through the perspectives and methods of inquiry. Science learning experiences for teachers must

- Involve teachers in actively investigating phenomena that can be studied scientifically, interpreting results, and making sense of findings consistent with currently accepted scientific understanding.

[1] *PI 34* is described in Chapter 4.

- Address issues, events, problems, or topics significant in science and of interest to participants.
- Introduce teachers to scientific literature, media, and technological resources that expand their science knowledge and their ability to access further knowledge.
- Build on the teacher's current science understanding, ability, and attitudes.
- Incorporate ongoing reflection on the process and outcomes of understanding science through inquiry.
- Encourage and support teachers in efforts to collaborate.

Standard B

Professional development for teachers of science requires integrating knowledge of science, learning, pedagogy, and students; it also requires applying that knowledge to science teaching. Learning experiences for teachers of science must

- Connect and integrate all pertinent aspects of science and science education.
- Occur in a variety of places where effective science teaching can be illustrated and modeled, permitting teachers to struggle with real situations and expand their knowledge and skills in appropriate contexts.
- Address teachers' needs as learners and build on their current knowledge of science content, teaching, and learning.
- Use inquiry, reflection, in science teaching.

Standard C

Professional development for teachers of science requires building understanding and ability for lifelong learning. Professional development activities must

- Provide regular, frequent opportunities for individual and collegial examination and reflection on classroom and institutional practice.
- Provide opportunities for teachers to receive feedback about their teaching and to understand, analyze, and apply that feedback to improve their practice.
- Provide opportunities for teachers to learn and use various tools and techniques for self-reflection and collegial reflection, such as peer coaching, portfolios, and journals.
- Support the sharing of teacher expertise by preparing and using mentors, teacher advisers, coaches, lead teachers, and resource teachers to provide professional development opportunities.
- Provide opportunities to know and have access to existing research and experiential knowledge.
- Provide opportunities to learn and use the skills of research to generate new knowledge about science and the teaching and learning of science.

Standard D

Professional development programs for teachers of science must be coherent and integrated. Quality preservice and inservice programs are characterized by

Professional development experiences that allow teachers of science to understand more fully how students learn science will result in a science program that is a standards-led science program.

Mark Klawaiter (Science Task Force member), 2000

The changes presented in the *NSES Professional Development Standards* are best illustrated in Table 6.1. This table articulates those changes in professional practices needed to support the K–12 standards-led science program. These changes must be a part of any professional-learning experience and all professional development strategies (NRC 1996, 72).

In addition to the *NSES Professional Development Standards*, professional development experiences should reflect the research about how students learn science (as presented in previous chapters). This notion has significant implications for the district team as they plan any type of staff professional development. The team must make sure that all staff professional development is consistent with how students learn science. For example, staff professional-learning experiences need to mirror the learning experiences desired for students. Teachers need to learn science in the same way students learn science. This is equally true for teachers of science when they make decisions about personal professional development.

What Staff Professional Development Experiences[2] Support a K–12 Standards-Led Science Program?

Relying on the *NSES Professional Development Standards* and understandings of how students learn science, the district team must map out plans for

[2] For the purposes of this guide, *PI 34* is emphasized in the context of individual teacher instruction and professional development. It is important for the district team to be aware of the influences of *PI 34* on staff professional development.

TABLE 6.1 **Changing Emphases**

In Professional Development Settings	In Professional Development Settings
Less Emphasis On	**More Emphasis On**
Transmission of teaching knowledge and skills by lectures	Inquiry into teaching and learning
Separation of science and teaching knowledge	Integration of science and teaching knowledge
Separation of theory and practice	Integration of theory and practice in school settings
Individual learning	Collegial and collaborative learning
Fragmented, one-shot sessions	Long-term coherent plans
Courses and workshops	A variety of professional development activities
Reliance on external expertise	Mix of internal and external expertise
Staff developers as educators	Staff developers as facilitators, consultants, and planners
Teacher as technician	Teacher as intellectual, reflective practitioner
Teacher as consumer of knowledge about teaching	Teacher as producer of knowledge about teaching
Teacher as follower	Teacher as leader
Teacher as an individual based in a classroom	Teacher as a member of a collegial professional community
Teacher as target of change	Teacher as source and facilitator of change

Reprinted with permission of National Research Council.

the staff professional development needed to support the K–12 standards-led science program. The team must take on a new role, that of professional development designers.

To assist the team with this role, the task force found useful the five principles taken from *Ideas That Work: Science Professional Development* (ENC 2000, 4). The principles were developed from the *NSES Professional Development Standards*. The district team should use these principles to guide their work as they develop the professional development plan. The principles presented by Loucks-Horsley[1] in *Ideas That Work: Science Professional Development* support the *NSES Professional Development Standards* and the research on how students learn science and should support the district team's vision of the K–12 standards-led science program. The following are the five principles:

1. *Professional development experiences must have students and their learning at the core—and that means all students.* Science education reforms—and the national, state, and local standards on which they are based—share a common commitment to high standards of achievement for all students and not just the few who are talented or privileged. This implies a different perspective on the content students should learn and the teaching strate-

[1] Note that the principles, design framework, and strategies for professional development in this publication are elaborated in *Designing Professional Development for Teachers of Science and Mathematics* by Susan Loucks-Horsley, Peter W. Hewson, Nancy Love, and Katherine E. Stiles, with Hubert M. Dyasi, Susan N. Friel, Judith Mumme, Cary I. Sneider, and Karen L. Worth (Thousand Oaks, CA: Corwin Press, 1998). The book is a product of the National Institute for Science Education, funded by the National Science Foundation.

gies that should be used by their teachers. To meet this challenge, all professional development resources, including teacher time, must be focused on rigorous content and the best ways to reach all students.

2. *Excellent science teachers have a very special and unique kind of knowledge that must be developed through their professional learning experiences.* Pedagogical content knowledge (Shulman 1987) involves knowing how to teach specific science concepts and principles to young people at different developmental levels. This kind of knowledge and skill is the unique province of teachers and distinguishes what they know from what scientists know. Knowledge of science content, although critical, is not enough, just as knowledge of general pedagogy is not enough. The goal of developing pedagogical content knowledge must be the focus of professional development opportunities for teachers.

3. *Principles that guide the improvement of student learning should also guide professional learning for teachers and other educators.* Professional developers must "walk their talk" because people tend to teach in ways in which they have learned. Engaging in active learning, focusing on fewer ideas more deeply, and learning collaboratively are all principles that must characterize learning for teachers if they in turn will apply these to helping their students learn.

4. *The content of professional learning must come from both inside and outside the learner and from both research and practice.* Professional development opportunities must honor the knowledge of the practicing teacher as well as draw on research and other sources of expertise outside schools and classrooms. Artful professional development design effectively combines theory and practice.

5. *Professional development must both align with and support system-based changes that promote student learning.* Professional development has long suffered because of its separation from other critical elements of the education system, with the result that new ideas and strategies are not implemented. Although professional development is not a panacea, it can support changes in such areas as standards, assessment, and curriculum, creating the culture and capacity for continuous improvement that is so critical for educators facing current and future challenges.

Eisenhower National Clearinghouse. (2000). "Ideas that Work: Science Professional Development." Reprinted with permission of Eisenhower National Clearinghouse; visit ENC Online (enc.org).

In *Ideas That Work: Science Professional Development*, a framework for staff professional development is presented (see Figure 6.1) (ENC 2000, 5). This framework describes the strategies the district team needs while designing a standards-led staff professional development program. This "design framework" supports the previous five principles and the K–12 standards-led science program. Following the description of the framework is an explanation of how it can be used to implement a staff professional development program. The district team should take advantage of this explanation when preparing the staff professional development program.

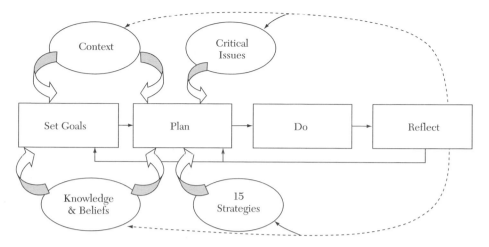

FIGURE 6.1 **A Framework for Designing and Identifying Professional Development Programs**[1]

Eisenhower National Clearinghouse, (2000). "Ideas that Work: Science Professional Development." Reprinted with permission of Eisenhower National Clearinghouse; visit ENC Online (enc.org).

With these five principles as a foundation (ENC 2000, 5–7), designers of effective professional development for science teachers need to proceed carefully and consider a number of different elements. Figure 6.1 illustrates a design framework that organizes these elements in ways that suggest both how to design a new program and how to analyze the design of an existing program.

The four boxes in Figure 6.1 represent a typical process of planning and action. This process reminds designers of professional development—which should include teachers, administrators, community and other resource people—of several important features of good programs:

1. There need to be goals, a set of clear and shared outcomes for the program. These goals must drive all other elements of the design.
2. There needs to be planning, careful consideration of how the pieces fit together and how to proceed over time.
3. The plan must be implemented.
4. There needs to be reflection on and evaluation of what happened that feed back into adjustment of plans and subsequent actions, as well as of goals.

This four-step cycle is meant to repeat itself, taking place over months as a program proceeds, or in the minutes it takes to monitor and adjust an ongoing event to increase its effectiveness.

In addition to the four central steps of the cycle, the design framework considers four inputs important to the design process. Designers of professional development need to draw upon:

[1]Illustration from: *Designing Professional Development for Teachers of Science and Mathematics* by Susan Loucks-Horsley, Peter W. Hewson, Nancy Love, and Katherine E. Stiles, with Hubert M. Dyasi, Susan N. Friel, Judith Mumme, Cary I. Sneider, and Karen L. Worth (Thousand Oaks, CA: Corwin Press, 1998). The book is a product of the National Institute for Science Education, funded by the National Science Foundation.

1. The existing base of knowledge and beliefs about learning, teaching, the nature of science, professional development, and the process of change.
2. An analysis of the context in which the teachers teach and their students learn.
3. Attention to a set of critical issues that will help them to be successful or foil their attempts if neglected.
4. A repertoire of fifteen strategies for professional learning that can be combined in different ways at different times to maximize different learning goals.

Knowledge and Beliefs

- Learners and learning
- Teachers and teaching
- The nature of science
- Professional development
- The change process

Current knowledge, remarkably strong in most cases, can form a firm foundation under professional development. Research suggests that learners construct their own understandings and that certain teaching strategies—such as building on prior knowledge and active exploration of concepts—can facilitate that learning.

Effective professional development involves active study, over time, of science content and pedagogy in ways that model effective learning and make direct connections with teachers' practices. Research on change indicates the importance of attending to individual teacher needs over time, providing learning opportunities tailored to those needs, and creating a climate of collegiality and experimentation and a capacity for continuous learning and support. These knowledge bases influence design decisions for effective professional development programs.

Context

- Students
- Teachers
- Practices
- Policies
- Resources
- Organizational culture
- Organizational structures
- History of professional development
- Parents and community

A thorough examination of factors in the context that participants bring to the program also assists in design. The needs and nature of the students; the backgrounds, needs, and teaching responsibilities of the teachers; the resources available and degree of community support; the organization, expectations, and current demands of the schools and districts—all are important considerations in the design of professional development for science teachers.

Critical Issues

- Ensuring equity
- Building professional culture
- Developing leadership
- Building capacity for professional learning
- Scaling up resources
- Garnering public support
- Supporting standards and frameworks
- Evaluating professional development
- Finding time for professional development

There are at least nine issues that designers of professional development must consider that carry the message: Ignore them at your peril! These may not require attention at the onset but should be considered as the initiative or program unfolds.

Ensuring equity and supporting new standards and frameworks through professional development promote high-quality learning for all students and maximize the likelihood that current improvement efforts will reach their goals. Such issues as building capacity, developing leadership, and scaling up influence the extent to which teachers change their practice. Only when they are addressed by a professional development program will changes made by individual teachers extend beyond their classrooms to the education system.

Attention paid to garnering public support and evaluating professional development helps ensure sustained commitment to a program that works effectively. All nine of the critical issues should concern professional developers at some time in their work.

Eisenhower National Clearinghouse. (2000). "Ideas that Work: Science Professional Development." Reprinted with permission of Eisenhower National Clearinghouse; visit ENC Online (enc.org).

Included in the design process are the strategies shown in Table 6.2; they each have a purpose and lend value to the overall K–12 science staff professional development process. The strategies are reprinted with permission from the Eisenhower National Clearing House (ENC) and provide examples of specific professional development approaches. The strategies are divided into categories and their purposes are explained. The strategies illustrate how the district team can use each strategy to support the K–12 standards-led science program, which, in turn, supports the basis for *PI 34*.

Summaries of the 15 strategies for staff development can be found in *Ideas That Work, Summaries for Professional Development* (ENC 2000, 8–9). These strategies are on the ENC Web site (http://www.enc.org). Details of these strategies can be found in *Designing Professional Development for Teachers of Science and Mathematics* (Loucks-Horsley et al. 1998). These strategies can be used in combination or individually in a general staff development setting.

TABLE 6.2 Strategies for Staff Professional Development

Strategies	Purposes				
	A Developing Awareness	**B** Building Knowledge	**C** Translating into Practice	**D** Practicing Teaching	**E** Reflection
Immersion					
1. *Immersion into Inquiry in Science:* Engaging in the kinds of learning that teachers are expected to practice with their students—that is, inquiry-based science investigations.	○	●			●
2. *Immersion into the World of Scientists:* Participating in an intensive experience in the day-to-day work of a scientist, often in a laboratory, industry, or museum, with full engagement in research activities.	○	●			
Curriculum					
3. *Curriculum Implementation:* Learning, using, and refining use of a particular set of instructional materials in the classroom.		○	○	●	
4. *Curriculum Replacement Units:* Implementing a unit of instruction that addresses one topic in a way that illustrates effective teaching techniques.		○	○	●	
5. *Curriculum Development and Adaptation:* Creating new instructional materials and strategies or tailoring existing ones to better meet the learning needs of students.		○	●		
Examining Practice					
6. *Action Research:* Examining teachers' own teaching and their students' learning by engaging in a research project in the classroom.		○			●
7. *Case Discussions:* Examining written narratives or videotapes of classroom events and discussing the problems and issues illustrated.	○	○			●
8. *Examining Student Work and Thinking, and Scoring Assessments:* Carefully examining students' work to understand their thinking so that appropriate instructional strategies and materials can be identified.	○	○	○		●
Collaborative Work					
9. *Study Groups:* Engaging in regular collaborative interactions around topics identified by the group, with opportunities to examine new information, reflect on classroom practice, and analyze outcome data.	○		○		●

TABLE 6.2 **Strategies for Staff Professional Development** (*continued*)

Strategies	Purposes				
	A Developing Awareness	**B** Building Knowledge	**C** Translating into Practice	**D** Practicing Teaching	**E** Reflection
10. *Coaching and Mentoring:* Working one-on-one with another teacher to improve teaching and learning through a variety of activities, including classroom observation and feedback, problem solving, and co-planning.		○	○	●	○
11. *Partnerships with Scientists in Business, Industry, and Universities:* Working collaboratively with practicing scientists with the focus on improving teacher content knowledge, instructional materials, and access to facilities.	○	●			
12. *Professional Networks:* Linking in person or through electronic means with other teachers to explore topics of interest, pursue shared goals, and address common problems.	○	●	○		○
Vehicles and Mechanisms					
13. *Workshops, Institutes, Courses, and Seminars:* Using structured opportunities outside the classroom to focus intensely on topics of interest, including science content, and learn from others with more expertise.	○	●	○		
14. *Technology for Professional Development:* Using various kinds of technology, including computers, telecommunications, video, and CD-ROMs, to learn content and pedagogy.	○	●	○		○
15. *Constructing Professional Developers:* Building the skills and deep understanding of content and pedagogy needed to create learning experiences.		○	○	●	○

● = Primary

○ = Secondary

A. Strategies that focus on **developing awareness** are usually used during the beginning phases of a change. The strategies are designed to elicit thoughtful questioning on the part of the teachers concerning new information.

B. Strategies that focus on **building knowledge** provide opportunities for teachers to deepen their understanding of science content and teaching practices.

C. Strategies that help teachers **translate new knowledge** into practice engage teachers in drawing on their knowledge base to plan instruction and improve their teaching.

D. Strategies that focus on **practicing teaching** help teachers learn through the process of using a new approach with their students. As teachers practice new moves in their classrooms, they deepen their understanding.

E. Strategies that provide opportunities to **reflect** deeply on teaching and learning engage teachers in assessing the impact of the changes on their students and thinking about ways to improve. These strategies also encourage teachers to reflect on others' practice, adapting ideas for their own use.

Table adapted from: Eisenhower National Clearinghouse. (2000). "Ideas that Work: Science Professional Development." Reprinted with permission of Eisenhower National Clearinghouse; visit ENC Online (enc.org). *Designing Professional Development for Teachers of Science and Mathematics* by Susan Loucks-Horsley, Peter W. Hewson, Nancy Love, and Katherine E. Stiles, with Hubert M. Dyasi, Susan N. Friel, Judith Mumme, Cary I. Sneider, and Karen L. Worth (Thousand Oaks, CA: Corwin Press, 1998). The book is a product of the National Institute for Science Education, funded by the National Science Foundation.

An alternative, yet similar model for organizing staff professional development, is found in *Professional Development, Learning from the Best, A Toolkit for Schools and Districts Based on Model Professional Development Award Winners* (NCREL 1999). Although this model is not specific to science, it provides a number of strategies that the district team may want to incorporate while designing the staff professional development program. The model emphasizes the following four steps for professional staff development:

1. *Designing professional development.* The "design" step takes the district team through elements of a complete professional development plan. The plan addresses what elements the district team should include as well as how the team should be organized. In summary, this plan includes preparing for implementation, evaluation, and idea sharing.

2. *Implementing professional development.* This step outlines factors essential for successful and effective implementation of professional development programs. These factors include staying current with research on teaching and learning, aligning district policies and practices with professional development implementation, providing adequate resources, and making sure professional development is part of the school culture.

3. *Evaluating and improving professional development.* This step recognizes the need for feedback to determine professional development effectiveness. Within the evaluation step, goals are established and used to keep the program on track and serve as the standard for measuring program success. As part of evaluation, detail is provided on who should collect data, what data should be collected, and when it should be collected. Finally, evaluation should reflect the program's effectiveness in improving teaching and increasing student understanding.

4. *Sharing professional development learning.* This step focuses on the importance of documenting the staff professional development process and decisions made about the overall professional development program. Through documentation, excellence in the program will be sustained even with changes in district personnel.

What Is Lifelong Professional Learning?

Teachers of science, through experiences, gradually learn about how students learn science (NRC 1996). This idea of "lifelong" professional learning embraces the *NSES* and *PI 34*.

As indicated earlier, lifelong professional learning begins with the acknowledgment that teachers of science are professionals, responsible for determining their professional learning and development and must continually increase and refine their scientific knowledge to parallel the continuous advances in science and technology. This view of lifelong professional learning, as supported in *PI 34*, represents an ideological shift from technical training for the acquisition of specific skills and short-term or one-shot activities to a profound appreciation of continual learning.

The *Professional Development Standards* of *PI 34* and the *NSES* stipulate that lifelong professional-learning experiences for teachers consist of a variety of opportunities, ranging from university courses to a variety of workshops.

The standards also include, as part of personal professional development, "classroom-based research, scientific research, collaboration with other science teachers, involvement in professional organizations, the use of professional journals, and many other experiences. These types of personal professional development experiences must be contextual, sustained, require participation and reflection, and applicable to the classroom" (NRC 1996, 58).

Teachers of science must plan out their own professional development using a personal professional portfolio, as described in *PI 34*. This portfolio establishes the plan that supports the standards-led science program and provides details of teachers' individualized professional development. The following suggestions are taken from *Pathways to the Science Standards, Middle School Edition* (NSTA 1998, 16–17). They represent suggestions that should be considered as part of a teacher's professional portfolio. Although the suggested professional development opportunities seem to duplicate opportunities incorporated in the overall staff professional development plan, they are presented here to assist teachers of science in the development of their portfolios. These opportunities may or may not be part of the overall district plan.

■ Graduate Courses

One of the most common ways to improve knowledge by enrolling in graduate courses. Some of these courses provide opportunities for additional learning in the laboratory, in research, and in teaching skills. They often discuss why some strategies work well in classrooms. Many colleges and universities give teachers the opportunity to design individualized programs around a set of courses to work toward an advanced degree.

■ Structured Inservice Programs

Today, many school systems allow staff committees to design departmental, building, or district inservice programs. Some local resources, such as science centers, museums, and industries, plan programs specifically for classroom teachers. Teachers attending these programs in teams, accompanied by a school administrator, become more effective in transferring what they have learned to the school setting. The most effective staff development programs are long-range (not one-shot workshops) that model the information.

■ Professional Associations

Thousands of teachers attend national and regional conferences sponsored by professional associations. NSTA sponsors one national and three regional conventions on science education/teaching each year. For the cost of registration, teachers can select from hundreds of workshops. In addition, the exhibits are expansive, and there are numerous opportunities to network with other teachers.

■ Journals

Membership in a professional association makes available professional journals (such as *Science & Children, Science Scope,* and *The*

Science Teacher from NSTA Press), newspapers, and newsletters that bring classroom science ideas and news to your doorstep.

■ Collaboration with Other Professionals
Teaching is no longer a private endeavor. Collaboration and team teaching are enriching instruction. Nonthreatening coaching by a fellow teacher of science can offer additional opportunities for discovering other styles, strategies, and options for teaching science. Mentoring (whether formal or informal) is another form of collaboration for giving and receiving feedback about the teaching and learning that occurs in classrooms.

■ Self-Reflection and Inquiry
Not all learning experiences need to involve structured meetings, nor do they need to be group-oriented. There is much value in reading, studying, and exploring on your own. In fact, an important component of any career-long professional development plan must be self-reflective inquiry. As we try new ideas, we might use journals, audio-tapes, and videotapes to track our progress.

■ Evaluation
Using evaluation as a vehicle for professional development will seem strange to most teachers. New, more reflective systems for evaluation, such as teacher portfolios, can become valuable opportunities for teachers to talk with other educators about classroom decisions involving curriculum, delivery, and climate. If evaluation is to be a tool for growth, however, teachers must be full partners in developing the evaluation system.

■ School Improvement for Professional Growth
Setting common goals can provide a school- or district-wide impetus for professional development. A shared direction (such as redesigning the science program) can prompt a group to determine what strategy or plan has the best hope of success. Most plans include regular evaluation of progress. Having a voice in the policies and procedures that affect their classrooms will certainly increase teachers' sense of ownership and dedication.

■ Other Possibilities
   a. Internships in industry or research establishments provide new perspectives for science teachers. Travel, either to scientific sites or to other classrooms, has long been considered one of the most motivating professional development resources.
   b. Exploration of the World Wide Web, including the NSTA Web site and online networks, can yield a wealth of resources and the opportunity to find answers to questions and share ideas with colleagues.

The possibilities for personal professional development are endless. The critical questions teachers of science must ask themselves are, "How does this experience move me toward my goal of becoming a lifelong professional learner?" "How does this experience increase my understanding of how students learn science?", and "How does this experience assist with my work on *PI 34?*"

Finally, as the district team designs the staff professional development program or teachers of science develop their professional development portfolios, the task force has provided two short vignettes. The vignettes model the essential elements of a standards-led classroom and are used to illustrate the teaching techniques that a professional development program must encompass. Table 6.3, which follows the vignettes, illustrates how each of the five principles described earlier can be used to guide professional development for both the staff and individual teachers. Each vignette was chosen by the task force because of its unique attributes. *So What* is an example of strong science content delivery through inquiry outside the traditional classroom. *Fast Plants* is an example of how attending a science teachers' convention can contribute significantly to lifelong professional learning.

Lifelong Professional Development in Action

Vignette 1: So What!

LeRoy Lee, a task force member, took a group of Wisconsin Academy Staff Development Initiative lead teachers in mathematics and science on a field trip. Acting as the facilitator, he first provided the lead teachers with background information on the geology of the greater Chippewa Falls area followed by a bus tour of the area.

During a series of stops at specific locations, groups of three to four teachers were asked to observe and describe to each other what they were seeing. They were also asked to answer simple questions.

- "What is it?" Observe and describe verbally with your partner(s) and then in writing or drawing.
- "How did it get there?" "What is your evidence?" Discuss with your partner(s) and then write or draw.
- "How has it and will it, change over time?" Discuss with your partner(s) and then write or draw.
- "So what?" What are the human implications of this feature?

Each location illustrated aspects of the presentation given before the bus trip, and each location became more complex geologically. The lead teachers were then taken to a site considered to be the most geologically complex. They were asked to describe the final site to each other, employing the questioning technique used throughout the bus trip. Each group was expected to draw upon the information gleaned from the prior locations to explain and describe the final site to each other. To assess, each group was asked to explain their thinking to the facilitator. He realized quickly that each group was able to describe the uniqueness and complexity of the geology in the area based on evidence and what they had collected while on the bus trip. Each group was able to answer the question of "So what?" by recognizing that Wisconsin has unique geology, that the geological past has contributed significantly to the present, and that those geological features have impacted the way humans use the land today.

Vignette 2: *Fast Plants* and Teachers of Science

At a recent Wisconsin Society of Science Teachers State Convention, Professor Paul Williams, a task force member, was one of the professional exhibitors. His booth displayed all of his work on the *Wisconsin Fast Plants*. Not wanting to just display his work and conduct a passive demonstration, he decided that the science teacher conference attendees would enjoy conducting a simple experiment using the Fast Plant seeds. Attendees were asked to conduct a simple investigation and answer this simple question: "Does a carbonated drink have any effect on seed germination?"

Each conference participant placed one seed in each of two microampules, and then placed a drop of water in one microampule and a drop of carbonated soda in the other one. Professor Williams gave each participant a card with the experimental question on it and further instructions. Participants then attached the card and microampules to their badges and observed

TABLE 6.3 **Relationship of Vignettes to the Five Principles**

	Principle	Vignettes
1.	Professional development experiences must have students and their learning at the core—and that means all students.	The facilitators were modeling how students learn science.
2.	Excellent science teachers have a very special and unique kind of knowledge that must be developed through their professional learning experiences.	The facilitators were incorporating "how to teach specific science concepts" into their overall teaching strategies. The facilitators were building the capacity for transferring this strategy into the classroom.
3.	Principles that guide the improvement of student learning should also guide professional learning for teachers and other educators.	The facilitators were "walking the talk" by focusing on one science concept.
4.	The content of professional learning must come from both inside and outside the learner and from both research and practice.	Through questioning, the facilitators were drawing upon the pre-existing knowledge of each learner.
5.	Professional development must both align with and support system-based changes that promote student learning.	While these vignettes do not directly support changes in the science education system, they clearly are illustrative of changes advocated in the *NSES* standards and *PI 34*.

the microampules for a period of time. Participants were asked to share their results with others as they were walking around and attending sessions at the conference. Finally, they were asked to report their findings on the Fast Plants Web site after the conference was over. Although the findings of the actual experiment are not known, be assured that this experiment led to many professional conversations about plant growth at the convention!

Conclusion and Implications

The professional development described in this chapter is fundamental to developing a K–12 standards-led science program. When used by the district team, the tools and design framework provide a road map for the staff professional development needed for the program. This chapter is fundamental to the success of the K–12 standards-led science program and should be approached with care. Simply stated, it is not easy to design staff professional development that is analogous to the standards presented in this chapter.

Teachers of science will find their lifelong professional development experiences easier by drawing upon this chapter while designing their personal professional development portfolios. Teachers of science will find this to be a worthwhile, rewarding, and even fulfilling experience because of ongoing opportunities to update their professional knowledge.

References

Eisenhower National Clearinghouse for Mathematics and Science Education (ENC). 2000. *Ideas that Work: Science Professional Development*. Columbus, Ohio: Eisenhower National Clearinghouse. pages 5–6 from Loucks-Horsley, Susan.et al. 1998. *Designing Professional Development for Teachers of Science and Mathematics*. Thousand Oaks, Calif.: Corwin Press

NCREL (North Central Regional Education Laboratory). 1999.*Professional Development Learning From the Best, A Toolkit for Schools and Districts Based on Model Professional Development Award Winners*. Oak Brook, Ill.: North Central Regional Laboratory.

NRC (National Research Council). 1996. *National Science Education Standards*. Washington, D.C.: National Academy Press.

NSTA (National Science Teachers Association). 1996. *Pathways to the Science Standards: Guidelines for Moving the Vision into Practice (High School Edition)*. Arlington, Va.: NSTA Press.

———. 1997. *Pathways to the Science Standards: Guidelines for Moving the Vision into Practice (Elementary School Edition)*. Arlington, Va.: NSTA Press.

———. 1998. *Pathways to the Science Standards: Guidelines for Moving the Vision into Practice (Middle School Edition)*. Arlington, Va.: NSTA Press.

Shulman, L.S. 1987. Knowledge and Teaching: Foundations of the New Reform. *Harvard Educational Review* 57: 1–22.

Teacher standards under s. PI 34.02, Wisconsin Administrative Code. Wisconsin Department of Public Instruction.

Additional Reading

ENC (Eisenhower National Clearinghouse for Mathematics and Science Education). 2000. *Ideas that Work: Science Professional Development*. Columbus, Ohio: Eisenhower National Clearinghouse.

Loucks-Horsley, Susan et al. 1998. *Designing Professional Development for Teachers of Science and Mathematics*. Thousand Oaks, Calif.: Corwin Press.

NSTA (National Science Teachers Association). 1997. *Pathways to the Science Standards: Guidelines for Moving the Vision into Practice (Elementary School Edition)*. Arlington, Va.: NSTA Press.

———. 1996. *Pathways to the Science Standards: Guidelines for Moving the Vision into Practice (High School Edition)*. Arlington, Va.: NSTA Press.

———. 1998. *Pathways to the Science Standards: Guidelines for Moving the Vision into Practice (Middle School Edition)*. Arlington, Va.: NSTA Press.

Wald, Penelope J., and Michael S Castleberry. 2000. *Educators as Learners: Creating a Professional Learning Community in Your School*. Arlington, Va.: Association for Supervision and Curriculum Development.

Chapter 7
Essential Components of a K–12 Science Program

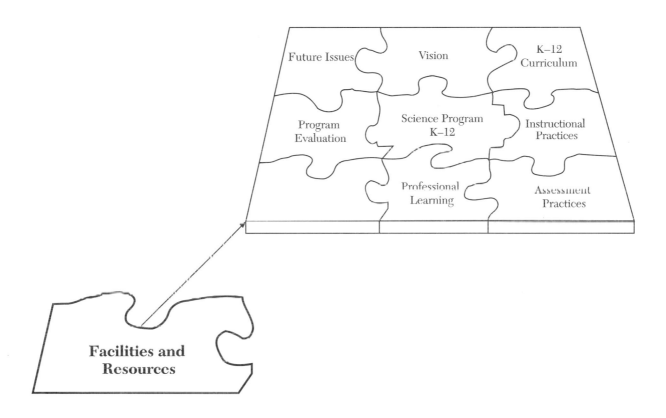

The figure illustrates the interlocking nature of the components of the standards-led science program. The power of the K–12 standards-led science program emerges when all the pieces of the program are present. Chapter 7 discusses the facilities and the resources teachers need to assist them with developing a scientifically literate classroom environment.

Science Task Force, May 2000

Implementation: What Support Is Needed to Implement a K–12 Standards-Led Science Program?

Facilities and Resources

Wetlands in the Pheasant Branch watershed near Middleton: Bruce A. Brown of the WGNHS. Wisconsin DNR photo.

Science classrooms in Wisconsin are places where students are excited and exploring, questioning, making observations, and discussing those observations with others. Teachers of science have created these classrooms. These teachers have embraced the state standards and have implemented the standards in their classrooms. However, some teachers may have fallen short of their personal and school goal of implementing the standards. Inadequate facilities and limited resources may have restricted their efforts to improve science education. The *district team* must recognize that developing a quality K–12 standards-led science program requires that careful attention be given to the facilities and resources necessary for the program to succeed.

They put safety goggles on. The Ziploc® bags were opened.

Paul Tweed (Science Task Force member), 2000 (safety step described by Tweed in the Introduction's vignette)

This chapter is divided into two sections. In the first section, the district team will become familiar with science facilities that support a K–12 standards-led science program. In the second section, discussion will focus on instructional resources that support a K–12 standards-led science program. The chapter will answer the following questions:

- What science facilities support a K–12 standards-led science program?
- What safety considerations are necessary in a K–12 standards-led science program?
- How does the district team select instructional resources that support a K–12 standards-led science program?

What Science Facilities Support a K–12 Standards-Led Science Program?

Before discussing the physical environment of a science facility, it is necessary to define what is meant by a science facility. A science facility is any location where science instruction is taking place and is a facility designed to support inquiry science. This most often is the classroom but may be outside of the classroom.

When planning the K–12 science facilities, the district team should form a member subcommittee or assemble a facilities committee. This committee should be responsible for science-facility planning, which entails discussions, investigation, and determination of what is needed for the physical environment of each classroom in the science program.

The facilities committee should create a statement of needs for each facility. The statement of needs should include educational specifications, accommodations for special needs, safety requirements, and technological design. The facilities committee must then develop a plan of action to implement the statement of needs. This plan of action should include immediate and long-range action steps necessary to meet the statement of needs. Obviously, budget is a major consideration during the implementation process.

As the facilities committee begins working on the statement of needs, the task force recommends "facilities that support a K–12 standards-led science program are facilities that allow for inquiry science" (DPI 1998, 2) be included in the statement of needs. Additionally, the statement of needs should include the National Science Teachers Association (NSTA) standards on class size and appropriate space and recommendations for the physical aspects needed in the facility. The NSTA recommends that science laboratory classes have no more than 24 students per teacher. The NSTA (2000) Position Statement on Safety and School Science Instruction further recommends that classrooms dedicated solely to labs provide a minimum of 45 square feet for every student. The state minimum guideline for a science labroom and classroom combined is 30 square feet per student or a maximum of 30 students in a classroom that is 900 square feet. To calculate the space needed per student, measure only free space; do not include space occupied by fixed furniture.

Physical features needed in a science facility will differ, depending upon the grade level. The task force provided some suggestions for these; however, the suggestions are not exhaustive, and it is highly recommended that the facilities committee seek other resources. One such resource is available from the NSTA Press, entitled *Guide to School Science Facilities*.

Elementary-level classrooms require access to water, sufficient electrical outlets, appropriate equipment, computer terminals, and proper lighting. Middle-level classrooms require more sophisticated science laboratories and equipment, including gas outlets, sufficient water, computer terminals, and appropriate lighting. High school classrooms require facilities and equipment, which include computer terminals, that allow for sophisticated scientific investigations.

A more detailed summary of the physical classroom description developed by the task force is outlined in Table 7.1. When developing this table, the task force used the NSTA recommendations on science classroom facilities and recommendations from *The Total Science Safety System, Wisconsin Version, Elementary and Secondary Editions* (DPI 1999).

What Safety Considerations Are Necessary in a K–12 Standards-Led Science Program?

Safety should be fundamental to teachers and students in science. When asking students to perform experiments, conduct demonstrations, work cooperatively, or engage in a field experience, safety must be the primary consideration. *Wisconsin's Model Academic Standards for Science* (WMASS) support the position that science classroom safety is an essential part of the K–12 standards-led program. As presented in *WMASS*,

> Teachers of science must know and apply the necessary safety regulations in the use, storage, and care of materials used by students. Safety while learning requires thorough planning, management, and continuous monitoring of student activities both at school and during any science-related activities. Students must also take responsibility for their own safety and perform experiments as instructed. (DPI 1998, 2)

The task force suggests that the district team assume the responsibility for districtwide K–12 science classroom safety by establishing a safety committee or by having the facilities committee act as the safety committee. The safety committee must become knowledgeable about existing state regulations, district personnel responsible for chemical hygiene and facilities management, and training needed to assure that those individuals, as well as K–12 classroom science teachers, are aware of and continually updated on safety issues.

A word of caution— inquiry science may result in a greater number of classroom accidents if teachers and students do not follow safe practice.

John Whitsett (Science Task Force member), 2000

TABLE 7.1 **Physical Aspects for K–12 Science Facilities**

Grade Level	Well-lit lab area with Natural Light	GFCI Electrical Outlets	Gas Jets with Cut-Off Master	Computer Terminal	Running Water	Sufficient Space (NSTA) Recommendations	General Storage	Teacher Prep Area	Proper Ventilation	Safety Exits	Communication Device	Appropriate Safety Equipment	Chemical Storage Area—Locked	Proper Disposal Methods (e.g., Proper planning for disposal of chemicals)	District Suggestions
Elementary	X	X		X	X	X	X	X	X	2	X	X	X	X	
Middle	X	X	X	X	X	X	X	X	X	2	X	X	X	X	
High School	X	X	X	X	X	X	X	X	X	2	X	X	X	X	

The next section, addresses information on developing a science safety plan and on classroom safety issues. To add more detailed information, the task force suggests the safety committee procure a customized software program designed for Wisconsin. *The Total Science Safety System* is available in both elementary and secondary editions and can be purchased from the Wisconsin Society of Science Teachers.

As the safety committee develops the science safety plan, they should include information about proper handling of materials, responsible behavior, techniques that minimize the potential for injury, and basic information on the inherent hazards of some materials. The safety committee should be aware that each district must currently have a chemical hygiene plan and a chemical hygiene officer (OSHA 29 CFR 1910 1450). It is important that the safety committee incorporate the policies found in the district's chemical hygiene plan into the science safety plan.

As part of the safety plan, the task force recommends that the committee provide adequate safety training for both teachers and students. Teachers need an operational knowledge of the hazards present with certain laboratory materials. Teachers also need to be properly trained on how to safely use materials. Students need to be instructed on the proper use of materials prior to conducting an investigation. Instruction should be specific to the materials being used, and students must be closely supervised.

Within the safety plan document, there should be a section describing classroom safety issues. The task force has provided general guidelines for consideration. Remember that these guidelines are not exhaustive, rather they set the framework for discussion. For greater detail, it is highly recommended that the software program previously mentioned be used. The general guidelines provided by the task force include the following:

1. Knowing the local, state, and federal policies, practices, regulations, and standards for science classroom safety
2. Knowing safe practices, including school safety, accident reporting, safety goggle legislation, disposal techniques, classroom use of plants and animals, and use of any potentially harmful substance, such as bacteria cultures
3. Knowing the location of all safety devices
4. Knowing what should be discussed with students about safe practices in the classroom
5. Developing a student/parent signed safety contract
6. Limiting class size to the number that can be safely supervised
7. Planning and allowing for sufficient time for students to complete activities
8. Knowing all emergency evacuation procedures
9. Knowing the location of all cut-off or shut-off valves for natural gas, electricity, and water
10. Knowing to never allow students to conduct unauthorized experiments or to work alone and unsupervised

How Does the District Team Select Instructional Resources that Support a K–12 Standards-Led Science Program?

This section is designed to help the district team select instructional resources that support the K–12 standards-led science program. The process the task force recommends for selecting materials is based on work by the National Science Foundation (NSF), the Third International Mathematics and Science Study (TIMSS) (USDOE 1997), and *Selecting Instructional Materials, A Guide to K–12 Science* (NRC 1999). The process, though used in a committee context for large-scale adoption of resources, can also be used by individual teachers to select materials for a specific grade or course. The selection process assumes the following:

1. The district team will establish a resource committee representative of district diversity to select the resources used in the K–12 science program.
2. A curriculum is in place that is part of and supports the K–12 standards-led science program.
3. Instructional resources are defined as materials for K–12 science programs and include multiple formats, such as textbooks, software, publications, Internet access, and materials for classroom activities.

The committee responsible for selection of resources should develop an action plan. As the committee begins the process of selection, a number of issues will arise, such as selecting a resource based on its being a teacher's favorite or that it has always been used. These, as well as other issues, can be problematic, but can be resolved by focusing on five criteria developed by the National Science Foundation's Division for Elementary, Secondary, and Informal Education. The five criteria developed from NSF are content, pedagogy, assessment, equity, and implementation. The task force then modified the criteria and developed short descriptions for each. (NSF 1997, 3–9)

(A) Strong Scientific Content

Science content includes important scientific concepts in life and environmental science, physical sciences, and earth and space sciences; opportunities for inquiry; and information on the history and processes of science. These are all part of *WMASS* and the *National Science Education Standards*. The content found in the instructional resources should be scientifically accurate, clearly presented, and appropriate for the age of the student.

(B) The Pedagogical Design

There are vastly different pedagogical designs for instructional resources in science, and the research used in developing those resources varies immensely. The pedagogical research used to design the resources must be consistent with and support the standards-led science program as described in this guide. Research strategies used for developing instructional resources should be clearly understood. Current research indicates that science materials should show a logical progression for development of conceptual understanding. Good instructional resources should offer suggestions for teachers, such as sequencing activities to achieve desired student learning, and should provide hints on working with diverse groups of students. These materials should be used to actively engage students in learning science content.

(C) Assessment

Assessment methods built into the resource must be consistent with the K–12 standards-led science program. Ideally, the assessment component is developed as the resource itself is being developed. The assessment component then is an integral part of the resource and can be used to inform instructional changes. If the resource contains no assessment component, then it should be examined to determine how easily assessment(s) could be developed and integrated.

(D) Equity

Resources should meet the needs of all students. The materials must be unbiased and free from stereotypical issues, such as gender or race. The resources must provide methodologies for meeting the needs of diverse learning populations, must show how to effectively use heterogeneous student groups, and must explain the importance of accommodating various learning styles.

(E) Implementation and System Support

Many resources may require extensive professional development for effective implementation. Strategies for district implementation, professional development, and for scaling up, as well as quality control and a replacement schedule should be an integral part of any resource-selection process.

Several national programs have evaluated instructional materials and resources. Examples of these national programs include Project 2061 by the American Association for the Advancement of Science, the National Science Resources Center, the NSF, the U.S. Department of Education, and the Center for Science, Mathematics, and Engineering Education. Each program has established criteria for evaluation and acquisition of instructional resources. The programs attempt to provide guidance to local school districts. To help guide their work, the resource committee should become familiar with these programs and their evaluation processes.

In the next section, two processes are described to assist the resource committee with their work. Both processes, although different in design, are based upon the five criteria previously described. The resource committee may want to adopt or adapt one of these processes or combine both processes to create a customized selection process unique to their school district's needs.

The resource committee should decide who will be the reviewers. Reviewers should include teachers of science, parents, and students representative of the diversity of the community. In addition, one or two scientists should be included to assist with evaluating the quality of the scientific content and processes. Prior to reviewing the resources, reviewers should be provided with current research on how students learn science, current research on implementation practices for certain materials and resources, and the purpose and goals of the district's science education program.

As part of the resource evaluation process, reviewers should be asked to provide evidence to support their judgments about the potential of the resources and how the resources support students learning science. Their review work should be done in narrative form. A narrative is essential because it allows the reviewers to articulate cogent and supportable statements about their work. Each narrative will help the resource committee as they come to consensus on the resource being evaluated (NRC 1999).

"Review Process Number One," illustrated in Figure 7.1 and the forms following the figure on pages 170 through 194, is presented by NRC in *Selecting Instructional Materials, A Guide for K–12 Science* (NRC 1999, 54–93). It asks each reviewer to focus on the content standards for the district, often the standards from the WMASS. Once the content standard is identified, each reviewer is asked to provide evidence about how the resource supports the content standard and meets the five criteria. In "Review Process Number One," the use of the term "instructional materials" is a synonym for "instructional resources." The NRC illustrates this process with a flow chart and provides several worksheets designed to answer questions about the five criteria. The flow chart and accompanying worksheets are being reprinted with permission from the NRC.

"Review Process Number Two" is an adaptation developed by the task force from *Review of Instructional Materials for Middle School Science* by National Science Foundation (NSF) (NSF 1997, 11–23). A more comprehensive version of the NSF document is found in *TIMSS As a Starting Point to Examine Curricula, Guidebook to Examine School Curricula* (USDOE, 1997). Each reviewer must answer questions and provide evidence about how the resource supports each of the five criterion. This process leads the reviewer through a series of detailed questions and rating scales to achieve a comprehensive evaluation of the resource.

Conclusion and Implications

This chapter emphasizes the important role of facilities and resources in supporting the K–12 standards-led science program. Having facilities that support teachers' reform efforts will contribute to the success of the program. Resources that are selected by the district with the standards in mind also support the reform efforts and equally contribute to the overall success of the science program. The time spent developing sufficient facilities and resources will be time well spent, worthwhile, and may lead to even greater expectations and excitement for the science program throughout the district.

Review Process Number One

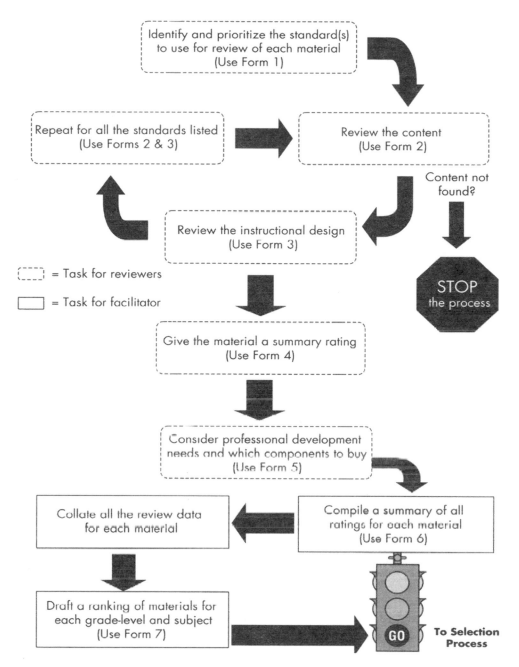

FIGURE 7.1 **Review Process Number One**
Reprinted with permission from NRC.

STANDARDS RECORD AND RATING SHEET   FORM 1

Title of Instructional Materials: _____

Name of Reviewer: _____

Use this sheet to record the standards you are using to review the instructional materials, and (after completing Forms 2 and 3) to record how well the materials meet each of those standards. List these standards in order of their priority, with the most important first.

Identify the source(s) for the standards used: _____

_____

	Grade Level	**Identify the Standard** *Write a short version and cite a page number from your standards document.*	**Summary Rating** *(From the end of Form 4).*
1			
2			
3			
4			
5			

Reprinted with permission from NRC.

CONTENT REVIEW

FORM 2

Title of Instructional Materials: _____

Name of Reviewer: _____

Use a separate set of Forms 2, 3, and 4 for each standard.

Standard # _____
from Form 1

Provide the complete text of the standard

2.1   Is the **content of the standard** found in the materials?
Provide specific evidence, examples, explanations, and references.

2.2 Is the content **scientifically accurate and significant**?
Provide specific evidence, examples, explanations, and references.

Note: *If the content of the materials does not match the standard or is inaccurate or trivial, there is no need to continue the review. Record "not at all" as your summary judgment on Form 4 and in the table on Form 1.*

INSTRUCTIONAL DESIGN REVIEW   **FORM 3**

Title of Instructional Materials: _____

Name of Reviewer: _____

Standard # _____
from Form 1

┌───┐
│ **Provide the complete text of the standard**   │
│   │
│   │
│   │
│   │
└───┘

3.1 Do the materials **actively engage** the students to promote their understanding of the subject matter of the standard?
*Consult the definition developed during review training. Provide specific
evidence, examples, explanations, and references. Be sure to consider
whether this material provides all students with the opportunity to be actively
engaged.*

Reprinted with permission from NRC.

FORM 3 (Continued)

3.2 Will the students develop a **depth of understanding** of the content of the standard through use of the materials?
Consult the definition developed during review training. Provide specific evidence, examples, explanations, and/or references. Be sure to consider whether this material provides all students with the opportunity to develop a depth of understanding.

Reprinted with permission from NRC.

Note: *SKIP item 3.3 if the standard you are using IS an inquiry standard.*

3.3   Is **scientific inquiry** taught, modeled, and practiced where appropriate? *Consult the definition developed during review training and the inquiry standards. Provide specific evidence, examples, explanations, and references. Be sure to consider whether this material can help all students achieve the standard.*

3.4 Do the materials provide informal and formal **assessments** for both the teacher and student to evaluate progress in achieving the standard? *Provide specific evidence, examples, explanations, and references. Be sure to consider whether the assessments will assist all students in achieving the standard.*

SUMMARY RATING   FORM 4

Title of Instructional Materials: _____

Name of Reviewer: _____

Standard # _____ *from Form 1*

Use this sheet to provide your summary rating on how well the materials under review will help all students achieve the standard.

_____ **Completely**

_____ **Almost Completely**
Please comment on modifications or additions needed for the material to meet the standard.

_____ **Incompletely**
Please comment on modifications or additions needed for the material to meet the standard.

_____ **Not at all**

Next steps:
- *Record your summary rating in the right-hand column on Form 1.*
- *Continue your review with the next standard on your list from Form 1. Use a new set of Forms 2, 3, and 4.*
- *When you are finished with all the standards on your list, complete Form 5 to finish your review of these materials.*

Reprinted with permission from NRC.

ADDITIONAL INFORMATION   FORM 5

Title of Instructional Materials: _____

Name of Reviewer: _____

Complete this after you have completed Forms 2, 3, and 4 with all the standards listed on Form 1.

How much and what kind of **professional development is likely to be needed** by the teachers in order to use these materials effectively?

Most materials are made up of several components (e.g., teacher's manual, materials kit, unit tests, videos, software, enrichment materials). **Which components of the materials under review should be purchased?**

Component	Must have	Optional, high priority	Optional, low priority	Not needed	Not examined

Comments:

REVIEW TEAM SUMMARY   FORM 6

Title of Instructional Materials: _____

Name of Reviewers:

1. _____

2. _____

3. _____

4. _____

To facilitate the selection process, complete a separate team summary for each unit or set of materials reviewed.

Standard	Rating of each reviewer			
	1	2	3	4

For ease in scanning the columns, use these codes:

C = completely

AC = almost completely

I = incompletely

N = not at all

SELECTION RECOMMENDATIONS   FORM 7

Grade Level and Subject: _____

(e.g., third grade physical science)

	Title and publisher	Comments
1		
2		
3		
4		
5		
6		
7		
8		
9		
10		
11		

Reprinted with permission from NRC.

COMPARATIVE COST WORKSHEET   FORM 8

Components Needed

Make a combined list of all the components mentioned by reviewers on Form 5 (e.g., teacher's manual, materials kit, unit tests, videos, software, enrichment materials). Then find out the current prices for all the components recommended for selection (for example, the "must have" and "optional, high priority").

Each component should be identified as a "class": either non-consumable (**NC**), completely consumable (**CC**), or a combination (**KIT**), because each is handled separately in estimating cost per student.

Component	Must have	Optional, high priority	Optional, low priority	Not needed	List price	Per	Class (NC, CC or KIT)

Computing Estimated Cost Per Student

Making a reasonable estimate of science material cost requires that you treat the following three categories separately: non-consumable components (textbooks, manuals, videos, software), combinations of consumable and non-consumable items, (kits, sets) and entirely consumable items (student tests, workbooks, chemicals). When materials and equipment are required but are not available from the publisher, you will need to estimate based on the materials list or substitute the cost of a similar package from another publisher.

This estimate is designed to be used for comparative purposes. For actual budget decisions, many more implementation factors need to be taken into consideration. For example, the reuse of a "science kit" implies a refurbishment system that may require new staff and space. Decisions about how to equip a classroom can depend on such teaching practices as cooperative learning or team teaching. Refurbishment costs can be significantly reduced if local bulk ordering eventually replaces buying from the publisher, and so on. The costs for replacing consumable items will also need to cover replacing lost and broken non-consumable items.

Non-consumable (NC) materials

Subtotals

1. List of the non-consumable components and their prices. For each, determine how many are needed to supply one classroom or one period. Multiply the cost by the number needed.

   Add these amounts to get (A) COST OF NC COMPONENTS. A _____

2. If the materials will be circulated or shared, divide A by the number of times that materials will be used in a year to obtain B. B _____

3. Divide B by the number of years you expect to use the materials to get (C) COST OF NONCONSUMABLES PER CLASSROOM PER YEAR. C _____

Combinations containing both consumable and nonconsumable materials (KIT)

4. List the prices of all the KITS used in one classroom in a year. Multiply each unit price by the number needed for each classroom—this is 1 if your class sizes match those provided for by

Reprinted with permission from NRC.

the supplier. (Large class sizes or teachers who teach more than 1 class perday may require the purchase of more KITS, as well as the purchase of more consumables.) Add all these products to find the Initial Cost of Kits.

D _____

5. Divide D by the estimated number of times each KIT will be refurbished and used in another classroom during one year. Then divide that number by the number of years the KITS will be used. This will give the approximate cost of the non-consumable part of the kits per classroom per year.

E _____

6. Estimate the cost of refurbishing each kit. Mutiply these costs by the number of a particular kit needed per classroom (usually 1). Add all these values to obtain the cost of refurbishment if there is no sharing.

F _____

7. Multiply F by the estimated average number of times each kit will be shared per year. This calculates the value for the total cost of reburbishment per class per year.

G _____

8. Add E and G.   This is the Total Cost of Kits Per Classroom Per Year.

H _____

Completely Consumable Components (CC)

9. Determine the number of consumables needed for one class-room or one period during one year. Multiply the cost of each by the number needed. Then add the cost of all consumable components to get (J) COST OF CONSUMABLE COMPO-NENTS PER CLASSROOM PER YEAR.

J _____

Total Cost per Student Per Year

10. Add C, H and J. Divide by the average number of students per classroom or period to get K.

K _____

This is an estimate of the cost per student per year of implementing this set of instructional material.

For more information on buying, refurbishing, and managing science instructional materials, contact the Association of Science Materials Centers listed in "Contact Information."

Reprinted with permission from NRC.

Review Process Number 2[1]

Title: _____

Author(s): _____

Publisher: _____ *Copyright date*: _____

Reviewed by: _____ *Date*: _____

1. **Descriptors**

   a. Write a brief description of the components of the curriculum upon which this review is based (e.g., teacher's guide, student books, hands-on materials, multimedia material).

   b. Write a brief description of the purpose and broad goals of these materials.

   c. What grade levels do the materials serve?

   ____   ____   ____   ____   ____

   d. Are the instructional materials designed to
   ____ provide a complete multi-year program for science.
   ____ provide a complete one-year course for science.
   ____ provide multiple modules or units that could be used to supplement other course materials for science.
   ____ provide a single module or collection of activities that could be used to supplement other course materials for science.
   ____ other (explain): _____

   e. What are the major domains/topics of content covered by these materials?

II. **Quality of the Science**

   Directions: For each question, please provide the appropriate answer.

   Does the content in the instructional materials align well with all eight areas of the Content Standards as described in the *National Science Education Standards (NSES)* and *Wisconsin's Model Academic Standards for Science?*

   _____
   _____
   _____
   _____

This framework is adapted from an instrument developed by Inverness Research under contract to the National Science Foundation.

a. Are the science concepts presented in the instructional materials accurate and correct? (Provide examples of major errors where they are evident. Attach extra page if necessary.)

_____

_____

_____

_____

b. Do the instructional materials adequately present the unifying concepts and adequately demonstrate and model the processes of science?

_____

_____

_____

_____

c. Does the science presented in the instructional materials reflect current disciplinary knowledge?

_____

_____

_____

_____

d. Do the instructional materials accurately represent views of science inquiry as described in the _National Science Education Standards_ and _Wisconsin's Model Academic Standards for Science?_

_____

_____

_____

_____

____ Not a focus of these materials (explain)

e. Do the instructional materials accurately present the history of science?

_____

_____

_____

_____

____ Not a focus of these materials (explain)

f. Do the materials emphasize technology as an area of study?

_____ Not a focus of these materials (explain)

g. Do the materials emphasize the personal and societal dimensions of science?

_____ Not a focus of these materials (explain)

h. Do the materials emphasize the content of life science?

_____ Not a focus of these materials (explain)

i. Do the materials emphasize the content of earth science?

_____ Not a focus of these materials (explain)

j. Do the materials emphasize the content of physical science?

_____ Not a focus of these materials (explain)

k. Do the instructional materials provide sufficient activities for students to develop a good understanding of key science concepts?

_____

_____

_____

_____

l. Do the instructional materials provide sufficient opportunities for students to apply their understanding of the concepts (i.e., designing of solutions to problems or issues)?

_____

_____

_____

_____

m. Do the instructional materials present an accurate picture of the nature of science as a dynamic endeavor?

_____

_____

_____

_____

n. Do the materials develop an appropriate **breadth and depth** of science content?

_____

_____

_____

_____

o. What is the overall quality of the science presented in the instructional materials?

1 .... 2............................... 3 .... 4............................... 5
Low   Medium   High

III.   The Pedagogical Design

a. Do the instructional materials provide a logical progression for developing conceptual understanding in science?

_____

_____

_____

_____

b. Do the instructional materials provide students the opportunity to make conjectures, gather evidence, and develop arguments to support, reject, and revise their explanations for natural phenomena?

_____

_____

_____

_____

c. To what extent do the instructional materials engage students in doing science inquiry?

_____

_____

_____

_____

d. To what extent do the instructional materials engage students in doing technology problem solving?

_____

_____

_____

_____

e. To what extent does the curriculum engage students in activities that help them connect science to everyday issues and events?

_____

_____

_____

_____

f. How would you rate the overall developmental appropriateness of the instructional materials, given its intended audience of **ALL** students at the targeted level(s)?

_____

_____

_____

_____

Implementation: What Support Is Needed to Implement a K–12 Standards-Led Science Program?

189

g. Do the materials reflect current knowledge about effective teaching and learning practices (e.g., active learning, inquiry, community of learners) based on research related to science education?

_____

_____

_____

_____

h. Do the instructional materials provide students the opportunity to clarify, refine, and consolidate their ideas, and to communicate them through multiple modes?

_____

_____

_____

_____

i. Do the instructional materials provide students the opportunity to think and communicate mathematically?

_____

_____

_____

_____

j. Do the instructional materials provide students with activities connecting science with other subject areas?

_____

_____

_____

_____

k. Are the instructional materials likely to be interesting, engaging, and effective for girls and for boys?

_____

_____

_____

_____

l. Are the instructional materials likely to be interesting, engaging, and effective for underrepresented and underserved students (e.g., gender, ethnic, urban, rural, with disabilities)?

_____

_____

_____

_____

m. Assessment has explicit purposes connected to decisions to be made by teachers (e.g., prior knowledge, conceptual understanding, grades).

_____

_____

_____

_____

n. Assessment focuses on the curriculum's important content and skills.

_____

_____

_____

_____

o. Do the instructional materials include multiple kinds of assessments (e.g., performance, paper/pencil, portfolios, student interviews, embedded, projects)?

_____

_____

_____

_____

p. Are the assessment practices fair to all students?

_____

_____

_____

_____

q. Do the instructional materials include adequate and appropriate uses of a variety of educational technologies (e.g., video, computers, telecommunications)?

_____

_____

_____

_____

r. What is the overall quality of the pedagogical design of these instructional materials?

_____

_____

_____

_____

V. Implementation and System Support

a. Will the teachers find the materials interesting and engaging?

_____

_____

_____

_____

b. Do the instructional materials include information and guidance to assist the teacher in implementing the lessons?

_____

_____

_____

_____

c. Do the instructional materials provide information about the kinds of resources and support systems required to facilitate the district implementation of the required science materials?

_____

_____

_____

_____

d. Do the instructional materials provide information about how to establish a safe science learning environment?

_____

_____

_____

_____

e. Do the instructional materials provide information about the kinds of professional development experiences needed by teachers to implement the materials?

_____

_____

_____

_____

f. Do the materials provide guidance on how to link the materials with the district and state assessment frameworks and programs?

_____

_____

_____

_____

g. Do the materials provide guidance and assistance for actively involving administrators, parents, and the community at large in supporting school science?

_____

_____

_____

_____

h. Overall, are the materials useable by, realistic in expectations of, and supportive of teachers?

_____

_____

_____

VI. Major Strengths and Weaknesses

a. In your opinion, what are the three major strengths of this curriculum?

_____

_____

_____

_____

b. In your opinion, what are the three major weaknesses of this curriculum?

_____

_____

_____

_____

VII. Overall Quality, Value, and Contribution

a. In your opinion, what is the overall quality of these materials relative to:

	low	high
• Turning students on to science?	1 ....2 ....3 ....4 5	
• Making students think?	1 ....2 ....3 ....4 5	
• Quality of science content?	1 ....2 ....3 ....4 5	
• Quality of pedagogy?	1 ....2 ....3 ....4 5	
• Quality of classroom assessments?	1 ....2 ....3 ....4 5	
• Pushing teachers to teach differently?	1 ....2 ....3 ....4 5	

b. In your opinion, what is the overall quality of these instructional materials?

1 ....2.............................3 ....4.............................5
Low   Medium   High

c. To what extent would you encourage the dissemination, adoption, and implementation of this curriculum?

_____

_____

_____

_____

Please provide an overall narrative to support your findings:

References

Buhle, James T., LaMoine L. Moty, and Sandra S. West. 1999. *Guide to School Science Facilities.* Alexandria, Va.: National Science Teachers Association Press.

NCES (National Center for Educational Statistics). 1997. *TIMSS Attaining Excellence as a Starting Point to Examine Curricula, Guidebook to Examine School Curricula.* Washington, D.C.: U.S. Dept. of Education.

NRC (National Research Council). 1999. *Selecting Instructional Materials: A Guide for K–12 Science.* Washington, D.C.: National Academy Press.

NSF (National Science Foundation). 1997. *Review of Instructional Materials for Middle School Science.* Arlington, Va.: National Science Foundation Division for Elementary, Secondary, and Informal Education. p. 214.

NSTA (National Science Teachers Association). 2000 *An NSTA Position Statement … Laboratory Science. NSTA Handbook 2000–2001.* Arlington, Va.: NSTA Press.

United States Department of Education. 1996. *National Science Education Standards.* Washington, D.C.: National Academy Press.

Wisconsin Department of Public Instruction. 1998. *Wisconsin's Model Academic Standards for Science.* Madison, Wis.: Wisconsin Department of Public Instruction.

———. 1999. *The Total Science Safety System, Wisconsin Edition, Elementary and Secondary Versions.* Waukee, Iowa: JaKel.

Additional Reading

Buhle, James T., L. Motz LaMoine, and S Sandra West. 1999. *Guide to School Science Facilities.* Alexandria, Va.: NSTA Press.

National Science Teachers Association. *An NSTA Position Statement … Safety and School Science Instruction. NSTA Handbook 2000–2001.* Arlington, Va.: NSTA Press.

Their, Herbert D. 2001. *Developing Inquiry Based Science Materials: A Guide for Educators.* Teachers College Press.

Wisconsin Department of Public Instruction. 1999. *The Total Science Safety System. Wisconsin Edition, Elementary and Secondary Versions.* Waukee, Ia.: JaKel, Inc.

Additional Reading about Science Facilities

Following is a list of science safety resources and federal and state statutes that apply to the typical science classroom and which teachers may want to know about. Further information can be found in *The Total Science Safety System, Elementary and Secondary Versions* and is also available from the Wisconsin Society of Science Teachers. These resources and information are available on the World Wide Web or by contacting the Wisconsin Department of Public Instruction.

- Occupational Safety and Health Association (OSHA). Hazard Communication Standard or Right-to-Know Legislation.
- OSHA. Chemical Hygiene Plan (29 CFR, 1910.1450).
- OSHA. The Lab Standard (29 CFR, 1910.1450).
- Wisconsin Department of Industry, Labor and Human Relations, Chapter ILHR 32, Public Employee Safety and Health.
- Wisconsin Department of Public Instruction, Chapter PI 8.01, School District Standards.
- PI 8.01 School District Standards. (1) (i) Safe and Healthful Facilities.
- Laws of Wisconsin 101.01(06) Frequenter Legislation.

- Laws of Wisconsin 255.30(1) Goggle Legislation.
- National Science Teachers Association Minimum Safety Guidelines for Presenters and Workshop Leaders.

Additional Information about Science Resources

Designs for Science Literacy by the American Association for the Advancement of Science Project 2061 recommends a process for reviewing science resources. Project 2061 has evaluated several science textbooks, and the results are available by contacting the project electronically.

The National Science Resources Center at the Smithsonian Institute in Washington, D.C. has evaluated science resources. Their work is available electronically.

The National Science Foundation has extensively evaluated their science resources. Contact them directly (NSF.gov) for information.

The U.S. Department of Education has evaluated science textbooks. Their work is available on the World Wide Web.

Chapter 8
Essential Components of a K–12 Science Program

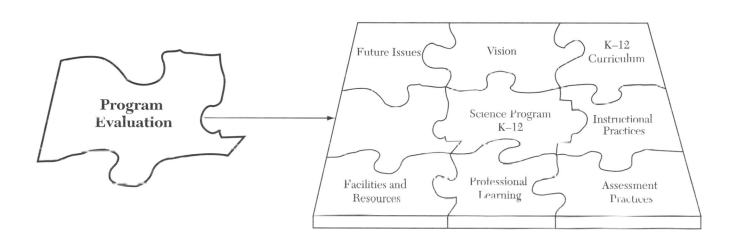

The figure illustrates the interlocking nature of the components of the standards-led science program. The power of the K–12 standards-led science program emerges when all the pieces of the program are present. Chapter 8 provides evaluation strategies for the science program.
Science Task Force, May 2000

Does the K–12 Science Program Achieve Scientific Literacy for All Students?

Evaluation and Evidence

Timber Coulee, a stream-cut valley in the driftless area: Bruce A. Brown of the WGNHS. Wisconsin DNR photo.

Science requires evidence and verification of data. Scientists must seek evidence by collaborating with others to verify their work. Seemingly immediate scientific breakthroughs have, in actuality, taken years because scientific breakthroughs rely on the systematic use of evidence and verification. Likewise, districts must rely on evidence to determine the degree to which the current K–12 standards-led science program is achieving its goal: scientific literacy for *all* students.

The purpose of this chapter is to help the *district team* evaluate the K–12 standards-led science program. Careful evaluation can measure the program's progress toward its goal of all students attaining scientific literacy. In assuming this responsibility, the district team must recognize program evaluation is not an occasion to place blame, but, rather, an opportunity for continuous program improvement and refinement leading to success.

How Does the District Team Evaluate the K–12 Standards-Led Science Program?

Science programs, no matter how well designed, should always be subject to systematic evaluation and refinement. Ongoing discoveries in science and technology, fluctuating social needs, more precise knowledge about how students learn science, and changing student needs necessitate periodic review and updating of all aspects of the science program. Program evaluation provides a solid basis for the decision to revise a portion of or even the entire science program.

The science program must have a built-in feedback mechanism so teachers and administrators readily know the extent to which each component of the program is contributing to its overall goals. Feedback will give the school district a more accurate picture of the K–12 standards-led science program and its strengths and weaknesses. The evaluation provides everyone interested in science with valuable evidence for modifying the entire science program or only identified aspects of the program in need of improvement.

Program-evaluation processes should be ongoing and consist of several data-collection strategies, each contributing information to help develop this clearer picture of the K–12 standards-led science program. The task force recommends that the district team convene a program-evaluation committee responsible for assembling, interpreting, and maintaining the program data. These steps provide evidence of program performance. The evaluation committee should consist of teachers, students, parents, administrators, and community members representative of school–community diversity.

As the evaluation committee begins planning data-collection strategies, they should realize that everything associated with the science program should be evaluated. As modeled in Figure 2.2 in Chapter 2, "A K–12 standards-led program is a program where all the pieces of the puzzle fit together." Rigorous program evaluation helps assure that the pieces of the science program do indeed fit together seamlessly, resulting in higher levels of student achievement. The task force recommends evaluating the following elements:

- District's vision about achieving scientific literacy
- Overall K–12 Science Program
- Curriculum
- Instructional practices
- Assessment practices
- Staff professional development
- Facilities and resources

To evaluate comprehensively the K–12 science program, the task force suggests a two-step process to collect and organize evidence from the science program. Important to note is that some of the data may overlap in both processes; however, each step for gathering the data is essential for contributing to the overall program evaluation.

Always evaluate with an end in mind.

Tim Peterson
(Science Task Force member), 2000.

The first step is for the evaluation committee to collect preliminary data about the K–12 science program. To assist the committee with their work, the task force has provided some guiding questions to help the committee gather the data, which are listed in Table 8.1. These questions are designed to assist committee members gather some of the necessary data about the scope of the K–12 science program. To respond to these questions, committee members should collect data from every grade and building in the district. The task force developed a sample framework for database design to compile and organize responses to these questions. The resulting data matrix provides a comprehensive horizontal and vertical picture of the K–12 science program across grades and buildings.

Step two includes collecting more detailed science data compiled from stakeholder perceptions, program data, performance data, and demographic data. As the evaluation committee assembles this data, the task force recognizes that each district has unique characteristics, resulting in a district-specific collection of data. In general, there are four kinds of data that can be gathered and examined (CESA 7 2000, 4).

TABLE 8.1 **Sample Framework for Scope of K–12 Science Database**

Question	K	1	2	3	4	5	6	7	8	9	10	11	12	**Preliminary Findings**
1. What evidence can be collected that indicates the students are learning science?														
2. How does the K–12 curriculum provide opportunities to learn science, including skills and processes?														
3. Is the WMASS evident throughout the K–12 science program?														
4. What levels of academic proficiency have the students achieved in science?														
5. What facilities and resources assist with students understanding science?														
6. How does the existing program support students learning science?														

Does the K–12 Science Program Achieve Scientific Literacy for All Students?

201

Perception data: Any type of survey or questionnaire about science education conducted in the district. These surveys may have been conducted with teachers, parents, students, or even community members about science education in the classroom or district.

Program data: Any type of data that illustrates a specific aspect of the K–12 science program, from standards to K–12 classroom curricula or course syllabi.

Performance data: Any type of data that indicates student achievement, from classroom assessment activities to overall district assessment results. Performance data can include classroom exams, district- and state-level testing, ACT and SAT results, and, if offered, AP examination results.

Demographic data: Any type of specialized data that describes the student population. This data may include information on ethnicity, socioeconomic status, disciplinary data, and specialized student populations.

Once the data gathering process is complete, it is time for the evaluation committee to analyze all the data and extrapolate what the data reveals. When examining the data, the evaluation committee should look for and uncover patterns and relationships among the data. The task force recommends that the evaluation committee create an additional database which organizes the patterns and relationships. A sample of the design of such a database is found in Table 8.2.

TABLE 8.2 **Patterns and Relationships Database**

	Patterns Within the Data	Relationships Among the Data
1. K–12 Science-Scope Data		
2. Perceptions Data		
3. Program Data		
4. Performance Data		
5. Demographic Data		

The evaluation committee must speculate on the reasons behind the patterns and relationships. To interpret this data, the committee must answer some simple questions that reveal evidence of program performance:

1. What interactions resulted in the current patterns and relationships?
2. Do the patterns and relationships produce a positive trend in the K–12 standards-led science program?
3. Why do the interactions produce these patterns and relationships?
4. What changes in the patterns and relationships, as well as in the underlying interactions, should occur to improve the overall K–12 standards-led science program?

Once interpretations have been made, the results must be applied to the science program. This is done through a process of goal setting. The goal setting process leads to implementation strategies throughout the K–12 standards-led science program.

As these goals are established and implementation strategies are developed, the committee should bear in mind that there will be physical and attitudinal barriers to address. Two examples of possible physical barriers are the facility needed for a quality science program and the amount of available money. Attitudinal barriers include the beliefs and attitudes of faculty, parents, or administrators. Each barrier must be analyzed to develop a strategy to overcome it. Strategies are usually so specific to local needs that it is impossible to outline general strategies in this document.

The findings, goals, and plans must be presented to the district team. The district team must then set the plan in motion by explaining the science-program evaluation process to everyone involved in school science. Everyone then must become actively engaged in implementing strategies developed by the evaluation committee.

The process of successful science program evaluation presented in this chapter is summarized in Figure 8.1. Each box in the diagram reflects back to a step essential for a thorough program evaluation. The committee can use the diagram to organize their work. The district team can use the diagram to communicate the evaluation process to others.

The following questionnaire, the task force decided, is an exemplary model and an example of a tool to collect teacher-perception data about the district science program. This tool uses a simple Likert scale to determine teacher attitudes on the status of the science program, including assessment of students, curriculum, instructional practices, professional development activities, and existing facilities and resources.

Conclusions and Implications

Are all students truly achieving scientific literacy? Answering this question requires the district team to engage in a rigorous process of data gathering and analysis. The answer to this question is essential for developing and maintaining a high-quality K–12 standards-led science program.

Does the K–12 Science Program Achieve Scientific Literacy for All Students?

203

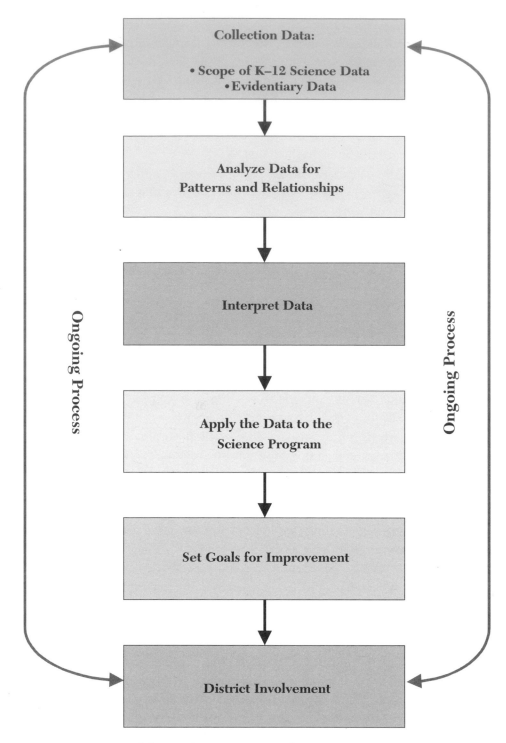

FIGURE 8.1 **Successful Science Program Evaluation**

Science

in our district

Facilities and Resources

Teaching and learning do not occur in a vacuum. The support of the science curriculum through appropriate facilities and resources is essential. The availability of scientific equipment and consumable materials, and the nature of the space in which instruction occurs, can either enhance or detract from the learning process.

Do the facilities and resources at _____

(fill in your school)

	A	F	S	N	NA*
1. receive ample and ongoing budgetary support in order to maintain and enrich all aspects of science instruction?					
2. ensure that all classrooms, laboratories, and other spaces conform to all pertinent safety considerations?					
3. meet safety and pedagogical needs for adequate instructional space and standard services (e.g., lab tables, venting hoods, water, gas, electricity, etc.)?					
4. comply with a Chemical Hygiene Plan that meets the federal and state mandates?					
5. receive oversight from a knowledgeable District Safety Officer?					
6. provide ample storage space capable of accommodating a variety of needs (e.g., acid storage cabinets, secure cabinets for expensive or fragile equipment)?					
7. have moveable furniture and flexible design to accommodate present and future instructional needs?					
8. accommodate special needs of a diverse population of students?					
9. provide for use of present and emerging technology, including adequate wiring, network computers, and easy access to audiovisual resources?					

Comments:

_____

A = Always   F = Frequently   S = Sometimes   N = Never   NA = Not applicable

Reprinted with permission of the Connecticut Academy for Education in Mathematics, Science & Technology, Inc., Middletown, Connecticut 06457-3769.

Science
in our district
Assessment

The evaluation of instruction, and ultimately of learning, provides teachers with feedback on their effectiveness, students with an appraisal of their achievement, and learning practices. Assessment also provides administrators and the community with information on the progress of children. Effective assessment instruments and procedures are crucial to an effective program because they can inform, illuminate, and improve teaching and learning.

Does the _____ School District science program . . .
(fill in your school)

	A	F	S	N	NA*
1. provide assessment data for students, teachers, parents, and administrators acquired through the use of a variety of evaluation instruments and techniques?					
2. require that students be provided with a clear statement of expectations regarding assignments, responsibilities, scoring rubrics, and criteria to be used to evaluate their performance?					
3. require students to demonstrate competence by authentic performance assessments in which students apply their knowledge and skills to real-life situations and practical applications?					
4. include assessments of students' prior knowledge and experiences?					

5. have assessments that:

• are directly linked to learning goals?					
• are learning experiences in themselves?					
• require students to produce high-quality products and/or performances?					
• provide tangible evidence of student learning?					

Comments:

_____

A = Always	F = Frequently	S = Sometimes	N = Never	NA = Not applicable

Reprinted with permission of the Connecticut Academy for Education in Mathematics, Science & Technology, Inc., Middletown, Connecticut 06457-3769.

Science
in our district
Professional Development

For teachers as well as students, learning is a life-long process. The explosion of knowledge requires districts to support teachers with ongoing professional development. This is particularly true in science, and thus life-long learning is the only option for teachers committed to excellence.

Does the professional development program for teachers of science in the
_____ School District . . .

(fill in your school)

	A	F	S	N	NA*
1. have a plan which guides the identification, selection, design, and implementation of effective professional growth opportunities?					
2. provide opportunities for teachers to remain current with advances in scientific knowledge, evolving educational trends, teaching strategies, and technologies?					
3. provide ample time during the school day for teams of teachers to meet, plan, collaborate, and engage in professional development?					
4. enable teachers to request professional development activities pertinent to their specific needs and interests?					
5. enable teachers to design individual plans to meet their specific needs?					
6. align with local curriculum expectations and revisions?					
7. utilize a planning committee which includes teachers, administrators, and resource persons?					
8. foster the collaborative efforts of teachers to reflect on their teaching practices in terms of the science philosophy and curriculum standards of the district?					
9. provide support for professional development opportunities outside of the school district?					
10. provide annual training for teachers to review safety procedures?					

_____
A = Always   F = Frequently   S = Sometimes   N = Never   NA = Not applicable

Reprinted with permission of the Connecticut Academy for Education in Mathematics, Science & Technology, Inc., Middletown, Connecticut 06457-3769.

Science
in our district
Curriculum

An important component of any instructional program is a carefully sequenced and articulated curriculum. This is particularly true in science where many topics and concepts need to be sequenced and developed over extended periods of time.

Does the _____ School District science curriculum . . .
(fill in your school)

	A	F	S	N	NA*
1. have an explicit philosophy that clearly delineates the major goals and values that guide instruction?					
2. provide an opportunity for every child to experience science every school day of every year?					
3. incorporate standards derived from contemporary reform initiatives (e.g., *Benchmarks, National Science Education Standards*)?					
4. have a coordinated sequence, with both vertical (K-12) and horizontal (across grade level) articulation?					
5. provide an equal emphasis on learning experiences in each of the sciences (physical, life and environmental, earth and space)?					
6. include effective strategies and materials that meet the diverse needs of the student population?					
7. ensure that all content is free of bias (e.g., age, culture, economic status, ethnicity, gender)?					
8. consist of developmentally appropriate content and skills?					
9. give students the opportunity to use scientific instrumentation and equipment (e.g., microscopes, calculator-based labs, etc.)?					
10. provide ongoing opportunities for experimentation and other hands-on/minds-on learning activities?					
11. emphasize scientific inquiry?					

A = Always   F = Frequently   S = Sometimes   N = Never   NA = Not applicable

Reprinted with permission of the Connecticut Academy for Education in Mathematics, Science & Technology, Inc., Middletown, Connecticut 06457-3769.

Science
in our district
Curriculum (cont.)

Does the _____ School District science curriculum . . .

(fill in your school)

	A	F	S	N	NA*
12. enable children to investigate important science concepts in depth over an extended period of time?					
13. include historical perspectives that illustrate the influence of science and technology on society as well as the connections between science and the students' present and future lives?					
14. infuse instructional technologies throughout the program (e.g., CD-ROMs, computers, calculators, Internet)?					
15. contain clear and easy-to-follow directions, references, and guidance for learning activities?					
16. provide teachers with helpful background information about the scientific concepts and skills to be learned?					
17. receive ongoing as well as periodic review and updating to ensure current and accurate science content?					

COMMENTS:

_____

A = Always   F = Frequently   S = Sometimes   N = Never   NA = Not applicable

Reprinted with permission of the Connecticut Academy for Education in Mathematics, Science & Technology, Inc., Middletown, Connecticut 06457-3769.

Science
in our district
Instruction and Learning Practices

Effective instruction and learning practices are the most fundamental ingredients of any instructional program. Science education is no exception. This section is based upon the assumption that teachers of science, like all teachers, already possess the basic teaching competencies.

Do YOU . . .

	A	F	S	N	NA*
1. implement teaching/learning standards aligned with contemporary reform initiatives (e.g., *Benchmarks*, *NSES*)?					
2. employ appropriate strategies to assure that all students have equal assess to high-quality science instruction and are encouraged to attain high standards of achievement?					
3. foster habits of mind that contribute to scientific literacy (e.g., respecting logic, basing decisions on empirical data, and applying appropriate skepticism)?					
4. model science as a way of thinking and learning about the natural world?					
5. model ethical values (e.g., honesty, fairness, respect) that guide scientists in their work?					
6. ensure that experimentation and other hands-on/minds-on learning activities are integral parts of instruction?					
7. provide the students with regular, ongoing opportunities to learn, practice, and apply process skills (e.g., measuring, observing, hypothesizing, and problem solving)?					
8. provide students with regular opportunities to collect data, and express and defend their results in a variety of ways?					
9. incorporate a learning cycle approach to guide instruction (e.g., engage, explore, explain, elaborate, and evaluate)?					
10. employ a variety of teaching/learning strategies responsive to the variety of learning styles of students and supported by contemporary research?					
11. provide opportunities for individual, cooperative, small-group, and large-group instruction?					

_____

A = Always   F = Frequently   S = Sometimes   N = Never   NA = Not applicable

Reprinted with permission of the Connecticut Academy for Education in Mathematics, Science & Technology, Inc., Middletown, Connecticut 06457-3769.

Science
in our district
Instruction and Learning Practices (cont.)

Do YOU . . .

	A	F	S	N	NA*
12. use scientific vocabulary to facilitate understanding rather than as an end in itself?					
13. make effective use of accessible instructional technologies (e.g., CD-ROMs, computers, calculators, internet)?					
14. make effective use of instructional technologies for lab interfacing, real-life data collection, and analysis?					
15. engage students in activities that enable them to appreciate and use the many connections within and between the sciences, and among science and other content areas?					
16. stimulate student interest in science?					
17. help students relate science learning to their daily lives?					
18. employ a variety of authentic assessment instruments and practices (e.g., portfolios, journals, research papers)?					
19. ensure that instructional practices are in compliance with the highest standards for safety?					
20. reflect on your teaching practices in terms of contemporary science, educational philosophy, and the curriculum standards of the district?					

COMMENTS:

A = Always   F = Frequently   S = Sometimes   N = Never   NA = Not applicable

Reprinted with permission of the Connecticut Academy for Education in Mathematics, Science & Technology, Inc., Middletown, Connecticut 06457-3769.

By using data, informed decisions can be made on program effectiveness and models for improvement exclusive of speculation and guesswork. As the district team finalizes their formal work on the K–12 standards-led science program, it is important to realize that their work is a dynamic process.

References

Sargent, Judy K. 2000. *Data Retreat Participant's Guide.* CESA 7. Green Bay, Wis.
Wisconsin Department of Public Instruction. 2000. *Task Force for Science Guide Discussions.* Madison, Wis.: Wisconsin Department of Public Instruction.

Additional Reading

Bernhardt, V. L. 1998. *Data Analysis for Comprehensive Schoolwide Improvement, Eye on Education.*
Sargent, Judy K. 2000. *Data Retreat Participant's Guide.* CESA 7. Green Bay, Wis.

Chapter 9
Essential Components of a K–12 Science Program

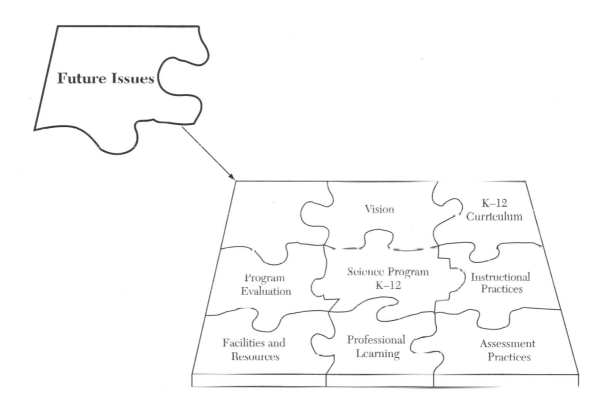

The figure illustrates the interlocking nature of the components of the standards-led science program. The power of the K–12 standards-led science program emerges when all the pieces of the program are present. Chapter 9 discusses the future of science education.

Science Task Force, May 2000

What Does the Future Hold for Science Education?

The Ending and the Beginning

A depression created by glacial erosion of the Maquoketa shale, Horicon Marsh: Bruce A. Brown of the WGNHS. Wisconsin DNR photo.

I n the publication *Inventing Science Education of the New Millennium*, Paul DeHart Hurd states "Since the 1940s, evolutionary changes have been developing in the sciences" (Hurd 1997, 33). He says these changes resulted from World War II. Using the "air age" as an example, he indicates that jet engines were designed to replace propellers, resulting in greater speed. Another example of an evolutionary change in the sciences Hurd refers to is the "atomic age." In all of his examples, he shows how these changes have significantly impacted contemporary science and the science curriculum. Turn to the publication for details on how the changes Hurd discusses have impacted the science curriculum. Because science continues to rapidly change, so must science education. This notion led the task force to leave the *district team* with one final question.

How Does the K–12 Standards-Led Science Program Include the Ever-Increasing Complexity of Science and Recent Advances in Science?

Although answering this question is not easy, the task force suggests the *district team* consider the following: Science teachers must continually seek ways to change their science curricula to reflect the ever-changing knowledge of science. An illustrative example comes from this vignette and course concepts from Ms. A., a high school science teacher in Wisconsin. Here is an excerpt from her molecular biology class.

First Day

On the first day of the new school year, students enthusiastically enter the classroom. They are busy learning how their friends spent the summer that has passed so quickly, when suddenly they hear "Welcome to a class where the goal is for you to develop a deeper understanding of your future. Welcome to Molecular Biology." Students look puzzled. One student responds, "Mrs. A., I can understand how this course is going to help me understand molecular biology, but how is this going to help me better understand my future?" Mrs. A. responds "You are in the midst of a new revolution—a bio-revolution. Molecular biology, often called the 'new biology', has significantly impacted the lives of many, and many don't even realize it. Think about a person who you know is diabetic. Thanks to molecular biology, that person can now get insulin, not as in the past from a pig, but rather from genetically-engineered bacteria cloned to produce human insulin. Remember the BGH milk controversy? The story was in the headlines of newspapers for weeks. Schools were developing policies to not accept milk from the cows injected with BGH. Advertising companies used the controversy to promote and market various products labeled 'BGH free'. During this time the Federal Food and Drug Administration (FDA) was busy explaining the nature of BGH and why they had approved it. Millions of federal dollars were invested to prove the safety of BGH. Across the nation, farmers, environmentalists, animal-rights activists and a whole host of other people claimed BGH was unsafe and posed health and economic threats. The story of BGH can go on and on, but I think I have made my point."

"Molecular biology impacts all our lives in a variety of ways. I am certain that molecular biology issues will directly impact each of you, as you become adults. By embracing this new revolution in science, you are choosing to be better informed and make decisions based on information and knowledge, not fear and speculation."

"In the case of BGH, people in the general population had to understand molecular biology concepts. Some of these nonscientists included the journalists reporting the story, technical writers describing the product, company investors, marketing and promotion personnel, grocery store managers making inventory decisions, farmers deciding if this is needed to keep their income steady, and even school board members wanting to make policy decisions on the type of milk to serve their students."

"This class is designed so you can explore the world of molecular biology, not only within the realm of science, but also understanding the impact of advances in molecular biology on our society. You will experience what it is to be a research scientist. Unlike the format of other courses where labs are set up and you perform a series of steps to reach or prove a conclusion, in this class you will assume the role of a researcher."

"You and a partner will be given the lab protocols. These lab protocols describe the procedures and provide the information needed to prepare all materials for the lab. When you receive these protocols, you will need to develop your own work plan outlining the schedule of events needed to carry out your procedure. You will assume all responsibilities for running the protocol and be expected to keep a record book documenting all aspects of the procedure. In the end, your team will be asked to report out findings, establishing the purpose behind each step and conclusions drawn. You will need to note any procedural experimental error and how to correct it. Finally you will be expected to extrapolate these findings to develop improved protocols or seek answers to new questions."

"As a class we will explore the impacts of this bio-revolution on our world. We will deal with bio-ethical issues that we disagree about and won't be able to come to consensus on. It's important for you to know that's OK. In the world of education, you have been taught that there are definite answers that are often either right or wrong. In the world of molecular biology we will face issues that will be neither right nor wrong, but simply there. Learning to understand various points of view, objectively analyzing information, debating issues, and yes—disagreeing—will be the cornerstone to the skills and abilities you will carry with you into your future. Come along and let's explore the wide range of molecular biology topics."

Molecular Biology Course Concepts[1] Ms. A.

1. Biotechnology/Molecular Biology Introduction
   - Define biotechnology
   - Uses of biotechnology through history
   - Distinguish between "old" and "new" biotechnology
   - Classify the areas of impact
2. Lab and Safety Techniques
   - Identify the location of first aid supplies.
   - Correlate the first aid supplies to the type of emergency encountered.
   - Describe proper personal protective equipment for laboratory work.
   - Interpret the information on a MSDS.
   - Contain and clean up a solid and liquid chemical spill.
   - Contain and clean up a biological material spill.
   - Understand the distinction between accuracy and precision.

---

[1] The course concepts only reflect "what" is being taught, not "how" the teacher is presenting the information. The teacher employs instructional practices described in this guide.

- Understand appropriate ways to measure mass and volume.
- Demonstrate skill in the use of pipetting techniques.
- Clean and prepare glassware properly.
- Prepare stock solutions.
- Describe the functions of basic laboratory instruments.
- Standardize a pH meter and determine the pH of a solution.
- Understand the function of a buffer and be able to prepare buffer solutions.
- Demonstrate proper technique for transfer of microorganisms.
- Streak an agar medium for isolated colonies of microorganisms.
- Understand the basic principles of spectrophotometry.
- Standardize a spectrophotometer and determine absorbency (or % transmittance) of a solution.
- Discuss the application of Baer's law for identifying the quantity of substance.

3. Basic Research Skills: Experimental Design and Communication
   - Understand the importance of effective communication in science and technology.
   - Discern between control and variables within an experiment.
   - Demonstrate familiarity with the scientific process.
   - Apply the principles of experimental design to basic laboratory protocols.
   - Write a protocol for a laboratory exercise.
   - Understand how to maintain a laboratory notebook.
   - Write a report in scientific format.
   - Present information or experimental results orally in a seminar format.
   - Present information or experimental results in a poster-session format.
   - Read articles in scientific journals and identify components of experimental design.

4. Basic Research Skills: Mathematics
   - Understand the metric system, scientific notation, significant digits, and logarithms.
   - Use basic proportions and ratios.
   - Understand and calculate percentages.
   - Understand dependent and independent variables and how to represent them graphically.
   - Understand basic statistical analysis: mean, standard deviation, correlation coefficients, and statistical significance.
   - Demonstrate an ability to understand statistical analysis of data in scientific literature.

5. Cell Biology Review (Part 1)
   - Differentiate between prokaryotic and eukaryotic cells.
   - Identify the intracellular structures in a cell diagram.
   - Discuss the function of organelles in the cell.
   - Differentiate between plant and animal cells.

6. Plant Tissue Culture
   - Demonstrate techniques for establishing and maintaining a sterile work area.

- Understand the concepts of totipotency and embryogenesis in plant-cell differentiation.
- Perform plant-cell culture to form callus tissue.
- Perform plant-cell culture to differentiate callus to the plantlet stage.
- Describe the role of plant hormones in plant tissue differentiation.
- Understand the use of tissue culture for clonal propagation and soma-clonal variation.

7. Animal Tissue Culture
- Demonstrate techniques for establishing and maintaining a sterile work area.
- Perform animal cell culture.
- Describe the role of nutrient requirements for animal tissue culture.
- Describe applications of an animal tissue culture.

8. Cell Biology Review (Part 2)
- Review the process of mitosis.
- Review the process of meiosis and sexual reproduction.
- Describe the structure of DNA and relate its structure to its function.
- Describe the process of DNA replication.
- Understand basic Mendelian genetics.
- Research and predict heredity disorders through pedigree analysis.
- Become familiar with some common genetic disorders.
- Demonstrate an understanding of the genetic code.
- Explain the central dogma of molecular biology.

9. Nucleic-Acid Techniques
- Describe the functions of nucleic acids.
- Isolate chromosomal DNA from plant or animal cells and partially purify it.
- Demonstrate an understanding of the principles of electrophoresis.
- Electrophorese DNA in agarose gels.
- Explain the role of restriction enzymes.
- Understand and use methods to visualize and photograph DNA in gels.
- Analyze patterns of DNA digested with restriction endonucleases on agarose gels.
- Identify specific sequences of DNA using restriction patterns.
- Calculate molecular weights of restriction endonuclease fragments.
- Use PCR to amplify DNA for purification and testing procedures.
- Describe hybridization techniques and perform blotting procedures.

10. Gene Cloning
- Explain the role of plasmids.
- Understand the concept of "gene cloning."
- Isolate, purify, and characterize plasmid DNA from bacterial cells.
- Prepare competent cells for DNA transformation.
- Use restriction enzymes and ligase to create a recombinant plasmid.
- Transform cells with recombinant plasmids.
- Understand the mode of action of antibiotics and the mechanism for antibiotic resistance.
- Understand the use of antibiotic resistance as a selectable marker.

- Understand the difference between selection and screening.
- Use selection/screening techniques to identify bacteria transformed with recombinant plasmids.

11. Protein Techniques
- Identify the molecular structure and characteristics of proteins.
- Understand the role of enzymes as biological catalysts.
- Demonstrate assays for measuring protein activity and quantity.
- Demonstrate skills in assaying enzyme activity (ELISA).
- Demonstrate skills in protein separation using gel electrophoresis.
- Understand the principles of different protein purification techniques.

12. Emerging Applications
- Animal Cloning
- Gene Therapy

Reprinted with permission of Albrecht (2001)

This vignette and the course concepts represent a science course that offers students opportunities to move beyond traditional science content. They represent the opportunity to explore and learn more about the bio-revolution. Courses like the one in this vignette center on new discoveries in science and incorporate the technological advances and applications found with these new discoveries. As the district team develops the K–12 standards-led science program, the team must consider the next generation of science courses and allow room for program growth that is reflective of the growth in the field of science.

Conclusion and Implications

The jigsaw puzzle below once again is illustrating how every piece of the K–12 science program is connected to every other piece of the program. Each chapter provides guidance to the district team for designing a standards-led science program. With each piece in place, the district will accomplish the overall vision of scientific literacy for all students within the district. However, remember the journey never really ends, but the journey is worth taking.

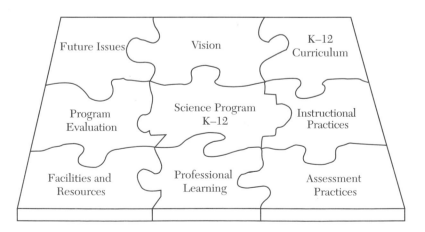

References

Albrecht, Lisa. 2001. *Molecular Biology Syllabus*. DeForest High School, DeForest Area Schools, DeForest, Wis.

Hurd, P. 1997. *Inventing Science Education for the New Millennium*. New York: Teachers College Press.

Additional Readings

Appendix E

Glossary

Assessment   Any systematic method of obtaining information from tests and other sources used to draw inferences about characteristics of people, objects, or programs (American Educational Research Association 1999, 172).

Brain-Based Education   The brain is an active processor that constantly looks for patterns and meaning. Isolation of facts and memorization without context do not provide adequate stimulation for the brain. Brain-based education involves (1) Designing and orchestrating lifelike, enriching, and appropriate experiences for learners and (2) Ensuring that students process experience in such a way as to increase the extraction of meaning (Caine and Caine 1991).

Concept   An idea or thought, especially a generalized idea of a class of objects, and abstract notion (Merriam-Webster 1993, 272). Concepts are organizing centers for connected curriculum that enable students to come to conclusions at higher levels of abstraction.

Connected Curriculum   Making connections between experiences in and out of school or between planned-learning experiences and previous learning or simply moving beyond the fragmented, separate subject or skill approach. Two major approaches to designing connected curriculum are the multidisciplinary and integrated approaches. The multidisciplinary model maintains distinctions between individual subjects while the integrated model does not.

Constructivism   A theory that assumes that students can create meaning and knowledge through their own explorations. This approach emphasizes active learning over memorization of facts. Constructivist theory is a theory of knowledge where students construct personal meaning by relating new information and concepts to past experiences. It also refers to teaching and learning where learners continue to build bodies of knowledge. "Constructivists are deeply committed to the view that what we take to be objective knowledge and truth is the result of perspective. Knowledge and truth are created, not discovered by the mind" (Schwandt 1994, 125).

Content Standard   A standard that specifies *what* students should know and be able to do.

Curriculum   Coherent and focused presentation of the district standards from kindergarten through twelfth grade.

District Team   Group of teachers, parents, students, community members, and others within a district or local building responsible for working on the K–12 standards-led science program.

Guiding (Essential) Question   A question that helps to ensure that curriculum connections are relevant and meaningful. A guiding question is probing and is answered through research and investigation.

Integrated Curriculum   Curriculum approaches that do not maintain the identities or separate subjects. Instead, educational activities organically integrate knowledge and skills from many subjects. Content and skills are taught, learned, and applied as the need arises in studying particular themes.

Interdisciplinary   See *multidisciplinary*.

Multidisciplinary   An approach based on an organizing center, such as a theme, topic, or problem. The organizing center allows connections between and among knowledge and skills drawn from various subjects. In a multidisciplinary framework, the separate subjects retain their identity and, typically, have separate time slots in the school schedule.

Performance Standard   Standards that specify *how* students will show that they are meeting a standard.

Personal Professional Development   Activities that contribute to an individual's professional lifelong learning, as called for in *PI 34*, that can be added to a personal professional development portfolio.

Professional Development Portfolio   A portfolio that contains information about the professional, including a plan for professional development, and leads to lifelong professional learning.

Proficiency Standard   Standards that indicate *how well* students must perform.

Project   A substantial student activity that addresses a theme, topic, problem, issue, or question. Projects are usually part of a learning experience requiring several weeks or more. They are intended to integrate knowledge from a variety of sources, and to culminate in a product or performance.

Science   An explanation of the natural and designed world.

Scientific Literacy Understanding of science concepts as defined in the *Wisconsin Model Academic Standards for Science* (DPI 1998), kindergarten through twelfth grade.

Service Learning A method of teaching and learning that combines academic work and community service. Students learn by doing, through a clear application of skills and knowledge, while helping meet needs in the school or greater community.

Staff Professional Development Overall staff activities that assist the staff with implementation of and changes to the standards-led science program.

Standards-Led A concept developed by the task force and based on the state or national science education standards.

Test An evaluative device or procedure where a sample of an examinee's behavior in a specific domain is obtained and subsequently evaluated and scored using a standardized process (American Educational Research Association 1999, 183).

Theme An organizing center for connected curriculum, such as a topic or subject, or a recurring, unifying subject or idea.

References

Caine, Renate Numela, and Geoffrey Caine. 1991. Making Connections: Teaching and the Human Brain. Alexandria, Va.: Association for Supervision and Curriculum Development.

Schwandt, T.A. 1994. Constructivist, Interpretivist Approaches to Human Inquiry. In *Handbook of Qualitative Research*. Edited by Norman K. Denzin, and Yvonna S. Lincoln. Thousand Oaks, Calif.: Sage Publications.

Wisconsin Department of Public Instruction. 1998. *Wisconsin's Model Academic Standards for Science*. Madison, Wis.: Wisconsin Department of Public Instruction.

Additional Resources

American Association for the Advancement of Science (AAAS). 1993. *Project 2061: Benchmarks for Science Literacy.* New York: Oxford University Press.

———. 1997. *Project 2061: Resources for Science Literacy–Professional Development.* New York: Oxford University Press.

———. 1997. *Resources for Science Literacy: Professional Development (CD-ROM).* New York: Oxford University Press.

———. 2000. Project 2061:2061 Today. *Science Literacy for a Changing Future* 10(1).

American Chemical Society. 1985. *Less is Better—Laboratory Chemical Management for Waste Reduction.* Washington, D.C.: American Chemical Society.

———. 1997. *Chemistry in the National Science Education Standards. A Reader and Resource Manual for High School Teachers.* Washington, D.C.: American Chemical Society.

Anderson, R., and H. Pratt. 1995. *Local Leadership for Science Education Reform.* Dubuque, Iowa: Kendall/Hunt.

Association of Science Materials Centers, c/o Science and Social Sciences Resource Specialist, Mesa Public Schools, Mesa, Az. (602) 898-7815.

Badders, B.L. et al. 1996. Journeys: A Collegial Study Group of Cleveland Teachers. Paper presented at the annual meeting of the National Science Teachers Association, St. Louis, Mo.

Ball, D.L. 1996. Teacher Learning and the Mathematics Reforms: What We Think We Know and What We Need to Learn. *Phi Delta Kappan* 77(7): 500–508.

Ball, D.L., and D.K. Cohen. 1995. Developing Practice. Developing Practitioners: Toward a Practice-Based Theory of Professional Education. Paper prepared for the National Commission on Teaching and America's Future.

———. 1996. Reform by the Book: What Is–Or Might Be–The Role of Curriculum Materials in Teacher Learning and Instructional Reform? *Educational Researcher* 25(9): 6–8, 14.

Bell, B., and J. Gilbert. (1996). *Teacher Development: A Model from Science Education.* London: Falmer.

Bender, W.N., G. Clinton, and D.S. Hotaling. 1996. Using Distance Learning in Staff Development. *Journal of Staff Development* 17(4): 52–55.

Bigelow, Bill et al. 1994. *Rethinking Our Classrooms. Teaching for Equity and Justice.* Rethinking Schools, Ltd.

Biological Sciences Curriculum Study (BSCS). 2000. *Making Sense of Integrated Science: A Guide for High Schools.* Colorado Springs, Colo: BSCS.

Boone, W.J., and H.O. Anderson. 1995. Training Science Teachers with Fully Interactive, Distance Education Technology. *Journal of Science Teacher Education* 6(3): 146–152.

Bowers, J. 1994. Scientists and Science Education Reform: Myths, Methods, and Madness. p. 123–130. *Scientists, Educators, and National Standards: Action at the Local Level, Forum Proceedings.* April 14–15. Research Triangle Park, N.C.: Sigma Xi, The Scientific Research Society.

Brown, M.I. 1995. Study Groups at Elder Middle School. *Journal of Staff Development* 16(3): 53.

Budnick, S. 1995. Study Groups at Mission Bay High School. *Journal of Staff Development* 16(3): 52.

Bybee, Rodger W. 1993. *Reforming Science Education–Social Perspectives & Personal Reflections.* New York: Teachers College Press.

Caccia, P.F. 1996. Linguistic Coaching: Helping Beginning Teachers Defeat Discouragement. *Educational Leadership* 53(6): 17–20.

Calhoun, E.F. 1993. Action Research: Three Approaches. *Educational Leadership* 51(2): 62–65.

———. 1994. *How to Use Action Research in the Self-Renewing School.* Alexandria, Va.: Association for Supervision and Curriculum Development.

CalTech Precollege Science Initiative (CAPSI). The Pasadena Modules Project: Modular Inquiries for Advanced Professional Development, David Hartney, Managing Director, Pasadena, Calif. (818) 395-3222.

Cambre, M.A., B. Erdman, and L. Hall. 1996. The Challenge of Distance Education. *Journal of Staff Development* 17(1): 38–41.

Carpenter, T.P. et al. 1989. Using Knowledge of Children's Mathematics Thinking in Classroom Teaching: An Experimental Study. *American Educational Research Journal* 26: 499–531.

Carter, S. et. al. 1995. Study Groups: The Productive 'Whole'. *Journal of Staff Development* 16(3): 50–52.

Center for Case Studies in Education, Rita Silverman and William Welty, Codirectors, Pace University, Pleasantville, NY. (914) 773-3879.

Center for Children and Technology (CCT), Education Development Center, Inc. 1995. On-Line Learning, On-Line Communities. *CCT Notes* 3(1): 1–6.

Charles, L., and P. Clark. 1995. Whole-Faculty Study Groups at Sweetwater Union High School. *Journal of Staff Development* 16 (3): 49–50.

Clewell, B.C., B.T. Anderson, and M.E. Thorpe. 1992. *Breaking the Barriers: Helping Female and Minority Students Succeed in Mathematics and Science.* San Francisco: Jossey-Bass.

Cobb, P.T. et al. 1991. Assessment of a Problem-Centered Second-Grade Mathematics Project. *Journal for Research in Mathematics Education* 22: 13–29.

Cognitively Guided Instruction Project. Directed by Elizabeth Fennema and Thomas P. Carpenter, University of Wisconsin–Madison, Madison, Wis.

Cohen, D.K. and H.C. Hill. 1991. *State Policy and Classroom Performance: Mathematics Reform in California. CPRE Policy Brief RB-23*. Philadelphia: Graduate School of Education, University of Pennsylvania.

————. 1998. *Instructional Policy and Classroom Performance: The Mathematics Reform in California (Research Report no. RR-39)*. Philadelphia: University of Pennsylvania, Consortium for Policy Research in Education.

Cole, M., and P. Griffin, eds. 1987. *Contextual Factors in Education: Improving Science and Mathematics for Minorities and Women.* Madison, Wis: Committee on Research on Mathematics, Science, and Technology Education, Wisconsin Center for Education Research.

Colorado College Integrated Science Teacher Enhancement Project (CC-ISTEP). Paul Kuerbis, Project Director, Colorado Springs, Colo. (719) 389–6147.

Committee on Biology Teacher Inservice Programs, Board on Biology, Commission on Life Sciences, National Research Council. 1996. *The Role of Scientists in the Professional Development of Science Teachers.* Washington, D.C.: National Academy Press.

Computer Supported International Learning Environments (CSILE). Ontario Institute for Studies in Education, Center for Applied Cognitive Science, Marlene Scardamalia and Carl Bereiter, Project Directors, Toronto.

Continuous Assessment in Science Project. 1996. Unpublished report to the National Science Foundation. Andover, Mass.: The NETWORK, Inc.

Costa, A., and B. Kallick. 1993. Through the Lens of a Critical Friend. *Educational Leadership* 51(3):49–51.

Costa, A., and R. Garmston. 1994. *Cognitive Coaching: Approaching Renaissance Schools.* Norwood, Mass.: Christopher Gordon Publishing.

Cusick, P.A. 1982. *A Study of Networks Among Professional Staffs in Secondary Schools.* East Lansing, Mich.: Institute for Research on Teaching, Michigan State University.

Danielson, C. 1996. *Enhancing Professional Practice: A Framework for Teaching.* Alexandria, Va.: Association for Supervision and Curriculum Development.

Darling-Hammond, K. 1993. Reframing The School Reform Agenda: Developing Capacity for School Transformation. *Phi Beta Kappan* June 90–92.

Decisions in Teaching Elementary School Science (videodiscs). Biological Science Curriculum Study (BSCS), Colorado Springs, Colo. (719) 531–5550.

Dempsey, E. 1995. IMPACT II: A Teacher-to-Teacher Networking Program. *Educational Leadership* 42(4): 41–45.

DiRanna, K., M. Osterfled, K. Cerwin, J. Topps, and D. Tucker. 1995. *Facilitator's Guide to Science Assessment.* California Department of Education; California Science Implementation Network; California Science Project; Scope, Sequence, and Coordination Project; and Santa Barbara County Office of Education Region 8.

Distance Learning Resource Network (DLRN). *Technology in Education Program.* San Francisco: WestEd.

Driscoll, M., and D. Bryant. 2001. *Getting Started with Teachers.* Washington, DC: National Research Council.

Duckworth, E. 1986. Teaching as Research. *Harvard Educational Review* 56(4): 481–495.

Dyasi, H.M. 1995. *The City College Workshop Center Program for Reculturing Teachers to Teach Inquiry-Based Science in the Elementary School.* Unpublished manuscript.

Eisenhower National Clearinghouse for Mathematics and Science Education. 1999. *Focus. A Magazine for Classroom Innovators* 6(1).

————. 1999. *ENC Focus. A Magazine for Classroom Innovators. Integrating Technology in the Classroom* 6(3).

Elementary Science Leadership Institutes, National Science Resources Center, Washington, D.C., (202) 287–2063.

Elliott, Stephen N., and Jeffery P. Braden. 2000. *Educational Assessment and Accountability for All Students. Facilitating the Meaningful Participation of Students with Disabilities in District and Statewide Assessment Programs.* Madison, Wis.: Wisconsin Department of Public Instruction.

Evans, C.S. 1993. When Teachers Look at Student Work. *Educational Leadership* 50(5): 71–72.

Far West Laboratory. 1990. *Case Methods: A Knowledge Brief on Effective Teaching.* San Francisco: Far West Laboratory.

Filby, N.N. 1995. *Analysis of Reflective Professional Development Models.* San Francisco: WestEd.

Flora, V.R. and J. Applegate. 1982. Concerns and Continuing Education Interests of Staff Developers. *Journal of Staff Development* 3(2): 45–53.

Fortier, John, Gary H. Cook, and Maggie Burke. 2000. *Wisconsin High School Graduation Test Educator's Guide.* Madison, Wis.: Wisconsin Department of Public Instruction.

Fullan, M.G. 1991. *The New Meaning of Educational Change.* New York: Teachers College Press.

Fullan, M., and S. Stiegelbauer. 1991. *The New Meaning of Educational Change.* 2d ed. New York: Teachers College Press.

Ganser, T. 1996. Preparing Mentors of Beginning Teachers: An Overview for Staff Developers. *Journal of Staff Development* 17(4): 8–11.

Gardner, April L., Cheryl L. Mason, and Marsha Lakes Matyas. 1998. *Equity, Excellence & 'Just Plain Good Teaching.'* Columbus, Ohio: Eisenhower National Clearinghouse.

Garmston, R. 1987. How Administrators Support Peer Coaching. *Educational Leadership* 44(5): 18–28.

Global Systems Science (GSS). Lawrence Hall of Science, Berkeley, Calif. (510) 642-9635.

Good, T.L., and D.A. Grouws. 1979. The Missouri Mathematics Effectiveness Project: An Experimental Study in Fourth-Grade Classrooms. *Journal of Educational Psychology* 71: 355–362.

Good, T.L., D. Grouws, and H. Ebmeier. 1983. *Active Mathematics Teaching.* New York: Longman.

Gottfried, S.S., C.W. Brown, P.S. Markovits, and J.B. Changar. Undated. *Scientific Work Experience Programs for Science Teachers: A Focus on Research-Related Internships.* Unpublished manuscript.

Great Explorations in Math and Science (GEMS), Lawrence Hall of Science, University of California, Berkeley, Calif. (510) 642–9635.

GroupSystems. Ventana Corporation, Tucson, Ariz. (520) 325-8228.

Guskey, T.R. 1986. Staff Development and the Process of Teacher Change. *Educational Researcher* 15(5): 6–12.

Hansen, A. 1997. Writing Cases for Teaching: Observations of a Practitioner. *Phi Delta Kappan* 78(5): 398–403.

Hassel, Emily. 1999. *Professional Development: Learning from the Best. A Toolkit for Schools and Districts Based on the National Awards Program for Model Professional Development.* Oak Brook, Ill.: North Central Regional Education Laboratory.

Hays, I.D. 1994. *Scientists, Educators, and National Standards Action at the Local Level: Forum Proceedings.* April 14–15. Paper prepared for Sigma Xi: The Scientific Research Society Forum. Raleigh, N.C.

Health and Safety Reference Service, American Chemical Society, Washington, D.C., (202–872–4515).

Holly, P. 1991. Action Research: The Missing Link in the Creation of Schools as Centers of Inquiry. In *Staff Development for Education in the '90s: New Demands, New Realities, New Perspectives.* Edited by A. Lieberman and L. Miller. New York: Teachers College Press.

Howe, Ann C., and Harriet S. Stubbs. 1997. Empowering Science Teachers: A Model for Professional Development. *Journal of Science Teacher Education* 8(3): 167–82.

Industry Initiatives for Science and Math Education. Lawrence Hall of Science, University of California, Berkeley, Calif. (415) 326–4800.

Joyce, B., and B. Showers. 1987. Low Cost Arrangement for Peer Coaching. *Journal of Staff Development* 8(1): 22–24.

———. 1988. *Student Achievement through Staff Development.* New York: Longman, Inc.

Just Think. Problem Solving through Inquiry (video series). Produced by the New York State Education Department, Office of Educational Television and Public Broadcasting. (518) 474–5862.

Kahle, Jane Butler. 1998. Measuring Progress Toward Equity in Science and Mathematics Education. *NISE Brief* 2(3).

Katz, M.M., E. McSwiney, and K. Stroud. 1987. *Facilitating Collegial Exchange Among Science Teachers by Writing: The Use of Computer-Based Conferencing.* Cambridge, Mass.: Harvard Graduate School of Education, Educational Technology Center.

Kennedy, M.M. 1998. *Learning to Teach Writing: Does Teacher Education Make a Difference?* New York: Teachers College Press.

Killion, J.P. 1993. Staff Development and Curriculum Development: Two Sides of the Same Coin. *Journal of Staff Development* 14(1): 38–41.

Kleinfeld, J. Undated. Ethical Issues and Legal Liability in Writing Cases About Teaching. Unpublished paper.

LaBonte, K., C. Leighty, S.J. Mills, and M.L. True. 1995. Whole-Faculty Study Groups: Building the Capacity for Change through Interagency Collaboration. *Journal of Staff Development* 16(3): 45–47.

Lampert, M. 1988. What Can Research on Teacher Education Tell Us About Improving the Quality of Mathematics Education? *Teaching and Teacher Education* 4: 157–170.

Lawrenz, F., and H. McCreath. 1988. Integrating Quantitative and Qualitative Evaluation Methods to Compare Two Inservice Training Programs. *Journal of Research in Science Teaching* 25: 397–407.

Lee, Shelley A. et al. 2000. *Beyond 2000–Teachers of Science Speak Out. An NSTA Lead Paper on How All Students Learn Science And the Implications to the Science Education Community.* Arlington, Va.: National Science Teachers Association Press.

Leonardt, N., and P. Fraser-Abder. 1996. Research Experiences for Teachers. *The Science Teacher* 63(1): 30–33.

Lewis, Anne, Willis D. Hawley, Donna C. Rhodes, and Robert McClure. 1999. *Revisioning Professional Development. What Learner-Centered Professional Development Looks Like.* Ann Arbor, Mich.: National Staff Development Council.

Lieberman, A. 1986. Collaborative Research: Working With, Not Working On. *Educational Leadership* 43(5) 28–32.

Lieberman, A., ed. 1988. *Building a Professional Culture in Schools.* New York: Teacher's College Press.

Lieberman, A., and M.W. McLaughlin. 1992. Networks for Educational Change: Powerful and Problematic. *Phi Delta Kappan* 73(9): 673–77.

Little, J.W. 1990. The Persistence of Privacy: Autonomy and Initiative in Teachers' Professional Relations. *Teachers College Record* 91(4): 509–36.

————. 1993. Teachers' Professional Development in a Climate of Educational Reform. *Educational Evaluation and Policy Analysis* 15(2): 129–51.

Loucks-Horsley, S. 1996. Professional Development for Science Education: A Critical and Immediate Challenge. In *National Standards and the Science Curriculum: Challenges, Opportunities, and Recommendations.* Edited by R.W. Bybee. Dubuque, Iowa: Kendall/Hunt Publishing Co.

Loucks-Horsley, S., C.K. Harding, M.A. Arbuckle, L.B. Murray, C. Dubea, and M.K. Williams. 1987. *Continuing to Learn: A Guidebook for Teacher Development.* Andover, Mass.: The National Staff Development Council.

Loucks-Horsley, S., R. Kapitan, M.D. Carlson, P.J. Kuerbis, R.C. Clark, G.M. Melle, T.P. Sachse, and E. Walton. 1990. *Elementary School Science for the '90s.* Andover, Mass.: The NETWORK, Inc.

Loucks-Horsley, Susan, Katherine Stiles, and Peter Hewson. 1996. Principles of Effective Professional Development for Mathematics and Science Education: A Synthesis of Standards. *NISE Brief* 1(1).

Loucks-Horsley, S., P.W. Hewson, N. Love, and K. Stiles. 1998. *Designing Professional Development for Teachers of Science and Mathematics.* Thousand Oaks, Calif.: Corwin Press.

Loucks-Horsley, S., P.W. Hewson, N. Levine, S. Mundry, E. Silver, M. Smith, M.K. Stein, and K. Stiles. 2000. *Case Studies of Professional Development Design for Teachers of Science and Mathematics.* Madison, Wis.: University of Wisconsin–Madison, National Institute for Science Education.

Lowery, Lawrence F. 1998. *The Biological Basis of Thinking and Learning.* Berkeley Calif.:University of California Press.

Makibbin, S. and M. Sprague. 1991. Study Groups: Conduit for Reform. Paper presented at the annual meeting of the National Staff Development Council, St. Louis, Mo.

Marek, E.A., and S.B. Methven. (1991). Effects of the Learning Cycle Upon Student and Classroom Teacher Performance. *Journal of Research in Science Teaching* 28: 41–53.

Martin-Kniep, G.O., E.S. Sussman, and E. Meltzer. 1995. The North Shore Collaborative Inquiry Project: A Reflective Study of Assessment and Learning. *Journal of Staff Development* 16(4): 46–51.

Mason, Cheryl. (1993). *Preparing and Directing a Teacher Institute.* Arlington, Va.: National Science Teachers Association Press.

Mason, D.A., and T.L. Good. (1993). Effects of Two-Group and Whole-Class Teaching on Regrouped Elementary Students' Mathematics Achievement. *American Educational Research Journal* 30: 328–60.

McKenzie, Jamieson A. 1993. *Power Learning in the Classroom.* Thousand Oaks, Calif.: Corwin Press.

————. 1999. *How Teachers Learn Technology Best.* Bellingham, Wash.: FNO Press.

————. 2000. *Beyond Technology. Questioning, Research and the Information Literate School.* Bellingham, Wash.: FNO Press.

Merseth, K. 1991. *The Case for Cases in Teacher Education.* Washington, D.C.: American Association of Higher Education and the American Association of Colleges for Teacher Education.

Miller, D.M., and G.J. Pine. 1990. Advancing Professional Inquiry for Educational Improvement through Action Research. *Journal of Staff Development* 11(3): 56–61.

Miller, L.D., and N.P. Hunt. 1994. Professional Development through Action Research. 296–303. *Professional Development for Teachers of Mathematics, 1994 Yearbook.* Edited by D.B. Aichele and A.F. Coxford. Reston, Va: National Council of Teachers of Mathematics.

Minstrell, Jim, and Emily H. Van Zee. 2000. *Inquiring into Inquiry Learning and Teaching in Science.*Washington, D.C.: American Association for the Advancement of Science.

Murphy, C. 1992. Study Groups Foster Schoolwide Learning. *Educational Leadership* 50(3):71–74.

————. 1995. Whole-Faculty Study Groups: Doing the Seemingly Undoable. *Journal of Staff Development* 16(3): 37–44.

NABT Policy on Vivisection and Dissection.1989, May 1. *Draft of The Responsible Use of Animals in Biology Classrooms.* On PSInet-CSSS (Science Computer Network).

National Commission on Teaching and America's Future. 1996. *What Matters Most: Teaching for America's Future.* New York: National Commission on Teaching and America's Future.

National Council of Teachers of Mathematics (NCTM} 1989. *Curriculum Evaluation Standards for School Mathematics.* Reston, Va: NCTM.

National Research Council. 1996. *Criteria for the Selection of Science Instructional Materials. State of South Carolina, Department of Education.* Washington, D.C.: National Academy Press.

National Research Council. 1996. *National Science Education Standards.* Washington, D.C.: National Academy Press.

National Research Council. In press. *Guidelines for Aligning Instructional Materials with the National Science Education Standards.* In Science for All Children *A Guide to Improving Elementary Science Education in Your School District.* Washington, D.C.: National Academy Press.

National Science Foundation. 1997. Inquiry—Thoughts, Views, and Strategies for the K–5 Classroom. A Monograph for Professionals in Science, Mathematics, and Technology Education. In National Science Resources Center. *Science for All Children: A Guide to Improving Elementary Science Education in Your School District.* Washington, D.C.: National Academy Press.

National Sciences Resources Center. 1997. *Science for All Children: A Guide to Improving Elementary Science Education in Your School District*. Washington, D.C.: National Academy Press.

————. *Science and Technology for Children*. Burlington N.C.: Carolina Biological Supply Company. (800) 334–5551.

National Science Teachers Asscociation (NSTA). 1992. *NSTA Standards for Science Teacher Preparation*. Arlington, Va.: NSTA Press. (Adopted by the National Council for Accreditation of Teacher Education [NCATE]).

————. 1998. *NSTA Pathways to the Science Standards: Guidelines for Moving the Vision into Practice, Middle School Edition*. Arlington, Va.:NSTA Press.

National Staff Development Council (NSDC) for information on professional development in peer coaching and mentoring, Oxford, Ohio (513) 523-6029.

National Teachers Enhancement Network (NTEN), Montana State University Extended Studies, Bozeman, Mont. (406) 994-6550.

North Central Regional Education Laboratory. In Press *Professional Development* (CD-ROM). Oak Brook, IL: North Central Regional Education Laboratory.

Newton, A.K., M. Bergstrom, M. Brennan, K. Dunne, C. Gilbert, N. Ibarguen, M. Perez-Selles, and E. Thomas. 1994. *Mentoring: A Resource and Training Guide for Educators*. Andover, Mass.: The Regional Laboratory for Educational Improvement of the Northeast and Islands.

Nichols, Sharon E., Deborah Tippins, and Katherine Wiseman.1997. A Toolkit for Developing Critically Reflective Science Teachers. *Journal of Science Teacher Education* 8(2): 77–106.

Oakes, J. 1990. Multiplying Inequalities: *The Effect of Race, Social Class, and Tracking on Opportunities to Learn Mathematics and Science*. Santa Monica, Calif.: RAND Corporation.

Oja, S.N., and L. Smulyan. 1989. *Collaborative Action Research: A Developmental Approach*. Philadelphia, Pa.: Falmar Press.

Otto, P.B., and R.F. Schuck. 1983. The Effect of a Teacher Questioning Strategy Training Program on Teaching Behavior, Student Achievement, and Retention. *Journal of Research in Science Teaching* 20: 521–28.

Parke, Helen M., and Charles R. Coble 1997. Teachers Designing Curriculum as Professional Development: A Model for Transformational Science Teaching. *Journal of Research in Science Teaching* 34(8): 773–89.

Participatory Oriented Planetariums for Schools (POPS), Lawrence Hall of Science, University of California–Berkeley, Berkeley,Calif., (510) 642–9635.

Phillips, M.D., and C.D. Glickman. 1991. Peer Coaching. Developmental Approach to Enhancing Teacher Thinking. *Journal of Staff Development* 12(2): 20–25.

Porter, A.C. 1989. A Curriculum Out of Balance: The Case of Elementary School Mathematics. *Educational Researcher* 18(5): 9–15.

————. 1993. School Delivery Standards. *Educational Researcher* 22(5): 24–30.

Projects STRO, Astronomical Society of the Pacific, San Francisco, Calif.

Prudent Practices for Handling Hazardous Chemicals in Laboratories. 1981. Washington, D.C.: National Academy Press. p. 227.

Rakow, Steven J.et al. 1998. *NSTA Pathways to the Science Standards. Guidelines for Moving the Vision into Practice. Middle School Edition*. Arlington, Va.: NSTA Press.

Regional Educational Laboratories. 1995. *Facilitating Systemic Change in Science and Mathematics Education. A Toolkit for Professional Developers*. Andover, Mass.: The Regional Laboratory for Educational Improvement of the Northeast and Islands.

Rhoton, Jack, and Patricia Bowers. 1996. *Issues in Science Education*. Arlington, Va.: National Science Teachers Association Press.

Riel, M., and J.A. Levin. 1990. Building Electronic Communities: Success and Failure in Computer Networking. *Instructional Science* 19: 145–69.

Roderick MacDougall Center for Case Development and Teaching. 1994. *Catalogue of K–12 Case Materials*. Cambridge, Mass.: Harvard Graduate School of Education.

Roseman, J.E., S. Kesidou, and L. Stern. 1996. Identifying Curriculum Materials for Science Literacy: A Project 2061 Evaluation Tool. Paper presented at National Research Council colloquium, Using the National Science Standards to Guide the Evaluation, Selection, and Adaptation of Instructional Materials.

Rowley, J.B., and P.M. Hart. 1996. How Video Case Studies Can Promote Reflective Dialogue. *Educational Leadership* 536: 28–29.

Roy, P. 1994. *A Primer on Study Groups*. Wilmington, Del.: Patricia Roy Company.

Rubin, R.L., and J.T. Norman.1992. Systematic Modeling Versus the Learning Cycle: Comparative Effects of Integrated Science Process Skill Achievement. *Journal of Research in Science Teaching* 29: 715–27.

Ruopp, R., S. Gal, B. Drayton, and M. Pfister. 1993. *LabNet: Toward a Community of Practice*. Hillsdale, NJ: Lawrence Erlbaum Associates.

Safety in Academic Chemical Laboratories, 5th ed. 1990. Washington D.C.: American Chemical Society.

Safety in the School Science Laboratory. 1977. Cincinnati, Ohio: U.S. Department of Health, Education, and Welfare; National Institute for Occupational Safety and Health.

Sagor, R. 1992. *How to Conduct Collaborative Action Research.* Alexandria, Va.: Association for Supervision and Curriculum Development.

San Francisco Exploratorium's Teachers Institute Program, San Francisco, Calif. (415) 561–0313.

Sargent, Judy K. 2000. *Data Retreat Participant's Guide.* CESA 7. Green Bay, Wis.

Schmidt, B.J., and S.L. Faulkner. 1989. Staff Development through Distance Education. *Journal of Staff Development* 10(4): 2–7.

Schwille, J., A. Porter, G. Belli, R. Floden, D. Freeman, L. Knappen, T. Kuhs, and W. Schmidt.1983. Teachers as Policy Brokers in the Content of Elementary School Mathematics. 370–91. *Handbook of Teaching and Policy.* Edited by L.S. Shulman and G. Sykes. New York: Longman.

Science Alive! A program sponsored by the Pacific Northwest Laboratory and the U.S. Dept. of Energy, funded by the National Science Foundation, Science Education Center, Richland, Wash. (609) 375–2820.

Science Education for Public Understanding Program (SEPUP). 1996. *Issues, Evidence and You.* Ronkonkoma, NY.: LAB-AIDS, Inc.

Science Scope 15(6).

Scientific Work Experience Programs for Teachers (SWEPT), Triangle Coalition for Science and Technology Education, College Park, Md. (301) 220–0870.

Sense Making in Science (video series). Edited by Ann S. Rosebery and Beth Warren. Published by Heinemann. (800) 541–2086.

Showers, B., and B. Joyce. 1996. The Evolution of Peer Coaching. *Educational Leadership* 53(6): 12–16.

Shulman, J., and A. Mesa-Bains. 1993. *Diversity in the Classroom: A Casebook for Teachers and Teacher Educators.* San Francisco: Casebooks from WestEd.

Shulman, J.H., and J.A. Colbert, eds. 1987. *The Mentor Teacher Casebook.* Eugene, Ore.: ERIC Clearinghouse on Educational Management, University of Oregon. Also San Francisco, Calif.: Far West Laboratory.

Shulman, J., and D. Kepner. 1994. *The Editorial Imperative: Responding to Productive Tensions Between Case Writing and Individual Development.* San Francisco, Calif.: Far West Laboratory.

Shulman, L.S. 1987. Knowledge and Teaching: Foundations of the New Reform. *Harvard Educational Review* 57: 1–22.

———. 1992. Toward a Pedagogy of Cases. 1–30. *Case Methods in Teacher Education.* Edited by J.H. Shulman. New York: Teachers College Press.

Smith, P.S. 1996. *Report of NTEN Evaluation Activities and Findings: January 1995–January 1996.* Durham, N.C.: Horizon Research.

Smylie, M.A. 1989. Teachers' Views of the Effectiveness of Sources of Learning to Teach. *The Elementary School Journal* 89: 543–58.

Sparks, D., and S. Loucks-Horsley. 1989. Five Models of Staff Development for Teachers. *Journal of Staff Development* 10(4): 40–57.

Sparks, D. 1982. Staff Developers: Where Have They Come From? And What Do They Know? *Journal of Staff Development* 3(2): 38–44.

———. 1995. A Paradigm Shift in Staff Development. In Professional Development (Theme Issue.). *ERIC Review* 3(3), 2–4. Available at http://www.aspensys.com/com/eric/ter/.

Sparks, G.M., and J.M. Simmons. 1989. Inquiry-Oriented Staff Development: Using Research as a Source of Tools, Not Rules. 126–39. *Staff Development: A Handbook of Effective Practices.* Edited by S.D. Caldwell. Oxford, Ohio: National Staff Development Council.

Spitzer, W., K., Wedding, and V. DiMauro. 1994. *Fostering Reflective Dialogues for Teacher Professional Development.* Cambridge, Mass.: TERC.

Stallings, J., and E.M. Drasavage.1986. Program Implementation and Student Achievement in a Four-Year Madeline Hunger Follow Through Project. *The Elementary School Journal* 87: 117–38.

Stevens, R.J., and Slavin, R.E. 1995. The Cooperative Elementary School: Effects on Students' Achievement, Attitudes, and Social Relations. *American Educational Research Journal* 32: 321–51.

Strycker, J. 1995. Science First. *Science and Children.* 32(7) 26–29.

Sussman, A., ed. 1993. *Science Education Partnerships: Manual for Scientists and K–12 Teachers.* San Francisco: University of California Press.

Sykes, G. ed. (in press). *The Heart of The matter: Teaching as the Learning Profession.* San Francisco: Jossey-Bass.

Systemic Initiative for Montana Mathematics and Science (SIMMS), Gary Bauer, Montana State University, Bozeman, Mont. (406) 994–7066.

Taylor, E.F., and R.C. Smith. 1995. Teaching Physics On Line. *American Journal of Physics* 53: 1090–96.

Teacher Enhancement Electronic Communications Hall (TEECH), TERC, Cambridge, Mass. (617) 547–0430.

Teacher Professional Development Institute (TAPPED IN), SRI Center for Technology in Learning, San Francisco, Calif. (415) 859–2881.

Teacher Research Associations (TRAC) Program, U.S. Dept. of Energy, Washington, D.C. (202) 586–0987.

Teachers Teaching with Technology (T3), University of Texas at Arlington, Arlington, Tex. (817) 272–5828.

The National Center for Improving Science Education. 1993. *Profiling Teacher Research Participation Programs: An Approach to Formative Evaluation.* Andover, Mass: The National Center for Improving Science Education.

Turner, P. 1995. Study Groups at Sarah Cobb Elementary. *Journal of Staff Development* 16(3): 53.

U.S. Dept. of Education. 1997. *Attaining Excellence: A TIMMS Resource Kit.* Washington, D.C.: Office of Educational Research and Improvement.

U.S. Dept.of Education. Office of Educational Research and Improvement. 1997. *Attaining Excellence. TIMSS as a Starting Point to Examine Curricula.* Washington, D.C.: U.S. Dept.of Education.

U.S. Dept. of Health and Human Services. 1980. *Manual of Safety and Health Hazards in the School Science Laboratory.*Washington, D.C.:U.S. Government Printing Office.

University Research Expeditions Program (UREP), University of California–Berkeley, Berkeley, Calif. (510) 642–6586.

Valdez, Gilbert, Mary McNabb, Mary Foertsch, Mary Anderson, Mark Hawkes, and Lenaya Raack. 1999. *Computer-Based Technology and Learning: Evolving Uses and Expectations.* Oak Brook, Ill.: North Central Regional Educational Laboratory.

Watkins, J. 1992. Speaking of Action Research. Paper adapted from a presentation to the Board of Overseers of the Regional Laboratory for Educational Improvement of the Northeast and Islands, Andover, Mass.

WestEd Eisenhower Regional Consortium for Science and Mathematics Education and Distance Learning Resource Network. 1996. *Tales from the Electronic Frontier.* San Francisco: WestEd.

WestEd. 1996. Scientists and Teachers Working Together. *SEABA Journal* (Fall) 9.

Wiggins, Grant, and Jay McTighe. 1998. *Understanding by Design.* Alexandria, Va.: Association for Supervision and Curriculum Development.

Wisconsin Department of Commerce. 1996. *Wisconsin Statutes, 1995–96. Chapter 101.* Department of Commerce-Regulation of Industry, Buildings and Safety.

Wisconsin Department of Public Instruction. *Wisconsin Knowledge and Concepts Examinations. An Alignment Study at Grade 4, 8, 10.* Madison, Wis: Wisconsin Department of Public Instruction.

———. 1995. *Wisconsin Statutes, 255.30. Safety Eye Protective Goggles,* Madison, Wis.: Wisconsin Department of Public Instruction.

———. 1996. *Wisconsin Administrative Code, Chapter PI 8, Wisconsin School District Standards.* Madison, Wis: Wisconsin Department of Public Instruction.

———. 1998. *Wisconsin's Model Academic Standards for Environmental Education.* Madison, Wis.: Wisconsin Dept. of Public Instruction.

Wood, P. 1988. Action Research: A Field Perspective. *Journal of Education for Teaching* 14 (2): 135–150.

Science Safety Resources

Chemical Catalogue/Reference Manual: 1988. Flinn Scientific, Inc., Batavia, Ill.

Contact Lenses in the Laboratory. 1998. *Chemical Health and Safety* May/June. Washington, D.C.: American Chemical Society.

Gerlovich, J.A. 1997. Safety Standards: An Examination of What Teachers Know and Should Know About Science Safety. *The Science Teacher* 64(3): 18–21.

———. 1999. *Secondary Wisconsin Edition Total Science Safety System.*Waukee, Ia.: JaKel, Inc.

Gerlovich, J.A., and G.E. Downs et al. 1981. *Better Science Through Safety.* Ames, Iowa: Iowa State University Press.

———. 1984. *School Science Safety: Secondary.* Batavia, Ill.: Flinn Scientific Co.

Gerlovich, J.A., and J. Miller. In press. Safe Disposal of Unwanted School Chemicals: A Proven Plan. *Journal of Chemical Education.*

State of Wisconsin. (1995). *Wisconsin Administrative Code, Chapter ILHR 32, Public Employee Safety and Health.* Department of Industry, Labor, and Human Relations.

Young, J. 1997. Chemical Safety: Part I Safety in the Handling of Hazardous Chemicals. *The Science Teacher* 64(3).

Guide to Appendixes

Appendix A

Appendix A is a compilation of professional development activities that the task force believes will be especially helpful for the *district team* when planning staff professional development described in Chapter 6. Each activity was selected because they address programmatic issues found in Chapters 1 and 2.

Activity 1.2, from the Eisenhower National Clearinghouse (ENC), is designed to "assess prior knowledge of the participants and to frame the focus on characteristics of a classroom where students learn effectively" (ENC 2000, 51).

Activity 1.3, again from (ENC), is designed to examine participants' beliefs and values about teaching and learning in science.

Activity 1.1, from the North Central Regional Educational Laboratory Regional Laboratory (NCREL), develops a common vocabulary for the term "equity".

Activity 1.2, from NCREL, continues to build a common understanding among participants of equity. Included is a consensus-building process.

Activity 1.3, from NCREL, focuses the participants on barriers to and indicators of equity.

Activity 1.4, from NCREL, develops equitable practices in science.
Each activity reprinted with permission.

Appendix B

Appendix B, reprinted with permission of the National Research Council, is a concept map for the *National Science Education Standards Structure of Matter Standard* and an example for the district team to use when developing concept maps for the district science curriculum described in Chapters 2 and 3.

Appendix C

Appendix C provides additional specificity to the methods for developing the science curriculum in Chapter 3 and was developed by John Fortier, who was the DPI assistant superintendent and is now retired.

Appendix D

Appendix D is a sample power point presentation the district team can use for the graphic organizer method for developing the science curriculum in Chapter 2. Professor Robert Hollen of the University of Wisconsin–Eau Claire's

Department of Curriculum and Instruction developed the presentation and granted permission to use it.

Appendix E

Appendix E is the complete vignette featured in Chapter 4.

References

Cook, C. and Christensen, M. 1999. Facilitation Tools I, Activities 1.2 and 3. p. 51–63. *Teacher Change: Improving K–12 Mathematics.* Berkeley, Calif.: Eisenhower National Clearinghouse (ENC). Reprinted with permission of ENC. Visit ENC online at http://enc.org

Facilitation Tools I
Activity 1.2

How Do We Describe Our Vision for Effective Learning?
Carousel Brainstorm Activity

Description and General Purpose of the Activity

The primary purposes of this activity are to assess prior knowledge of the participants and to frame the focus on characteristics of a classroom where students learn effectively. In addition, the sharing process will build a common vocabulary as the group moves toward consensus about effective learning.

Participants will first reflect on their vision of such a classroom and then move carousel fashion around the room as a group. They will be asked to describe the role of teacher, the role of students, the nature and type of activities, and ways learning might be assessed in an ideal classroom. The carousel can also serve as a warm-up for an agenda.

This activity, like Activity 2.2, uses the Indicators of Engaged Learning as described in NCREL's *Plugging In: Choosing and Using Educational Technology. Plugging In* was developed to give educators a framework to determine how well technology supports certain goals for teaching and learning such as increased interaction among students and between students and teachers. The Engaged Learning Indicators have been included here because they are useful for looking at more than technology. The text of the indicators is included in the electronic portion of this project. See connections from this activity under Framing the Context: Facilitation Tools I.

Activity Set-up and Materials Needed

Set-up:
• Four or more easels with chart paper placed around the room.
• Participants seated at tables of four to six.

Materials:
• Set of guidelines for brainstorming on overhead/chart or facilitator may elicit these from the group
• Chimes, markers, masking tape, and chart paper

- Transparency/easel page of the flow of the activity
- Copies of the Engaged Learning Indicators or *Plugging In* (Note: The table of Engaged Learning Indicators from *Plugging In* is reproduced electronically with permission of NCREL. To order hard copies, see the Facilitator Readings and Information below.)
- Each of four carousel questions written on easels (see below).

Time:
- Total time about 45 minutes
- Introduction and directions - 5 minutes
- Carousel - 15 minutes
- Original station analysis - 10 minutes
- Sharing and summary - 15 minutes

Activity Process and Notes for the Facilitator

1. With participants seated at their tables, explain the process and timing of the carousel.

2. Assign participants to groups of four to six and have each group move to an easel. Groups should be about the same size.

3. Each group will begin by responding to the question on their easel. One person, arbitrarily chosen, is given a colored marker and asked to be the recorder for the group, keeping the same colored marker as the group moves to each new station.

4. After two to four minutes, ring the chimes to signal the participants to move to the question (and easel) to their right; the last group will move to the first question in the set. Repeat the process until each group responds to each of the questions.

5. After all questions have been answered by all groups, participants will return to the question where they began their brainstorming. Have them take a few minutes to analyze the responses, looking for and highlighting common themes and big ideas.

6. Ask the participants to move back to tables in their groups. Distribute copies of the Carousel Brainstorm Questions handout for participants to use in recording important ideas from each group.

7. Each group will take two minutes to report to the whole group their insights and big ideas from the carousel activity.

8. The facilitator will moderate and summarize, highlighting important insights for each of the questions.

Carousel Questions

1. Quality Tasks: What are some of the characteristics of high quality tasks that actively engage students in learning?

2. Teacher Roles: How would you describe a teacher who effectively engages students in learning?

3. Student Roles: How would you describe a student who is engaged in learning?

4. Assessment: What are some examples of effective strategies for finding out what students know and are able to do?

Distribute copies of or display the Indicators of Engaged Learning table from *Plugging In* at the conclusion of the activity. Explain that this list is drawn from the research and the four indicators used in this activity have been found to correlate highly with improved student learning.

Facilitator Readings and Information

• *Plugging In: Choosing and Using Educational Technology* is available as a print document or as a free Adobe Acrobat file from NCREL. To access the Acrobat file, visit http://www.ncrtec.org/capacity/plug/plug.htm. To order the print version, #ED-PLUG-95, call NCREL toll-free at (800) 356-2735. The print version costs $7.95.

These activities were developed by Cathy Cook and Marv Christensen, Midwest Consortium for Mathematics and Science Education at NCREL, as part of their professional development program, Facilitating Professional Learning: A Set of Interactive Strategies Using TIMSS.

How Do We Describe Our Vision for Effective Learning?

Carousel Brainstorm Questions

Quality Tasks: What are some of the characteristics of high quality tasks that actively engage students in learning?

Teacher Roles: How would you describe a teacher who effectively engages students in learning?

Student Roles: How would you describe a student who is engaged in learning?

Assessment: What are some examples of effective strategies for finding out what students know and are able to do?

Facilitation Tools I
Activity 1.3

Beliefs and Values: A Four Corners Activity

Description and General Purpose of the Activity

In this activity, participants will have the opportunity to examine and take positions on several statements related to beliefs and values about teaching and learning that can be explored through the lens of the TIMSS data. This activity could be used in a variety of other contexts.

Activity Set-up and Materials Needed

Materials:

- Chimes, markers, easels, and chart paper
- Projection device for PowerPoint slides or transparencies
- Four corners signs
- Copies of the Beliefs and Values statements for each participant
- Staff Analysis Tool for each participant

Time:
- 40 minutes to an hour

Activity Process and Notes for the Facilitator

1. Values and Beliefs Statements

A. Create and post the four corners signs around the room so they are visible. The four corners statements are Strongly Agree, Agree, Disagree, Strongly Disagree.

B. Using PowerPoint or overhead transparencies, project a statement from the Beliefs and Values set. Each of these statements starts with "All Children Can Learn."

- All children can learn based on their ability.
- All children can learn if they take advantage of the opportunity to learn.
- All children can learn and we will establish high standards of learning that we expect students to achieve.

• All children can learn except when there are factors beyond our control.

C. As you project each statement, ask participants to go to the corner that best signifies their belief about the statement.

D. After the participants have taken a position with a group near one of the signs, ask them to briefly discuss why they made that choice with at least one other person in the group.

E. Ask members of each group to quickly share their rationale. Summarize and test for consensus in the groups. Allow participants to change corners at any time if, upon reflection and hearing what the consensus is for the group, they don't want to stay with their original choices.

F. Relate TIMSS data to the statement through slides, verbal statements, or transparencies. This step requires the facilitator to do some background reading and preparation. See the Facilitator Readings and Information for sources.

G. Repeat this entire process for all four statements beginning with "all students can learn."

2. Staff Analysis Tool

A. Encourage participants to reflect individually on the issues that surface during part one. Ask them to use the Staff Analysis Tool provided to record their thoughts on these issues. This tool asks participants to rate the percentage of staff members in their school or district who would agree with each of the beliefs and values statements.

B. After a few minutes, ask participants to share at their table the prevailing attitudes in their district or school. Ask each group to appoint a recorder to capture their insights on the easel paper provided.

C. Take a few minutes to hear from the different groups. Encourage participants to add to their individual worksheets from the ideas presented.

D. Ask this question to debrief: How might you incorporate these ideas in your school or district-wide improvement plan?

Reprinted with permission from ENC.

Facilitator Readings and Information

While this activity could be used in many different contexts, the facilitator will need a familiarity with TIMSS in order to bring the data in at relevant points in the group discussion. The Learning from TIMSS section of the electronic portion of this project contains the TIMSS achievement data, test items, and curriculum analysis. The specific documents listed here provide a good start to understanding TIMSS.

- This project's Introduction to TIMSS gives an overview of the study and of the other TIMSS documents contained as part of this project.

- *Pursuing Excellence: A Study of U. S. Fourth-Grade Mathematics and Science Achievement in International Context*

- *Pursuing Excellence: A Study of U. S. Eighth-Grade Mathematics and Science Achievement in International Context*

- *Pursuing Excellence: A Study of U. S. Twelfth-Grade Mathematics and Science Achievement in International Context*

Each volume of *Pursuing Excellence* provides an introduction to TIMSS and a summary of the achievement data for the specific level covered. The information is given in a question-answer format; the preface to each document includes a brief overview of the study design and research team.

This activity was developed by staff of the Eisenhower Regional Consortium at SERVE for the professional development program Developing Resource Capacities Using TIMSS.

STRONGLY AGREE

Appendix A

Reprinted with permission from ENC.

DISAGREE

Reprinted with permission from ENC.

Reprinted with permission from ENC.

Staff Analysis Tool

Record next to each box what percent of your faculty operates at each interpretation of the All Children Can Learn statements that you have been discussing.

All children can learn and we will set high standards of learning we expect of ALL students.

All children can learn except when there are factors beyond our control.

All children can learn if they take advantage of their opportunities.

All children can learn but how much they can learn depends on their ability.

What is the current mindset in your district (or of your staff) regarding the belief that All Children Can Learn? What evidence do you have?

What shift in mindset needs to occur to help staff set high standards & expectations in order that All Children Can Learn? How might you initiate this shift?

All Children Can Learn

Based on Their Ability

All Children Can Learn

If They Take Advantage of the Opportunity to Learn

All Children Can Learn

Except When There Are Factors Beyond Our Control

All Children Can Learn

And We Will Establish High Standards Of Learning That We Expect All Students To Achieve

Activity 1.1

"WHEN I SEE OR HEAR . . ."

Introduction and Purpose

This activity is for educators who are responsible for facilitating reform and developing equitable practice in mathematics and science education. As a warm-up, Activity 1.1 facilitates interaction among and between these educational leaders by encouraging them to get to know each other and start building a common vocabulary around the content and concepts of a learning experience. It is a great activity to use initially with a group to access individuals' prior knowledge and experience.

Objectives

- To help individuals and the group begin to define equity and build a common vocabulary around equity issues

- To facilitate individual reflection upon personal beliefs and to learn about the beliefs of others in the group

Materials

Equipment:

- 6 to 10 posters (one for every 3 to 4 people in the group) with a "magnetic word" written on each of the posters—a word that will either be attractive or repellent to the participants in this session

Suggested Time

- 20–30 minutes (with larger groups it will take a little longer)

Facilitator Notes and Process

Post 6 to 10 of the following words (or others) on the walls around the room:

> Equity, Access, Equal, Quality, Cooperative Learning, Individual Choice, Inclusion, Capacity Building, Diversity, Multiculturalism, Special Services, Inequity, Intervention, Heterogeneous Grouping, Special Treatment, Pull-Out Classes, Enrichment

1. Introduce this activity as one that will help build community and a common vocabulary within the group as well as one that will integrate participants' prior knowledge and beliefs about equity issues.

2. Ask participants to stand by a word that either attracts or repels them (forming a group of at least two people), to introduce themselves, and to discuss the following questions:

   - *What attracts or repels you about this word?*

   - *What brought you to this professional development session?*

3. As the small-group discussion draws to a close (about 10–15 minutes, depending on the size of the groups), begin with one group and "whip" or move in a clockwise circle around the room, asking participants to introduce one person in their group who will summarize the group's discussion of the magnetic word. Use effective question techniques. Rephrase and connect group responses with the goals of the professional development session as participants begin to build a common vocabulary.

Reprinted with permission from NCREL.

"TO US EQUITY MEANS . . ."

Introduction and Purpose

This activity is primarily aimed at helping to increase participants' knowledge base and understanding of equity issues in mathematics and science education and to build a shared definition of equality, excellence, and equity. Participants will be asked not only to explore and come to consensus on definitions for these three terms, but to consider the significant differences among the terms and the implications for setting an equitable classroom/school environment that supports learning for all students.

Objectives

- To assist individuals and the group in beginning to define equality, excellence, and equity and the relationships among them, and to build a common vocabulary

- To assist participants in identifying and understanding equity issues

- To facilitate the exploration of changes in school and classroom practice that move toward the achievement of equity

Materials

Equipment:

- Copy of "Did You Know . . ." cut into strips (could be cardstock and laminated)

- Chart paper and markers

Transparencies:

- Pyramidal Process for Reaching Consensus

- Equality

- Excellence

- Equity

Reprinted with permission from NCREL.

Handouts:

- "Did You Know . . ."
- Answers to "Did You Know . . ."
- The Pyramidal Process for Reaching Consensus
- Rules for Building Consensus

Suggested Time

- 3 hours—can be divided into two parts

Facilitator Notes and Process

Part 1 - Startling Statements

1. In preparation for this activity, cut a copy of the **"Did You Know . . ."** handout into strips, one question per strip. Before starting the activity, explain that this exercise is intended to increase participants' awareness of equity issues in science and mathematics education. It also will increase their knowledge of the status of academic preparation of underserved and underrepresented groups at all levels of schooling for scientific, mathematics, and technology careers. Note: This kind of exercise was originally developed by the Lawrence Hall of Sciences at Berkeley in the EQUALS project.

2. Roam the room, taping one question on each participant's back. Several participants may have the same question, depending upon the number present. Have the participants stand, walk around the room, and ask five other participants for the answer to the questions on their backs. Note: The participants do not know what questions is taped to their backs. Once each participant has five answers, he or she should sit down and find the average and range of the five answers.

3. Distribute the **"Did You Know . . ."** handout. Read a question and asks who thinks they had that question on their back. Have them share why they think they have the question, and ask them to give their answer and range. Then give the correct answer. Continue until all of the questions have been answered. Distribute the **Answers to "Did You Know . . ."** handout.

4. In debriefing Part 1 of this activity, discuss who is underrepresented and underserved, as well as the patterns of inequity that were discovered in this exercise. This can be done with the whole group or as a Think-Pair-Share (see Section 1-page 73) in small groups.

Part 2 - Defining Equality, Excellence, and Equity

5. Introduce the idea of consensus and the pyramidal process by using the **Pyramidal Process for Reaching Consensus** transparency and/or handout and the **Rules for Building Consensus** handout. In groups of two, ask participants to share their meanings for *equality, excellence,* and *equity.* Have them record their answers on chart paper with markers, using words, pictures, or a metaphor, and reflect on the relationships they see among them.

6. Next, combine the groups into groups of four and ask them to come to consensus on the three definitions. Continue combining groups until the entire room is working together and shares a common definition of the three terms. Record the definitions on chart paper once the large group has reached consensus.

   Note: This process by which consensus is reached in small groups and then combined until all groups have reached agreement is a style of decision making used by many cultural groups. It closely parallels the governing style of the Iroquois Nation and several other Native American groups.

7. Use the **Equality, Excellence,** and **Equity** transparencies to discuss each term and some examples of each. Relate these to the definitions participants previously developed and ask for additional examples.

8. Discuss in whole group or as a Think-Pair-Share in small groups, the implications for designing the school/classroom environment to achieve equity.

"Did You Know..."

1. In 1994, 48 percent of white high school graduates completed four years of English and three years each of social studies, mathematics, and science. What percentage of African American, Native American, and Hispanic high school graduates completed these curriculum areas?

   African American _____   Native American _____   Hispanic _____

2. In 1992, 35 percent of African American students completed high school Algebra II and geometry. What percentage of white, Native American, and Hispanic students completed these courses?

   White _____   Native American _____   Hispanic _____

3. In 1992, 25.9 percent of white students completed high school physics. What percentage of African American, Native American, and Hispanic students completed this course?

   African American _____   Native American _____   Hispanic _____

4. In 1995, 13 percent of African American children in married couple families lived in poverty. What percentage of African American children in single parent families headed by females lived in poverty?

   % living in poverty _____

5. In 1995, 28 percent of Hispanic children in married couple families lived in poverty. What percentage of Hispanic children in single parent families headed by females lived in poverty?

   % living in poverty _____

6. In 1994, how did females score in comparison to males on the National Assessment of Educational Progress (NAEP) mathematics and science tests?

   Math _____   Science _____

7. In 1996, 9.6 percent of white high school students were taking calculus. What percentage of African American, Native American, and Hispanic students were also taking this course?

   African American _____   Native American _____   Hispanic _____

8. In 1996, 22.7 percent of white high school students were taking biology, chemistry, and physics. What percentage of African American, Native American, and Hispanic students were also taking these courses?

   African American _____   Native American _____   Hispanic _____

9. In 1996, 92 percent of white males age 25-29 had received a high school diploma or equiv-alency certificate. What percentage of African American and Hispanic males in this age group had done the same?

   African American _____   Hispanic _____

10. In 1996, the difference between the percentages of white and Native American eighth grade students who met the standard in science was 13 percentage points. How many percentage points separated white and African American students and white and Hispanic students respectively?

    African American _____   Hispanic _____

11. In 1990, the gap between African American and white eighth graders who met the stan-dard in mathematics was 14 percentage points. How large was this gap in 1996?

    1996 gap _____

12. In 1990, the gap between Hispanic and white eighth graders who met the standard in mathematics was 14 percentage points. How large was this gap in 1996?

    1996 gap _____

13. In 1993, the average score of African Americans was 91 points lower than that of whites on the verbal component of the SAT. How did these groups compare on the mathematics component of the SAT?

    Point gap _____

14. From 1982 to 1995, how did female's SAT scores on the mathematics component compare to those of males?

    Point gap _____

15. In 1995, the drop-out rate for grades 10-12 of white students was 10.2 percent. What were the percentages for African American and Hispanic students?

    African American _____   Hispanic _____

16. In 1995, of the 64 percent of nonminority student in grades 9-11 who reported that they had been encouraged by their teachers to take more math and science, what percentage were African American, Native American, and Hispanic students?

    African American _____   Native American _____   Hispanic _____

"Did You Know..." Answers

1. In 1994, 48 percent of white high school graduates completed four years of English and three years each of social studies, mathematics, and science. What percentage of African American, Native American, and Hispanic high school graduates completed these curriculum areas?

   African American **45%**   Native American **30%**   Hispanic **35%**
   Source: The National Center for Education Statistics. (1997). *The Condition of Education.*

2. In 1992, 35 percent of African American students completed high school Algebra II and geometry. What percentage of white, Native American, and Hispanic students completed these courses?

   White **53.1%**   Native American **35.7%**   Hispanic **41.9%**
   Source: The Education Trust. (1996). *Education Watch: The 1996 Education Trust State and National Data Book.*

3. In 1992, 25.9 percent of white students completed high school physics. What percentage of African American, Native American, and Hispanic students completed this course?

   African American **17.6%**   Native American **13.3%**   Hispanic **15.7%**
   Source: The Education Trust. (1996). *Education Watch: The 1996 Education Trust State and National Data Book.*

4. In 1995, 13 percent of African American children in married couple families lived in poverty. What percentage of African American children in single parent families headed by females lived in poverty?

   % living in poverty **62%**
   Source: Federal Interagency Forum on Child and Family Statistics. (1997). *America's Children: Key National Indicators of Well-Being.*

5. In 1995, 28 percent of Hispanic children in married couple families lived in poverty. What percentage of Hispanic children in single parent families headed by females lived in poverty?

   % living in poverty **66%**
   Source: Federal Interagency Forum on Child and Family Statistics. (1997). *America's Children: Key National Indicators of Well-Being.*

6. In 1994, how did females score in comparison to males on the National Assessment of Educational Progress (NAEP) mathematics and science tests?

   Math **5 point lower**   Science **11 points lower**
   Source: National Center for Education Statistics. (1997). *The Condition of Education.*

7. In 1996, 9.6 percent of white high school students were taking calculus. What percentage of African American, Native American, and Hispanic students were also taking this course?

   African American **3.8%**   Native American **3.8%**   Hispanic **6.0%**
   Source: National Center for Education Statistics. (1997). *The Condition of Education.*

8. In 1996, 22.7 percent of white high school students were taking biology, chemistry, and physics. What percentage of African American, Native American, and Hispanic students were also taking these courses?

   African American **13%**   Native American **8%**   Hispanic **13.4%**
   Source: National Center for Education Statistics. (1997). *The Condition of Education.*

Reprinted with permission from NCREL.

9. In 1996, 92 percent of white males age 25-29 had received a high school diploma or equivalency certificate. What percentage of African American and Hispanic males in this age group had done the same?

African American **87.9%**   Hispanic **59.7%**

Source: National Center for Education Statistics. (1997). *The Condition of Education*.

10. In 1996, the difference between the percentages of white and Native American eighth grade students who met the standard in science was 13 percentage points. How many percentage points separated white and African American students and white and Hispanic students respectively?

African American **32%**   Hispanic **26%**

Source: National Education Goals Panel. (1997). *The National Education Goals Report: Building a Nation of Learners*.

11. In 1990, the gap between African American and white eighth graders who met the standard in mathematics was 14 percentage points. How large was this gap in 1996?

1996 gap **27%**

Source: National Education Goals Panel. (1997). *The National Education Goals Report: Building a Nation of Learners*.

12. In 1990, the gap between Hispanic and white eighth graders who met the standard in mathematics was 14 percentage points. How large was this gap in 1996?

1996 gap **22%**

Source: National Education Goals Panel. (1997). *The National Education Goals Report: Building a Nation of Learners*.

13. In 1993, the average score of African Americans was 91 points lower than that of whites on the verbal component of the SAT. How did these groups compare on the mathematics component of the SAT?

Point gap **African American students were 106 points lower**

Source: *The Educational Progress of Black Students: Findings From "The Condition of Education 1994,"* No. 2, May 1995.

14. From 1982 to 1995, how did female's SAT scores on the mathematics component compare to those of males?

Point gap **Females scored 45.5 points lower**

Source: Karp, K., & Shakeshat, C. (1997). Restructuring Schools to Be Math Friendly to Females. *NASSP Bulletin*, 81, 84-93.

15. In 1995, the dropout rate for grades 10-12 of white students was 10.2 percent. What were the percentages for African American and Hispanic students?

African American **12.3%**   Hispanic **23.4%**

Source: U.S. Bureau of the Census. (1995). *Table 4-A. Annual High School Dropout Rates by Sex, Race, Grade, and Hispanic Origin: October 1967 to 1995*.

16. In 1995, of the 64 percent of nonminority student in grades 9-11 who reported that they had been encouraged by their teachers to take more math and science, what percentage were African American, Native American, and Hispanic students?

African American **49%**   Native American **48%**   Hispanic **53%**

Source: NACME. (1995, June). Uninformed Decisions: A Survey of Children and Parents About Math and Science. *NACME Research Letter*, 5(1).

Survey compiled by Annette Reimers, Barry University

Reprinted with permission from NCREL.

Pyramidal Process for Reaching Consensus

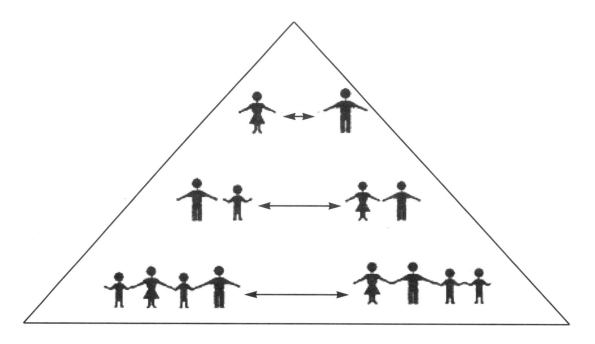

PAIR: Share ideas/opinions/responses. Come to consensus on one statement.

PAIRS PAIR: Share ideas. Come to consensus on one statement.

QUADS PAIR: Share ideas. Come to consensus on one statement.

The size of the consensus group can grow until one statement is developed with which all participants agree.

Source: Arbuckle, M. A., & Murray, L. B. (1989). *Building systems for professional growth: An action guide.* Andover, MA: Laboratory for Educational Improvement of the Northeast and Islands.

Pyramidal Process for Reaching Consensus

The process is most useful when a group needs to come up with a single position, definition, or statement. For example, it has been used effectively for developing mission statements.

1. Thoroughly introduce and discuss the task at hand. For example, if the group is working on a mission statement, the characteristics of a well-written mission should be discussed and agreed to. Make sure everyone has a good grasp of what the final product will look like.

2. First, ask individuals to write their own version of whatever is being developed.

3. After each person has written his/her own draft, pairs are formed. Their task is to reach a consensual agreement on one statement which satisfies them both. Note: At this stage, it is often necessary to review the "rules" of reaching consensus.

4. Each pair is then joined by another pair and the consensus-building process begins again.

5. The size of the consensus-building groups continues to grow until one product/statement is arrived at with which every member of the group can agree.

Notes:

This process is seldom completed in a day. Often it is possible to arrive at two or three versions of whatever is being developed in the first session. It is useful for people to have some time to think about the various versions before trying to reach a consensus on the one and only. Often three or four sessions are necessary to complete the task.

If the group appears to be stalemated—unable to agree on one version or another—the discussion and negotiation process can be speeded up by using a "fish bowl." The spokespersons form a circle of chairs in the middle of the room, with everyone else seated around them. They continue negotiations while the rest of the group observes; thus a "fish bowl" is formed. An empty chair or two should be provided in the circle for the observers to temporarily join the negotiations whenever they want to make a particular point or put forth a particular argument.

Source: Arbuckle, M. A., & Murray, L. B. (1989). *Building systems for professional growth: An action guide*. Andover, MA: Laboratory for Educational Improvement of the Northeast and Islands.

Rules for Building Consensus

Consensus is based on the term "to consent" as in "to grant permission." To arrive at consensus is to give permission to go along with the total group (the majority). The implication of consensus is that an individual can negotiate the terms by which he or she will grant his or her permission. Each individual has the right and obligation to make his or her terms known.

Consensus Means . . .

- All group members contribute
- Everyone's opinions are heard and encouraged
- Differences are viewed as helpful
- All members share in the final decision
- All members agree to take responsibility for implementing the final decision

Consensus Does NOT Mean . . .

- A unanimous vote
- The result is everyone's first choice
- Conflict or resistance will be overcome immediately

Assumptions

- All people are choosing beings
- All people are free to disagree and voice an opinion
- Freedom means he/she engages in action by choice
- Compromise is not necessary

Commitments/Procedures

- I will explain my perception of the issue
- I will discuss my feelings
- I will discuss my needs/goals concerning the issue
- I will listen and respect other opinions
- I will grant permission to the majority, with a minority report
- I will implement the decision

Source: Arbuckle, M. A., & Murray, L. B. (1989). *Building systems for professional growth: An action guide.* Andover, MA: Laboratory for Educational Improvement of the Northeast and Islands.

Copyright © 1989 Learning Innovations, a division of WestEd. Reprinted with permission.

Equality

Treating all students the same

Examples:

- Same required courses

- Same assignments

- Same assessment criteria

- Same disciplinary actions

Source: Laboratory for Educational Improvement of the Northeast and Islands. (1995). Activity 2: Science and mathematics for all. In *Facilitating systemic change in science and mathematics education: A toolkit for professional developers* (pp. 2.16). Andover, MA: Author.

Excellence

Achieving at the highest level

Examples:

- High expectations

- High standards

Source: Laboratory for Educational Improvement of the Northeast and Islands. (1995). Activity 2: Science and mathematics for all. In *Facilitating systemic change in science and mathematics education: A toolkit for professional developers* (pp. 2.17). Andover, MA: Author.

Copyright © 1995 Learning Innovations, a division of WestEd. Reprinted with permission.

Reprinted with permission from NCREL.

Equity

Treating students fairly by considering differences

Examples:

- Different ways to demonstrate mastery

- Handicaps for sports

- More teacher time and help

Source: Laboratory for Educational Improvement of the Northeast and Islands. (1995). Activity 2: Science and mathematics for all. In *Facilitating systemic change in science and mathematics education: A toolkit for professional developers* (pp. 2.18). Andover, MA: Author.

"IN AN EQUITABLE SCHOOL I'D SEE . . ."

Introduction and Purpose

Equity means many things to many people. This simulated walk through a school helps participants better understand some of the barriers to and indicators of equity. This activity is also helpful for gaining greater understanding of the needs of the learners and helps a facilitator access the prior knowledge and experience of the group.

Objectives

- To help participants define their own notions of equity and learn how others view and define equity
- To build a greater understanding of equity and equity issues

Materials

Equipment:

- A sheet of chart paper and marker for each group to record discussion

Handout:

- The Equitable School Walk

Suggested Time

- 60–90 minutes

Facilitator Notes and Process

1. Ask participants to be seated at a small table or in circles of chairs to facilitate discussion. Divide the participants into groups of 5 or 6.

2. Set the stage with this scenario:

For the next half hour or so, I am going to ask you to become equity consultants. Your first job is to visit a school that is considered to be a model equitable school. Other consultants who have been there before have praised it on many counts and say that students, teachers, and all school personnel are treated equitably. The school attempts in many ways to overcome the harmful results of gender, ethnic group, and disability bias and discrimination. You are being paid well for your time so plan to take good notes about what you see in this school. In order to get a frame of reference, picture a school you are familiar with, perhaps one you attended as a child, or one that you currently work with or in. You may want to give the school a name. Decide on the grade level of the students in this building.

3. Assign each group 2 of the 11 parts on **The Equitable School Walk** handout. Instruct them to read the prompt and discuss what they would see and hear in this school that is a model of equity. Have them write as many things as they can on a large sheet of chart paper and use it as a visual when they describe their component to the rest of the group. Give the groups about 15–20 minutes to discuss the first prompt and then another 15–20 minutes to discuss the second prompt.

4. As a large group, have each small group read its prompt and describe what they would see and hear.

5. In small groups, have each group write its own definition of equity. Listen to the presentation from each group, looking for similarities and differences among the definitions.

6. Ask the whole group to discuss what they learned about equity and equity issues and the implications for teaching and learning.

Variation

Each group might take the entire equity school walk before writing their own definition of equity, presenting their vision and definition to the group, and debriefing points from their small-group discussions.

The Equitable School Walk

1. As we walk up to the building and through the set of double doors, the first thing you see is a large display area and bulletin board. It extends the length of the hall, which is about the length of this wall. Considering that this school is a model of equity, what have you noticed that gives you the immediate impression that this school is truly a model of equity?

   (Physical Environment)

2. As we continue our tour of the building, we meet two students who talk excitedly about a class they are taking. You ask them to describe it to you. As they talk, you think that this is an excellent way to help students understand the negative effects of stereotyping. Describe this class that gives students an experience of being equitable.

   (Curriculum)

3. You ask if you could attend the class with them. The students say yes and get the teacher's permission. What do you notice about who is in the class?

   (Student Assignments)

4. You are now scheduled to attend a staff meeting. As you enter the meeting room, you are introduced to the staff and you can see that the staff is also a model of equity. What is the staff like?

   (Role Models)

5. The staff meeting ends on time and we are once again in the halls heading for the lunch room. On our way we stop to visit a classroom that is having a visitor. Who is the visitor? Why is this person here? What is the topic being discussed?

   (Role Models)

6. You are in the lunch line waiting to make your salad (this school is also conscious of nutrition) and you hear a boy making derogatory sexist remarks to a girl nearby. If you are in a junior high or high school, this remark is overtly sexual in nature. There are other students and teachers who overhear the incident. You are curious about how this situation is gong to be handled. You are surprised. Describe what happens.

   (Behavior Management)

7. Over lunch you have the opportunity to listen to a group of students who are excited by an extracurricular event that they are participating in. You ask them about it and discover that all the students seem to be involved in some type of extracurricular or cocurricular activities. What are some of the extracurricular or cocurricular activities that this model of equity has available for its students?

(Extracurricular and Cocurricular Offerings)

8. After lunch you have an appointment with a guidance counselor. During the interview, a student comes in who is quite agitated and asks if the counselor could see him right away. The counselor, with the student's permission, asks you to sit in. This is apparently the second time that this students has come to see this counselor to complain about racist attitudes of a teacher he has. He has tried step one, which was talking to the teacher. How is this situation handled?

(Student Support)

9. Another student has come to talk about her situation and again you have an opportunity to listen in. She is a Hispanic student who wishes to drop out of math. She says, "Please get me out of this class, I just can't do the work. Please get me into something easier." What happens here?

(Student Support)

10. At the end of the school day, you meet with the administrative team. They show you the school handbook for students and staff and discuss what efforts they have undertaken and supported to help this school become a model of equity. What do you notice about the make-up of the administrative team? What are some of the administrative efforts that have helped this school become a model of equity?

(Administrative Oversight)

11. You have completed your day at a model of an equitable school and have returned to your hotel room. As you relax, you pick up the local newspaper that the hotel has kindly put in your room. As you leaf through, you notice some articles about the school you have just visited. What is in the newspaper?

(Any component is possible here)

Source: The Network Inc. (1992). *The equitable school walk.* Andover, MA: Author.

"EQUITY IS MORE LIKE . . ."

Introduction and Purpose

This activity is for educators who are responsible for facilitating reform and developing equitable practice in mathematics and science education. It will help a group to cultivate both personal and organizational metaphors. It is great for a warm-up activity and will assist the facilitator(s) in understanding the beliefs and accessing the prior knowledge and experience of the group.

Objectives

- To assist participants in thinking about their own beliefs related to equity

Materials

Equipment:

- Round tables and chairs for group of 4 to 6 participants to be seated at each table
- Center and front facilitator area (for easel and overhead projector, etc.) that is easily visible by all participants
- Easel, chart paper, and good-smelling markers
- Overhead projector, markers, and a blank transparency

Suggested Time

- 15–20 minutes

Reprinted with permission from NCREL.

Facilitator Notes and Process

1. Draw a four-box grid on a chart or overhead transparency. Elicit examples of everyday objects (or examples from any context or content area) from the group and label the boxes as the ideas are given (e.g., toaster, chair, thermometer, egg beater).

2. The *topic at hand* is then compared with each object. Say and write on an easel or overhead transparency the following:

    " Equity is like a _____ because . . ."

    OR

    "Equity is more like a _____ than a _____ because . . ."

    For example: Equity is more like a thermometer than a chair because you need to probe and gauge the inside rather than just view it from the outside.

3. Have small groups generate four to six ideas and then select their one or two favorites to report to the larger group.

4. Ask participants to discuss how this activity might be used with students or other adult educators. For example, if one of the goals of the day for a group of elementary science teacher-leaders is to focus on teaching inquiry-based science, then the *topic at hand* can be *"teaching science* is like/more like . . ."

Reprinted with permission from NCREL.

Activity 1.5

"SURVEY SAYS . . ."

Introduction and Purpose

This activity is for educators who are responsible for facilitating reform and developing equitable practice in mathematics and science education. It will stimulate discussion and increase the knowledge base of these educational leaders about who can learn mathematics and science and about the value of mathematics and science for all students. Participants examine their beliefs and check them against research results. The activity helps facilitators become more aware of participants' beliefs and access participants' prior knowledge and experience.

Objectives

- To stimulate discussion among participants about who can learn mathematics and science and the value of mathematics and science to all students

- To involve participants in examining their beliefs and checking them against research results

Materials

Handouts:

- Awareness Survey
- Awareness Survey Answers

Suggested Time

- 30–60 minutes

Facilitator Notes and Process

1. Distribute the **Awareness Survey** and ask participants to record their answers for each question. As participants finish, give them a copy of the answer sheet to read.

2. In small groups, have participants discuss their reactions to the survey. Ask them to talk about their reactions to the answers to survey questions. Have them respond to the following:

    ■ *What items were interesting or surprising to you?*

3. In whole-group debriefing, ask each group to tell the others about its discussion of the survey.

4. Some groups will continue to meet as a long-term learning community. Suggest that they or individuals in their groups do more research on areas of interest and share the information with others.

Awareness Survey

1. In the 21st century in America, most of the 10 highest ranked jobs will be directly related to what subject?

   a. mathematics   b. biology   c. chemistry   d. language arts

2. Kindergarten through sixth grade U.S. teachers, when surveyed, reported spending approximately 60 minutes on mathematics each day. How much time per day was spent on science?

   a. 60 minutes   b. 45 minutes   c. 30 minutes   d. 20 minutes

3. The Hispanic population increased from 9 percent in 1980 to 14 percent in 1996. By 2020, how many children in the U.S. will be Hispanic?

   a. 16 percent   b. 18 percent   c. 20 percent   d. 22 percent

4. Between 1994 and 2005 the employment growth rate for men is expected to be 8.5 percent. What is the expected growth rate for women?

   a. 6.3 percent   b. 8.5 percent   c. 12.4 percent   d. 16.6 percent

5. In 1994, women made up 16.7 percent of the architects in the U.S. What percentage of engineers were women?

   a. 4.1 percent   b. 8.5 percent   c. 10.2 percent   d. 14.3 percent

6. Between 1995 and 1996, how much did women who worked full-time make for every dollar made by men also working full-time?

   a. 66 cents   b. 74 cents   c. 83 cents   d. 92 cents

7. What percentage of senior managers in the nation's largest corporations are women?

   a. 0.5 percent   b. 5 percent   c. 10 percent   d. 15 percent

8. Of the total number of Ph.D.'s awarded to men in 1994, 13.7 percent were in the physical sciences. Of the total number of the Ph.D.'s awarded to women in 1994, what percentage was in the physical sciences?

   a. 4.8 percent   b. 5.3 percent   c. 6.1 percent   d. 8.0 percent

9. Of the total number of Ph.D.'s awarded to men in 1994, 20 percent were in engineering. Of the total number of Ph.D.'s awarded to women in 1994, what percentage was in engineering?

   a. 4.0 percent   b. 6.7 percent   c. 7.3 percent   d. 9.2 percent

10. In 1991, females represented 10 percent of the Ph.D faculty in chemistry departments. What percentage of Ph.D. faculty members in engineering departments were female?

    a. 4 percent   b. 6 percent   c. 8 percent   d. 10 percent

11. Nearly 30 percent of K-12 students in the U.S. are minorities. What percentage of U.S. teachers are minorities?

    a. 9 percent   b. 13 percent   c. 21 percent   d. 32 percent

12. In 1990, what percentage of classroom teachers were African American and Hispanic?

    a. 6.5% and 0.9%   b. 6.8% and 1.6%   c. 8.4% and 2.4%
    d. 9.2% and 3.1%

13. How much will the demand for teachers rise by the year 2000?

    a. 10 percent   b. 14 percent   c. 21 percent   d. 28 percent

14. In 1994, the median annual income for a female high school dropout working full-time was $15,133. What was the median annual income for women who earned a bachelor's degree or higher?

    a. $23,727   b. $26,952   c. $28,064   d. $35,378

15. In 1995, the median annual income for white females age 25-34 with a bachelor's degree or higher was $26,800? What was the median annual income for African American and Hispanic women of equivalent educational standing?

    a. $22,492 and $21,578   b. $23,053 and $26,176
    c. $25,585 and $28,436

16. During the 1990-91 academic year, 38.5 percent of mathematics bachelor's degrees were awarded to white women. What percentage was awarded to African American and Hispanic women?

    a. 3.0% and 1.1%   b. 7.4% and 3.2%   c. 9.8% and 3.3%
    d. 9.4% and 5.3%

Awareness Survey Answers

1. **a. mathematics.** *Source*: Karp, K., & Shakeshat, C. (1997). Restructuring schools to be math friendly to females. NASSP *Bulletin*, 81, 84-93.

2. **c. 30 minutes.** *Source*: National Institute for Science Education. (1997, June). NISE B*rief*, 1(3), 1.

3. **c. 20 percent.** The Hispanic population has increase more rapidly than other racial and ethnic groups. *Source*: Federal Agency Forum on Child and Family Statistics. (1997). *America's Children: Key National Indicators of Well-Being*, pp. 7-9.

4. **d. 16.6 percent.** *Source*: U.S. Department of Labor Women's Bureau. (1997, May). *Facts on Working Women*. Available: http://gatekeeper.dol.gov/dol/wb/public/wb_pubs/hotjobs/htm

5. **b. 8.5 percent.** Engineering and architecture are considered nontraditional occupations for women; women make up less than 25 percent of the total employment in these fields. In 1992, Congress passed two pieces of legislation to increase opportunities for women in nontraditional fields: the Nontraditional Employment for Women (NEW) Act and the Women in Apprenticeship and Nontraditional Occupations (WANTO) Act. *Source*: U.S. Department of Labor Women's Bureau. (1997, May). *Facts on Working Women*. Available: http://gatekeeper.dol.gov/dol/wb/public/wb_pubs/hotjobs/htm

6. **b. 74 cents.** *Source*: Housing and Household Economics Statistics Division, U.S. Census Bureau. (1997, September 29). *Press Briefing on 1996 Income, Poverty, and Health Insurance Estimates*. Available: http://www.census.gov/hhes/poverty/poverty96/pv96cst1.html

7. **a. 0.5 percent.** Unfortunately, many qualified people are still being denied the opportunity to compete for and hold executive-level positions in the private sector. *Source*: Women in Engineering Program Advocates Network. (1996, Fall). WEPAN *News*, 5(1), 3.

8. **c. 6.1 percent.** *Source*: National Center for Education Statistics. (1997). *The Condition of Education*. Washington, DC: Author.

9. **a. 4.0 percent.** *Source*: National Center for Education Statistics. (1997). *The Condition of Education*. Washington, DC: Author.

10. **a. 4 percent.** *Source*: Center for the Education of Women, University of Michigan. (1996, January). Percentage of Women Ph.D. Faculty by Field, 1991. In *The Equity Agenda*: *Women in Science, Mathematics, and Engineering*. Ann Arbor, MI: Author.

11. **b. 13 percent.** *Source*: National Teachers Forum. (1997). *Making Teaching a True Profession*: *Background Paper and Questions*. Available: http://www.ed.gov/MailingLists/EDinfo/0293.html

12. **d. 9.2 percent and 3.1 percent, respectively.** Over 40 percent of U.S. schools do not have a minority teacher on their faculty. *Source*: ERIC Clearinghouse on Teaching and Teacher Education. (1996). *Supply and Demand for Teachers of Color*. Washington, DC: Author.

13. **c. 21 percent.** *Source*: ERIC Clearinghouse on Teaching and Teacher Education. (1996). *Supply and Demand for Teachers of Color*. Washington, DC: Author.

14. **d. $35,378.** *Source*: U.S. Department of Labor. (1996, September). Table 8: Median Income of Persons, by Education Attainment and Sex, Year-Round, Full-Time Workers, 1994. In *Women's Bureau Fact Sheet*. Washington, DC: Author.

15. **b. $23,053 and $26,176, respectively.** *Source*: The National Center for Education Statistics. (1997). *The Condition of Education*. Washington, DC: Author

16. **a. 3.0 percent and 1.1 percent, respectively.** *Source*: Center for the Education of Women, University of Michigan. (1996, January). Percentage of Science and Engineering Degrees Awarded to Women by Degree Level, Field, and Race/Ethnicity. In The *Equity Agenda: Women in Science, Mathematics, and Engineering*. Ann Arbor, MI: Author.

Survey compiled by Annette Reimers, Barry University

Appendix B

MAPPING THE *NSES* FOR STRUCTURE OF MATTER (K-12)

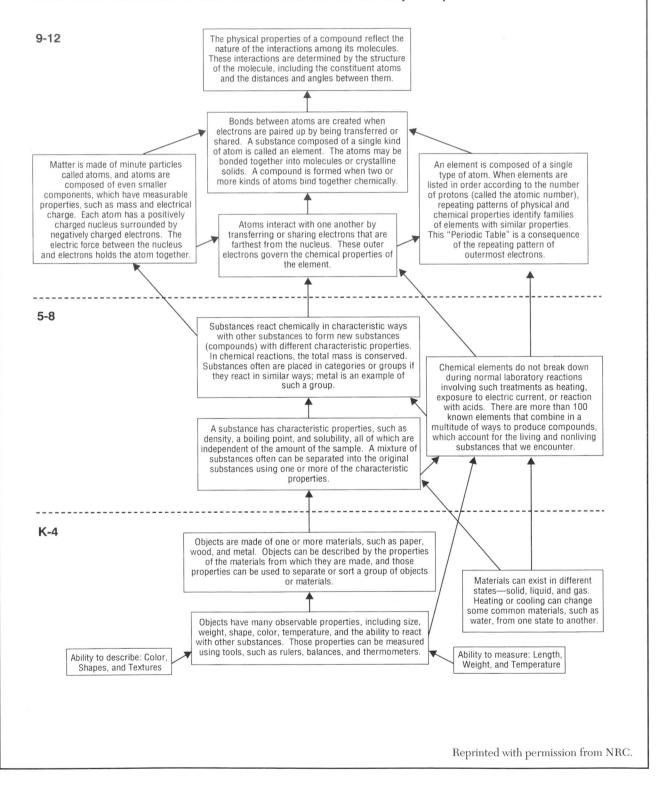

9-12

The physical properties of a compound reflect the nature of the interactions among its molecules. These interactions are determined by the structure of the molecule, including the constituent atoms and the distances and angles between them.

Bonds between atoms are created when electrons are paired up by being transferred or shared. A substance composed of a single kind of atom is called an element. The atoms may be bonded together into molecules or crystalline solids. A compound is formed when two or more kinds of atoms bind together chemically.

Matter is made of minute particles called atoms, and atoms are composed of even smaller components, which have measurable properties, such as mass and electrical charge. Each atom has a positively charged nucleus surrounded by negatively charged electrons. The electric force between the nucleus and electrons holds the atom together.

Atoms interact with one another by transferring or sharing electrons that are farthest from the nucleus. These outer electrons govern the chemical properties of the element.

An element is composed of a single type of atom. When elements are listed in order according to the number of protons (called the atomic number), repeating patterns of physical and chemical properties identify families of elements with similar properties. This "Periodic Table" is a consequence of the repeating pattern of outermost electrons.

5-8

Substances react chemically in characteristic ways with other substances to form new substances (compounds) with different characteristic properties. In chemical reactions, the total mass is conserved. Substances often are placed in categories or groups if they react in similar ways; metal is an example of such a group.

Chemical elements do not break down during normal laboratory reactions involving such treatments as heating, exposure to electric current, or reaction with acids. There are more than 100 known elements that combine in a multitude of ways to produce compounds, which account for the living and nonliving substances that we encounter.

A substance has characteristic properties, such as density, a boiling point, and solubility, all of which are independent of the amount of the sample. A mixture of substances often can be separated into the original substances using one or more of the characteristic properties.

K-4

Objects are made of one or more materials, such as paper, wood, and metal. Objects can be described by the properties of the materials from which they are made, and those properties can be used to separate or sort a group of objects or materials.

Materials can exist in different states—solid, liquid, and gas. Heating or cooling can change some common materials, such as water, from one state to another.

Objects have many observable properties, including size, weight, shape, color, temperature, and the ability to react with other substances. Those properties can be measured using tools, such as rulers, balances, and thermometers.

Ability to describe: Color, Shapes, and Textures

Ability to measure: Length, Weight, and Temperature

Reprinted with permission from NRC.

Appendix C

An Additional Method for Developing
Grade-by-Grade Standards

Developed by John Fortier, Former Assistant
Superintendent, Wisconsin Department
of Public Instruction

A Working Example

To assist the *district team* tailor curriculum to the state standards, this appendix uses one concept from the physical science standards as an example. The appendix shows how to arrive at a curriculum that ensures students meet the benchmarks at the three target grades: 4, 8, and 12. Several steps are presented.

1. The district team should be familiar with how the standard is treated within the standards at each of the three benchmark levels.
2. The district team should review what is known about the concept as it is framed at each level. The team should determine what students will need to know about the concept to meet the benchmark level. (The team may wish to review how other groups and programs have treated the concept.)
3. Within each grade range (K–4, for example), the district team should determine the sequence and grade level at which various subconcepts identified in Step 2. should be introduced. Again, reviewing other group's or program's work may be helpful.
4. The team should consider how to assess the concept at the benchmark grades, Grade 4 for example. This will include at least two considerations. First, what is known about how the concept will be assessed on large-scale state tests? Second, how will the concept be assessed in classrooms?
5. The district team should consider to what extent teachers expected to provide instruction in the targeted concepts are actually familiar with the concept. The team may need to plan for inservice activities to fill any perceived knowledge gaps.
6. Finally, the district team may wish to recommend activities, resources, and time allocations that may enable students to learn the concepts. The team may wish to consider how these concepts may be taught in relationship to other concepts.

For the purposes of illustration and detail, the performance standard dealing with the properties of earth materials (matter) has been chosen.

The first step is to determine how the concept is treated in the state standards at each benchmark level. At Grade 4, *Wisconsin's Model Academic Standards for Science* treats this concept under the title "Properties of Earth Materials" It is divided into the following performance standards:

D.4.1 Understand that objects are made of more than one substance, by observing, describing, and measuring the properties of earth materials, including properties of size, weight, shape, color, temperature, and the ability to react with other substances.

D.4.2 Group and classify objects and substances based on the properties of earth materials.

D.4.3 Understand that substances can exist in different states–solid, liquid, or gas.

D.4.4 Observe and describe changes in form, temperature, color, speed, and direction of objects, and construct explanations for the changes.

D.4.5 Construct simple models of what is happening to materials and substances undergoing change using simple instruments or tools to aid observations and collect data.

At Grade 8, the standards treat the concept under the title "Properties and Changes of Properties in Matter." It contains four performance standards:

D.8.1 Observe, describe, and measure physical and chemical properties of elements and other substances to identify and group them according to properties such as density, melting points, boiling points, conductivity, magnetic attraction, solubility, and reactions to common physical and chemical tests.

D.8.2 Use the major ideas of atomic theory and molecular theory to describe physical and chemical interactions among substances, including solids, liquids, and gases.

D.8.3 Understand how chemical interactions and behaviors lead to new substances with different properties.

D.8.4 While conducting investigations, use the science themes to develop explanations of physical and chemical interactions and energy exchanges.

At Grade 12, the standards treat the concept under two titles: "Structure of Atoms and Matter", having three performance standards, and "Chemical Reactions", having another three.

Structure of Atoms and Matter

D.12.1 Describe atomic structure and the properties of atoms, molecules, and matter during physical and chemical interactions.

D.12.2. Explain the forces that hold the atom together and illustrate how nuclear interactions change the atom.

D.12.3 Explain exchanges of energy in chemical interactions and exchange of mass and energy in atomic and nuclear reactions.

Chemical Reactions

D.12.4. Explain how substances, both simple and complex, interact with one another to produce new substances.

D.12.5 Identify patterns in chemical and physical properties and use them to predict likely chemical and physical changes and interactions.

D.12.6. Through investigations, identify the types of chemical interactions, including endothermic, exothermic, oxidation, photosynthesis, and acid/base reactions.

It is important to recognize that *Wisconsin's Model Academic Standards in Science* intend to include what *all* students should know and be able to do at the various levels. The *district team* will have to consider how students will be exposed to the concepts around matter that is being presented. Will, for example, all students at Grade 12 know the properties of atoms and molecules?

The district team must consider what the standards at Grade 4 expect students to know and be able to do as it relates to matter. Students are expected to recognize the properties of matter and be able to measure them. Specifically mentioned as properties are size, weight, shape, color, temperature, solubility, and ability to react. They are expected to be able to classify materials by properties and to recognize that matter has gas, liquid, solid, and solid states. They must know that properties change under certain conditions and should be able to provide simple models to show what happens during change.

Second, the district team needs to talk about these expectations outlined in the standards and consider whether there are any unstated assumptions about what students need to know if they are to master the standards identified. This activity is best performed by teachers who work with the standard at the relevant benchmark grade or level and by any science specialists who may be working with the group. Sample questions should include the following:

- What unstated knowledge would help students to learn the contents of the last paragraph?
- Would it help them to know that measurement requires three elements: sample, energy source, and detector?
- What system of measurement is each student expected to use: metric or English?
- How complex are the classification systems they are expected to use and at what level?
- What kinds of changes in properties should be addressed?
- To what degree does it help to explain the causes of change?

At Grade 8 what will students need to know about atomic theory and molecular theory to "describe physical and chemical interactions among substances, including solids, liquids, and gases?" The standard does not specify that. At this point, the group may wish to examine materials from other sources to see to what extent they have addressed this question. We include the following discussion of how the issue of matter and its properties are treated in a number of sources. The same process can be used for grades 9 through 12.

Examples of Various Treatments of the Structure and Properties of Matter

This list of examples is by no means intended to be exhaustive.

(1) Marzano, R. and J. Kendall, *Essential Knowledge*, (McCrel, 1999). Mid-Continent Regional Educational Laboratory drew its standards from the work of several states and from the national discipline standards. They probably represent the most thorough compilation of U.S. standards in any one place.

(2) Core Knowledge Foundation, *Core Knowledge Sequence*, (Core Knowledge Foundation, 1995). The Core Knowledge Standards were developed based upon the work of E.D. Hirsch, the author of *Cultural Literacy*. The Core Knowledge program is used by a large number of schools and is known for its detail and specificity—much closer to an entire curriculum than to a set of standards. They are provided at each grade through Grade 6. Since this document was developed, standards have been added for Grades 7 and 8.

(3) Bosher, Wm., Science Standards of Learning for Virginia Public Schools, (Commonwealth of Virginia, Board of Education, 1995). The Virginia Standards of Learning are also pegged for each grade level and include extensive detail.

(4) Hazen, R. and J. Trefil, *Science Matters: Achieving Scientific Literacy*. (Carnegie Institution of Washington, 1991) *Science Matters* differs from the other sources in being a book sponsored by the Carnegie Institute and not really a set of standards laid out by grade or by range of grades. Instead, it develops the concepts that its authors believe a person who is scientifically literate would be familiar with.

(5) *Benchmarks for Science Literacy,* Project 2061. This project provides details on science standards and was one of the documents most used to develop the *National Science Education Standards*.

Many state documents can be found either in print form or on the World Wide Web.

Appendix D

Power Point Presentation Graphic Organizers Method for Science
Curriculum Development

April 1, 2000

Wisconsin Model Academic Standards for Science

- Based on NSES, Benchmarks, other States
- Broad involvement by educators, scientists, business, and community

A bright idea

WI_DPI http://badger.state.wi.us/agencies/dpi/

Standards - Related Issues

- Concerns of stakeholders
- Course-taking patterns
- Student performance on high stakes measures of success

Improvement Goals

- Link standards, curriculum, assessments
- Improve reading and writing
- Build on successes in elementary to improve middle and high schools
- More high performing students in math, science, reading and writing, and social studies

Wisconsin Model Academic Standards

By August 1, 1998, each school board shall adopt pupil academic standards in mathematics, science, reading and writing, geography, and history.

118.30 Wis. Stats.

Key Links in Wisconsin...

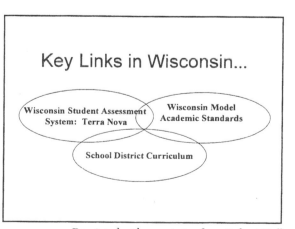

Wisconsin Student Assessment System: Terra Nova

Wisconsin Model Academic Standards

School District Curriculum

Reprinted with permission from Robert Hollon.

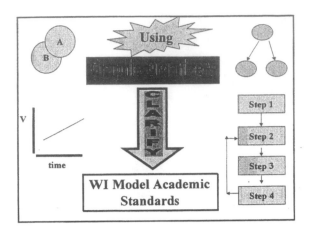

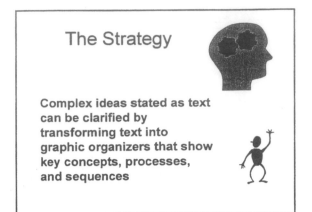

An Example from Science

E.4.4   Identify celestial objects (stars, sun, moon, planets), noting changes in patterns of those objects over time.

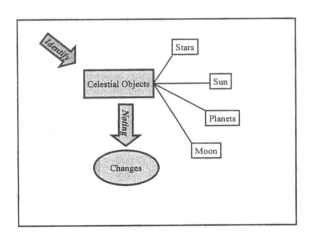

Let's Critique An Example from Mathematics

B.8.3
Generate and explain equivalencies among fractions, decimals, and per cents

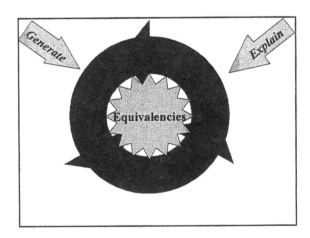

Reprinted with permission from Robert Hollon.

How Did it Happen???

Science Standard
E.12.4

Analyze* the benefits, costs, and limitations of past, present, and projected use of resources and technology and explain* the consequences to the environment

---

Analyze the Standard for

- Key ideas
- Actions or processes (verbs...)
- Causal statements
- Words that link or separate ideas
- Sequences

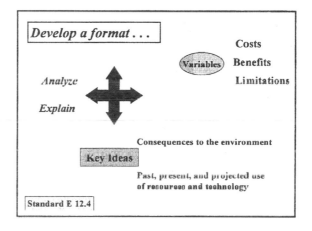

Create the Organizer!

- No single "right" way
- Focus on the meaning as written!
- Don't "over-interpret"

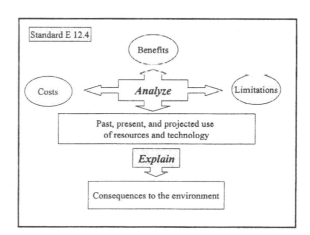

Reprinted with permission from Robert Hollon.

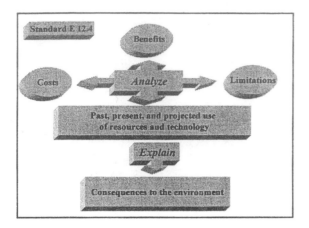

The Invitation...

- Form a **group** of 3 people
- **Select** a 4th or 8th grade science or math content standard
- **Discuss** the important ideas, processes, and sequences that give it meaning
- **Create** a graphic organizer that represents the intent of the Standard *as written*
- **Hang** the organizer in the appropriate spot

Reporting Strategies

- Group reporting about standards
- Interpreting another group's map
- Themes within groups
- Themes that cut across groups

Reflections on the Activity

- How did the process of creating a graphic organizer help you clarify the intent of the standard?

- How could you use this activity to show connections among standards, curriculum and instruction, and assessment?

Some Potential Planning Questions from the Literature

- What do you want students to know?
- What thinking should students exhibit?
- How will you assess learning?
- What will quality performance look like?
- How will you find out what students already believe?
- What activities will you use to help students construct knowledge?

Analyzing
A Classroom Example

Reprinted with permission from Robert Hollon.

Your Ideas   Your Ideas

Your Ideas

Your Ideas   Your Ideas

Your Ideas   Your Ideas

Your Ideas

Your Ideas   Your Ideas

Your Ideas   Your Ideas

Your Ideas

Your Ideas   Your Ideas

The final question for this morning

What are some of your next steps working with science standards??

Thank you for participating in WASDI!

Reprinted with permission from Robert Hollon.

Appendix E

The first science class after Christmas is unusually full of energy. Mr. L.'s students are informally surveying their classmates to see what research project they are interested in doing. Mr. L.'s second semester classes are not unlike other introductory biology classes where the topics of genetics, protein synthesis, evolution, taxonomy and the like assume major curricular importance.

However, Mr. L. wants to go further. He wants to design an educational setting, in the confines of a freshman introductory biology curriculum, where his students can demonstrate their ability to apply the information and experiences they gained in the first semester to a new educational situation in the second semester. The students will build on their first semester experience of growing *Wisconsin Fast Plants* to model the actions and thought processes of a scientific researcher.

The chatter in the room today tells Mr. L. that these additional challenges of designing and conducting research utilizing the Fast Plants has more than a few students a little nervous. He collects the vacation assignments—write a question and design a controlled experiment to attempt to answer your question—avoiding the pitfall of discussing them. Written feedback will be provided on their ideas the very next class period. The feedback is the first in a number of "scientific dialogues" that will take place between student and teacher throughout the semester where students can reference and build off of their Fast Plants experiences as well as any other relevant materials that have been covered in the scope of the biology course. Class then focuses on the new topic at hand, genetics.

The next day, students receive their "corrected" assignments and quickly notice that there are many questions and comments written on their papers: "How are you going to control this variable?" "What is your sample size?" "How will this be monitored on the weekend?" "Do we have equipment that you would like to use?" Mr. L. quells the chaos by informing the students that he will be glad to meet individually to spend time discussing their specific concerns. Many students set up appointments to see him during their free time—study hall, lunch, before and after school.

Even with individual consultations, many students remain unsettled. These students, like many others, are used to traditional laboratory work where the teacher hands out a lab sheet and the student follows the direction to the prescribed outcome. However, Mr. L. has subtly been preparing his students for this experience by discussing the experimental design of the "cookbook" labs and encouraging his students to come up with a laboratory procedure for a lab before handing out the laboratory sheet. Up to this point, many just considered this an additional component of their laboratory work. Now they are putting those critical thinking skills to work on their own, very real experimental design problems.

The next two weeks are very hectic. Mr. L. has entered into five to ten minute "scientific dialogues" with many of the student groups, frequently sending the group away with additional questions, ideas to consider, and background information to research. He is very sensitive to the students' frustration levels and is recording the progress or lack of progress for each of the groups. These dialogues are a key component of the evaluation process. By the end of the second week, a fair number of the groups are given permission to conduct the research, and Mr. L's role shifts from teacher to research director. As research director, Mr. L. monitors the equipment use, room use, and safety issues. He also requests periodic verbal progress reports. These reports provide an opportunity to engage students in conversations regarding their project, revealing their understanding of their work.

Mr. L. encourages collaboration with students in different sections who are conducting similar experiments. Often students search the internet for other schools conducting similar studies. With these collaborators, students can discuss particular challenges, surprising results and can sometimes pool data to address the issue of sample size and number of trials in their studies. This process in and of itself is educationally rich. Mr. L. has observed students discussing issues of controlling variables, defining operational terms, collecting data, and analyzing data with fellow students. A few years back, Mr. L. arranged for his students to link up with two schools: one in Connecticut and the other in California conducting the same type of project.

The process of refining the question and experimental design takes some student groups longer than others, which serves to reduce the immediate demand on materials and laboratory space. So, with many of the projects underway, Mr. L. devotes his energies to the students that haven't started their research. Occasionally class time will be devoted to a research team that is having particular difficulty with their research and the class brainstorms solutions and ideas. By the end of week four every research group is making progress. The projects range from using time-lapse photography to record the life cycle of *Brassica rapa*, to determining the effects of soil composition on plant growth and development, to developing age appropriate curricular material for use in the preschool and elementary classroom, to determining the effects of plant hormones on plant growth and development. In the role of Research Director, Mr. L. keeps tabs on all the groups.

Towards the end of the third quarter the students are provided with some class time to set up and enter data on computer spread sheets. Many utilize this time to begin writing the initial sections of their laboratory report—introduction, background information, materials, procedure, safety—in preparation for their presentations during the final exam week in the fourth quarter. Mr. L. fields many of their questions by asking students how they handled a particular issue on a past lab or by directly relating their question to their experiences of writing the Fast Plants laboratory report in the first semester.

Time management issues always seem to lie just below the surface throughout this project. The students are aware that these plants take about 38 days to complete their life cycle, and that the laboratory reports are due toward the end of the fourth quarter, some nine weeks away. But the unexpected does arise. The beginning of the fourth quarter, a full seven weeks into the project for many of the students, reveals the rare research group facing a perceived insurmountable obstacle—dead plants or lost data. Always cognizant of the students' frustration level, Mr. L. provides these groups with options to conduct "mini" research projects on germination and cotyledon development, which can be completed in roughly ten days. While these students engage in intensive discussions with Mr. L. to define their new question, they are still accountable for demonstrating ownership of their "new" research focus. They must clearly articulate the methodology utilized, background information and experimental design. These groups are now faced with writing two reports, one reflecting on the progress and end point of their initial research and the second, focusing on their mini research project.

With all of the groups on track and just two weeks before the final exam, Mr. L. distributes a Fast Plants Presentation-Scoring rubric and sets the due date for the Fast Plants laboratory report. Most of the students find that the process of development and revision of the more traditional Fast Plants lab report in the first semester was sufficient to eliminate the mystery of writing this report. The preparation of the oral presentation, on the other hand, is quite a different story. In an effort to reduce student anxiety, Mr. L. shows videotapes from previous years and spends a period or two of class time discussing presentation details such as eye contact, reading from note cards, speed of the presentation, size of the visuals used, body language, and so forth. This seems to reduce at least some of the anxiety.

The presentation day arrives. The school's professional library is the location for this symposium of Fast Plants research. The audience for these presentations includes parents, administrators and fellow student researchers. Some of the students have spent their free periods over the past couple of days setting up computers for Power Point presentations, while others have arranged for slide projectors, easels, or overheads to aid in their presentations. Mr. L. arrives with refreshments and a printed presentation schedule. Mr. L. is especially interested in the students use of vocabulary and how they field the questions based on their research.

It has become very clear by the students' performances that they have gone beyond just completing another course requirement. They have integrated and internalized many of the major themes in science; asking questions, controlling variables, understanding the limits of your experiment, communicating ideas, showing biological connections. In essence they have satisfied Mr. L.'s goals of having students doing science instead of having science done to them.

This vignette was developed by Professor Emeritus Paul Williams, Wisconsin Fast Plants, under a contract with the Department of Public Instruction.